5 9 95

THE DYNAMICS OF
RACIAL PROGRESS

THE DYNAMICS OF RACIAL PROGRESS

ECONOMIC INEQUALITY AND RACE RELATIONS SINCE RECONSTRUCTION

ANTOINE L. JOSEPH

M.E.Sharpe
Armonk, New York
London, England

Library of Congress Cataloging-in-Publication Data

Joseph, Antoine L., 1951–
    The dynamics of racial progress : economic inequality and race relations since
Reconstruction / Antoine L. Joseph.
        p. cm.
Includes bibliographical references and index.
ISBN 0-7656-1271-2 (hardcover : alk. paper)
 1. United States—Race relations. 2. United States—Race relations—Economic aspects.
3. United States—History—1865– 4. United States—Economic conditions. I. Title.

E184.A1J66 2005
323.173′09′04—dc22   2004027363

Printed in the United States of America

The paper used in this publication meets the minimum requirements of
American National Standard for Information Sciences
Permanence of Paper for Printed Library Materials,
ANSI Z 39.48-1984.

BM (c)   10   9   8   7   6   5   4   3   2   1

Contents

Acknowledgments

I wish to thank Zachary Schiffman, Michael Hobart, and the members of the 1994 NEH seminar Cultural Pluralism and the Nation-State directed by M. Crawford Young for reading and commenting on early portions of the manuscript. Jack Bloom also generously read and commented extensively on an early version of the manuscript. My greatest debt is to three individuals who were essential in the development of the manuscript. First, the late C. Eric Lincoln sparked my interest in writing a book on American race relations. Second, my colleague Judy McDonnell painstakingly read and commented on several versions of the manuscript in its entirety. She was especially helpful in recommending revisions essential to the final version of the manuscript. Finally, my friend and mentor William Julius Wilson, who happens to be the leading race relations analyst and scholar of the last half century, took the time to read and discuss several versions of the manuscript, going far beyond what would ordinarily be expected of a former graduate advisor. I would also like to thank Andrew Gyory, PhD, and Niels Aaboe, the former and current senior social science editors respectively at M.E. Sharpe; Esther Clarke, M.E. Sharpe editorial assistant; and the anonymous reviewers for M.E. Sharpe. Most importantly, I would like to dedicate this book to the memory of my late mother, Lorraine F. Joseph, who was herself a writer and teacher. Her encouragement and support were essential in my becoming a writer and teacher as well.

Introduction

A recent national election was marred by political violence and efforts to disfranchise opposition supporters through intimidation, changes in election laws, and shifts in the distribution of polling places. Western observers had no trouble recognizing the deficiencies of the election held in Zimbabwe on March 13, 2002.[1] This election has been roundly and rightfully condemned by international observers as fraudulent. But consider that on November 7, 2000, more than 100 million Americans went to the polls to cast their votes. Most notably in Florida, but in other states as well, serious questions have emerged concerning whether some Americans—especially black and brown Americans—were able to vote without intimidation.

Is it possible that in 2000, thousands of Americans might have been prevented from exercising their right to vote? Ultimately the U.S. Supreme Court, slightly more than a month after the election, cast the decisive vote, ruling 5 to 4 that recounts of the Florida vote were violations of the Fourteenth Amendment's equal protection clause, thereby awarding victory to George W. Bush, the Republican candidate. Yet the Supreme Court's declaration only increased the speculation—did George W. Bush really win the vote among the electorate, or did he merely win the vote in the Court? As legal scholar Ronald Dworkin points out, "it is therefore difficult to find a respectable explanation of why all and only the conservatives voted to end the election in this way, and the troubling question is being asked among scholars and commentators whether the Court's decision would have been different if it was Bush, not Gore, who needed the recount to win—whether, that is, the decision reflected not ideological division, which is inevitable, but professional self-interest."[2]

Certainly the differences between the American presidential election of 2000 and the Zimbabwean of 2002 outweigh the similarities. But the willingness of the winners to use means that many find to be questionable is similar. The commitment to win at almost any cost is clear in each case.

Among the most serious questions surrounding the American election of 2000 were those that concern the treatment of minority voters. It was reported that an unknown number of blacks were prevented from voting in Florida once they arrived at the polls. In the words of *New York Daily News* reporter Juan Gonzales, "some people were discouraged, intimidated, and even prevented from voting."[3] There were reports that blacks were routinely stopped and asked for identification while whites were allowed to remain in the voting lines without showing any identification. A predominantly black precinct in Duval County had a long line of people waiting to vote. Meanwhile, police began to hand out tickets for loitering. Some polling places were shut at the official closing time even though black voters were still in line.[4]

The above irregularities alone are sufficient to cast serious doubt upon the fairness of the election and the potential recount of the votes in Florida. However, the heart of the case of unequal treatment of black voters rests upon more tangible evidence, evidence that cannot easily be dismissed as anecdotal. In part these differences were due to arbitrary decisions to void ballots, especially in majority black voting districts, which ignored clear and unambiguous evidence of the intent of the voter. According to journalists Andres Viglucci, Geoff Dougherty, and William Yardley, "Ballots in majority black precincts were voided at a rate three times higher than those in non-black precincts. Nearly one in every ten ballots in majority black precincts went unrecorded. In majority white precincts, the discard rate was less than one in 38. A prime reason, a higher proportion of black voters live in counties that use error-prone punch card machines."[5] Predominantly black areas were plagued with technological deficiencies in their election apparatus. Reporter Noel Rubinton believes "heavily Democratic and African-American neighborhoods in Florida lost many more presidential votes than other areas because of outmoded voting machines and rampant confusion."[6] It may never be possible to fully answer whether disparate racial treatment on Election Day changed the outcome of the election.

Problems of a substantial racial gap in voided votes emerged in other states as well, where there were also substantial differences in the rates of voided ballots by race. According to a study by the House Committee on Government Reform, "voters in low-income, high minority congressional districts throughout the country were three times more likely to have their votes for president discarded than those in more affluent, low-minority districts." Harvard University's Civil Rights Project detected a substantial relationship between ballot spoilage and the size of the black population. Essentially, as the black population in a county increases, so does the spoiled ballot rate: "Examining the 100 counties with the worst (highest) spoilage rates nationwide, 67 percent have black populations above 12 percent."[7] In predominantly black Fulton County, which includes Atlanta, one of every sixteen ballots was invalidated. In nearby Cobb and Gwinnett counties, which are predominantly white and Republican, and use modern equipment, the invalidation rate was one in 200. In Chicago's Cook County, which normally has a nullified vote rate of 2 percent, the void rate in the 2000 election was 5 percent. A prominent reason for this dramatic increase in voided ballots was that Republican majorities in the state legislature passed a new election law that prevented voters from voting straight party tickets. Consequently, in Chicago's Cook County voters confronted a ballot with 400 candidates that was twenty-one pages long. The result was that the rate of disqualified ballots was one in twelve for Cook County precincts that were more than 70 percent black but only one in twenty in precincts that were less than 30 percent black. Furthermore, the Republican-dominated state legislature refused to allow Cook County to use ballot counting machines, which would catch many errors, even while nearby counties were allowed to use similar technology to reduce their error rate. As a result, 120,000 ballots in Cook County—70,000 in Chicago and 50,000 in surrounding communities—did not count.[8]

Thus in numerous counties in key states, the first presidential election of the twenty-first century was conducted in a manner far more suited to the fraudulent elections of the nineteenth century. The clock appears to have been turned back to the time when southern Democrats used every means at their disposal to frustrate poor, often illiterate voters—both black and white. How did the nation come to this result, that in 2000, the Republican Party, the self-proclaimed party of Lincoln would resort to such devices? Was not the type of chicanery used to undermine the political power of black voters in 2000 outlawed by the 1965 Voting Rights Act, the crown jewel of the Second Reconstruction era (1954–65)?

And finally, why were Republicans willing to jeopardize the legitimacy of the leadership of the "world's oldest running experiment in democracy" simply to secure a temporary partisan advantage? Why were so many Republicans on the Supreme Court, in Florida's and other states' legislatures, among Florida election officials and the rowdy demonstrators in Miami-Dade, so willing to win at all costs, by any means necessary? Why did none of these partisans weigh the consequences of adding to the nation's tensions, both racial and otherwise? A key reason is that the American electorate has become more racially polarized over the last twenty years and black Americans are an insignificant Republican constituency. But was not racial polarization supposed to have declined, due to the considerable advances achieved in race relations during the 1960s and 1970s?

There are certainly those who regard the messy circumstances of the 2000 election as atypical. Yet consider other evidence: in 1966 Edward Brooke was elected to the U.S. Senate. He was the first black to be directly elected to the Senate, and also the first to serve in the Senate since the end of Reconstruction. It would not be until 1992 that a second black American, Carol Moseley-Braun, would be elected to the Senate. Only one black, L. Douglas Wilder, was elected to the governor's office in any state during the twentieth century. Qualified and promising black Americans have found their electoral careers ended by a "race ceiling." Twenty-five years after the passage of the Voting Rights Act there were only five black Democrats out of 116 southern representatives. The doors to the pinnacles of state and national political power have usually been shut to blacks. There is, however, some evidence of progress. The number of African-Americans in the House of Representatives grew from twenty-six to thirty-nine during the 1990s, while membership in state legislatures grew from 430 (5.8 percent) to 557 (7.5 percent) over the same period.[9] Moreover, the number of black elected officials increased from 1,469 in 1970 to 8,936 by 1999. Yet, most black Americans are elected as local politicians in majority black districts. The list of talented black leaders facing a "race ceiling" when they seek higher office includes both titans of the civil rights struggle, such as Andrew Young, to quieter moderates, such as Harvey Gantt and Tom Bradley.[10] Each failed when seeking office beyond the confines of majority black congressional districts or cities with large black populations.

It was only a quarter century ago that the evidence of dramatic racial progress was clear. The near revolutionary breakthroughs made by black Americans in employment and political power supported the position that the significance of racism was declining, as argued in William Julius Wilson's landmark work, *The Declining Significance of Race*. Yet such dramatic racial progress is only one part of the evolving story of American race relations. Since the end of Second Reconstruction (1954–65), America has also witnessed a resurgence of racial polarization, racial conflict, and racial controversy.

The Dynamics of Racial Progress: Economic Inequality and Race Relations Since Reconstruction argues that these seemingly contradictory assessments are both on target. In essence, both the long-term declining significance of race and the more recent resurgence of racial conflict reflect the ongoing historical social construction of race. The central proposition of this analysis is that advances and setbacks in race relations have been strongly shaped by broad trends in economic and political inequality. Moreover, political and economic equality are highly interdependent, meaning that developments favorable to economic and political equality or alternatively to economic and political inequality generally move in tandem. In other words, growing economic equality promotes political equality, creating a climate favorable to progress in race relations. Conversely, growing economic inequality promotes political inequality, slowing the pace of race relations progress. Long-term changes in economic and political inequality thus influence the tenor of race relations by at times advancing racial progress, and at other times by impeding it.

The major intent of this book is to outline, analyze, and explain the key forces responsible for the broad contours of change in race relations in American society. The analysis focuses specifically on the interrelation between economic and political factors. It will not attempt to provide a comprehensive study of race relations or of racial developments over the last 120 years. Nor will it attempt to supplant analyses that focus primarily on ideology, social and cultural factors, political mobilization, or political theory.

This work emphasizes the relationship between blacks and whites in terms of the way their interaction has shaped the contours of the American economic and political experience over the last 120 years. This is not to say that the experiences of other racial groups, Native American, Hispanic, and Asian, have been insignificant. But the black-white experience has been uniquely central to both the advances and declines in the democratic character of American society.

THE DYNAMICS OF
RACIAL PROGRESS

1

The Resurgence of
Racial Conflict

Examining the impact of contemporary political and economic forces upon American race relations leads me to conclude that the dramatic increase in racial polarization during the 1970s and 1980s was a consequence of the growing economic inequality of the last generation. In this context, affirmative action has helped to fan the flames of racial discord. Affirmative action can be defined as a set of policies that use preferences to aid distinct groups. The most controversial preferences have been racial, but ethnicity, gender, and language have also defined groups eligible for favored treatment. According to political scientists Donald Kinder and Lynn Sanders, in 1986, 85 percent of whites opposed preferential hiring for blacks, while 70 percent opposed college quotas for blacks. According to an October 1995 NBC/*Wall Street Journal* poll, 50 percent of whites opposed affirmative action while 36 percent supported it. In comparison, 76 percent of blacks favored affirmative action versus 16 percent opposed. A January 2003 NBC News/*Wall Street Journal* poll reported 26 percent in favor of using race as a factor in admissions compared to 65 percent opposed. A June 2003 Gallup poll found 44 percent of non-Hispanic whites favoring affirmative action polls versus 49 percent of non-Hispanic whites opposed. In comparison, 70 percent of blacks favored affirmative action while 21 percent opposed it.[1]

Ironically, affirmative action's very existence testifies to the dramatic changes that have taken place in the United States in the past century. In particular, affirmative action tells us that white supremacy is no longer a dominant feature of American society. When Reconstruction ended in the 1870s, it was inconceivable that the policies of the U.S. government, or of any of its branches, or of any state or local government, would have considered the substantial reduction of racial disparities to be an important goal. By comparison, Edward Bellamy's *Looking Backward*, a popular work of the late nineteenth century that foresaw a socialist United States by the year 2000, depicted a more plausible future.[2] True, the Socialist Party's electoral support peaked at 5 percent in the presidential election of 1912, but there was no visible electoral support for racial equality.

During the final decades of the nineteenth century few black Americans were in a position to take advantage of economic or educational opportunities. As recently as fifty years ago a majority of Americans might well have favored affirmative action policies, but only to safeguard the privileged positions of white Americans. More than half of those surveyed in the late 1930s and 1940s believed that whites should be preferred over blacks for employment. In 1940, 98 percent of white southerners supported segregation.[3] By the late 1940s educational and economic upgrading of the black population had proceeded far enough to stimulate the dawning of a civil rights movement. However, the relatively few blacks graduating from the nation's best-known institutions were likely to find their employment options severely limited.

A personal example may illustrate the dramatic changes that have occurred in the last half-century. Out of the handful of blacks (fewer than ten) graduating from one of the nation's most prestigious law schools in Chicago between 1948 and 1952 (of which my father was one), not one received an offer to join any of the city's major (or even minor) law firms. My father found it necessary to continue working at the post office for several years after receiving his law degree. Perhaps best placed was future mayor Harold Washington, whose father had sufficient political connections to place him in a city job. The others were forced to start their own law firms and to operate as sole practitioners.

Although affirmative action is not popular today, its existence suggests that economic and educational opportunities are increasingly accessible to qualified blacks (or at least that the barriers to their entry are substantially smaller than in the past). Since the 1978 Supreme Court ruling in *Regents of University of California v. Bakke*, opposition to affirmative action has exploded. In 1989, in *City of Richmond v. Croson*, the Supreme Court struck down a plan that set aside 30 percent of city contracts for minorities. In 1996, California voters passed Proposition 209, which forbade consideration of race in hiring or school admissions.

Still, the very existence of affirmative action is a sign of progress. If the United States remained a society fully steeped in white supremacy, affirmative action not only would not exist, it would be unthinkable. Second, the existence of policies promoting affirmative action suggests that there has been substantial growth in the pool of blacks capable of utilizing such opportunities.

However, the controversy over affirmative action also shows that even as

American society is more open to black advancement, such advance promotes racial tensions. Affirmative action's visibility and controversial nature resonates so strongly because conflicting interpretations of principles of merit and fair play are embedded into the economic structure of American society. Finally, affirmative action heightens racially charged anxieties stemming from the intensifying competition for economic security in a rapidly changing economic order.

Progress in race relations has occurred in large measure due to broad trends favoring increasing economic and political equality between the late 1940s and the 1970s. Affirmative action policies were a consequence of both the improving racial climate and the existence of positive economic expectations about the future. Americans were generally confident about their economic future. They believed the economic pie was increasing and would continue to do so. Such "generosity of the spirit" paved the way for the kind of redistribution of opportunity that affirmative action symbolized. The initial policies targeting aid to racially disadvantaged groups commenced with the Civil Rights Act of 1964. According to sociologist John Skrentny, pragmatism was the paramount reason for using numerical targets to assess the success of nondiscrimination policies in education and employment.

Affirmative action policies became more pronounced during the Nixon years. The Philadelphia Plan required federal contractors to establish goals for minority hiring. Originally based on an executive order from President Lyndon Johnson, the Philadelphia Plan was implemented by President Richard Nixon's Department of Labor in 1969. Its purpose was to increase the number of minorities, especially blacks, employed in high-paying skilled trades. Such trades, which include ironworkers, electricians, and carpenters, were seen as opening a pathway into the middle class. Skrentny believes the Philadelphia Plan had ulterior motives. Its purposes were: first of all, to rebut the charge that Nixon's "southern strategy" meant the administration was forming an alliance with southern racists; and second, to sow discord among key Democratic constituencies. Accordingly, the Philadelphia Plan demonstrated the Nixon administration's commitment to civil rights enforcement while simultaneously functioning as a Trojan horse designed to divide unionized white workers from the civil rights movement. Affirmative action was further legitimized by the 1971 Supreme Court decision in *Griggs v. Duke Power Company*. In this decision, the Court ruled that employers were required to scrutinize their practices to ensure that they did not "freeze the status quo of prior discriminatory employment practices."[4]

The dramatic expansion of the black middle class and the widespread entry of black Americans into higher status occupations were clear indicators of black economic progress. Such trends suggest that black Americans have achieved a considerable measure of formal legal and political equality with white Americans. Such positive indicators also suggest that educated blacks are more competitive in employment and education than they have been at any previous time. Hence, compelling indicators bolster the view that the significance of race has declined (a decline that is not really debatable the longer the time span considered).[5]

But as economic conditions soured by the mid- to late 1970s, the continued racial polarization of voting, the continued underrepresentation of black Americans in the nation's political and economic elite, and the concurrence of racially charged incidents suggest the need for a reexamination of the declining-significance-of-race thesis. The decline in racial antagonisms has not been a straightforward, linear phenomenon, and further gains have been more gradual.

Racial Polarization Amid Surging Inequality

There were many signs of growing racial polarization in American politics. During the 1960s, George Wallace was unexpectedly successful in northern primaries in 1964 and he received an impressive share (13 percent) of the popular vote in 1968. Richard Nixon employed a southern strategy, appealed to a silent majority, and emphasized law and order, which was little more than a thinly veiled recasting of obsessions regarding race and crime. During his presidency, Nixon reached out to racial conservatives, appointing judges who viewed segregation favorably and voiced opposition to school desegregation. The election of Ronald Reagan in 1980 was historic, because of Reagan's role in creating a dominant majority coalition. This subject will be covered in detail in Chapter 2. Other indications of rising racial tensions in American politics lay in the polarizing conditions surrounding Harold Washington's election as mayor of Chicago in 1982. During the campaign, his Republican opponent, Bernard Epton, who ironically had been considered a liberal, ran advertisements that said "Vote for Epton before it's too late." One can hardly ignore Jesse Helms's 1990 campaign against Harvey Gantt for the U.S. Senate. The Helms campaign ran a now infamous political advertisement that showed a pair of white hands crumpling a rejection letter for a job given to a black applicant based on racial quotas.

A prime example of increased racial polarization in the 1980s and early 1990s was the growing prominence of David Duke. His campaigns highlighted the effectiveness with which affirmative action could be used as a device to build political support. The serious economic depression in southern Louisiana, due to the oil industry's decline in the mid-1980s, spurred a blending of economic and racial frustrations. For Republicans, David Duke eventually came to be an unwanted poor relation, one who served as an ever-present reminder that their efforts to exploit racial tensions through code words and oblique references were not far removed from more straightforward racist appeals. Duke received 57 percent of the white vote in the 1990 U.S. Senate primary election.

> More common than slurs against blacks is a sense that white people are being victimized by affirmative action and minority contracting programs. It is the centerpiece of Mr. Duke's speech and perhaps his most effective issue with voters. "We don't have the same rights as black people," said Jay Louviere, a 29-year-old lumberyard worker. "Duke's the only one standing up for white people." But critics say that the issue has more basis in emotion than economics, that programs like affirmative action evoke particular resentment from white people facing their own economic problems. . . . "I don't think there are 500 people in Louisiana that have either been adversely affected or benefited by affirmative action," said Mr. Edwards, the former governor. "But everyone who doesn't have a job or whose son cannot get into law school believes it's because of affirmative action." Real or not, it taps into a powerful vein of anger that can seem the ultimate extension of the politics of sex and ethnicity. . . . To some observers, what is most disturbing about Mr. Duke's campaign is that frustrated and angry white people seem willing to forget his extremism while embracing his more mainstream views on racial issues.[6]

Perhaps most notorious of all was the infamous Willie Horton advertisement, which highlighted George Bush's successful 1988 race for the White House. The Bush campaign successfully merged anxieties about crime with already prevalent racial antagonisms. They used Willie Horton as a symbol to appeal to less affluent whites who might have otherwise responded to Bush's elitist upbringing with skepticism. The success of such campaign tactics showed that the appeal of racially charged sentiments was alive nationwide and could be effectively used within mainstream political discourse. The extent to which the political resurgence of Republicans since the 1960s has been built upon their use of racially charged sentiments will be explored more fully in Chapter 2.

During this era, black progress promoted white backlash. But why in the 1970s and 1980s, after so much progress in the previous two decades? I believe that the answer lies in the more difficult economic circumstances that emerged after 1973. William Julius Wilson's *The Bridge Over the Racial Divide* highlights this observation.

> During the first half of the 1990s, a period of heightened economic anxiety as the country was staggering from the effects of the 1990–92 recession, . . .

the poisonous rhetoric of certain highly visible spokespersons ... increased racial tensions and channeled frustrations in ways that divided groups in America. Instead of associating citizens' problems with economic and political changes, these divisive messages encouraged groups to turn on each other—race against race and citizens against immigrants.[7]

To understand why racial polarization was a dominant political theme during this era we need to explore the economic trends of the last generation. Essentially, the greater economic difficulties of the 1970s and 1980s soured the formerly positive economic expectations of many Americans. Heightened economic insecurity drove political polarization, exacerbating a deteriorating racial climate. Perhaps to no one's surprise, as economic insecurity increased, the spirit of generosity declined, and affirmative action programs became decidedly less popular.

Growing Economic Inequality

Perhaps the most significant economic reality of the last generation has been the stagnation in living standards for the average American. Frank Levy once termed the years from 1973 to 1984 a "quiet depression."[8] He believes this era of economic stagnation was due in large measure to the declining proportion of jobs capable of sustaining middle-class living standards. Economist Lawrence Summers has also spoken of this era as one of "a quiet depression in living standards." A median family income of approximately $35,000 in 1990 was no longer sufficient to sustain what is regarded as a middle-class standard of living.[9]

According to Levy, since the early 1970s the economic standing of black men has been determined by a number of factors. Educational attainment determines which forces are most influential in shaping the economic destiny of particular segments of black men. First of all, involvement in criminal activities and incarceration diminished the employment prospects of black male high school dropouts. Second, restructuring of manufacturing depressed the economic environment faced by black high school graduates. Finally, a disproportionate growth in the number of college graduates and the backlash against civil rights and affirmative action undermined the economic environment for black male college graduates. Overall then, slow wage growth, the falling demand for less-skilled men, involvement in criminal activity, and the decline of affirmative action policies combined to slow substantially the progress of black males.[10] Levy's view is shared by economists Sheldon Danziger and Peter Gottschalk, who also believe that since the early 1970s the economic environment has soured for less-skilled workers.[11]

However, the role of declining demand for less-skilled men is a topic of controversy. Economists William Darity and Samuel Myers dispute the view that increasing racial inequality is adequately explained by the deteriorating fortunes of low-skilled workers. They believe that "independent of the relative quality black males present to the labor market, processes persist that exclude them from comparable participation with non-black males with similar productivity linked characteristics. To put it bluntly, discrimination in a comprehensive sense lies at the core of matters, not just at the point of employment but throughout an entire range of stages that affect labor market outcomes."[12] Economist James Galbraith also questions the significance of the declining demand for low-skilled workers. He argues that "unemployment, the exchange rate, inflation, economic growth and the minimum wage—account for nearly 90 percent of the variation in wage inequality over time." Thus in his view, declining demand for low-skilled labor is at best a subordinate, rather than a dominant, cause of increasing inequality.[13]

Under any circumstances, by the end of the 1970s economic inequality had begun to rise significantly. Such rising inequality has been a long-term, rather than a cyclical, phenomenon. According to William Julius Wilson, "in the early 1970s, economic growth slowed and the distribution of inflation-adjusted income became more unequal. Whereas average income gains from 1974 to 1997 continued for the higher quintiles, especially in the top fifth, the lowest quintile experienced annual declines in income during this period, and the second lowest experienced stagnating incomes."[14] Ever since, a large percentage of American households have been losing ground. In fact, U.S. Census surveys show that as many as one-third of all full-time jobs pay less than $20,000 per year.[15] These are jobs that will not allow most of those raising children on one income to elevate their families out of poverty.

Quite clearly, rising economic inequality has played a substantial role in slowing the economic progress made by black Americans. Certainly, the deteriorating circumstances of lower-income blacks is to blame for much of the worsened condition of black Americans as a group.[16] High unemployment rates are the culprit for much of this worsened condition. The kinds of jobs many less-skilled black workers are qualified for are not as plentiful. Moreover, many of these jobs are inaccessible to blacks living in inner city communities, who must also overcome employers' reluctance to hire them. Many employers would rather not hire young black men if alternatives were available. Among the recent studies that corroborate this point are the audit studies conducted by the Urban Institute. Pairs of black and white men between the ages of 19 and 25 who were looking for entry-level jobs were matched. They were sent out to apply for work, after training to minimize differences in the way they presented themselves. The tests were conducted in Chicago and Washington, D.C. The results were that black men were turned down three times as often as white men. Comparable results were found in an audit study directed by the Fair Employment Council of Greater Washington, Inc. Whites were 10 percent likelier to receive interviews than blacks. Fifty percent of white interviewees received job offers, compared to only 11 percent of black interviewees.[17]

The deterioration of living conditions of black youths is due as well to the declining fertility of married black women, and the declining proportion of black women who marry. Because fewer black women are getting married, and married black women are having fewer children, a larger percentage of births are by unmarried black women. In 1960, approximately 20 percent of the children born to black women were to single mothers; by 1991, 68 percent of the births to black women were to single mothers. By 1999, 68.9 percent of black births were to single mothers.[18] Single black mothers are typically younger and poorer. As a result, a larger percentage of black children grow up in poverty, experiencing inferior living conditions and life chances.

Yet, more-affluent blacks have not been insulated from the effects of economic and political retrenchment. The highest education levels show the largest income disparities between black and white men. Growing racial disparities in monetary returns for additional years of schooling has slowed the progress of middle-income blacks.[19] Second, political assaults on public sector employment have limited the progress made by educated black Americans. Third, middle-income blacks are rarely as insulated as middle-income whites from the conditions of the disadvantaged. By 1978, for example, 11 percent of black men in their economic primes (25–55 years of age) reported no earned income, double the late 1960s figure. Given the tightening of public assistance, these men most likely survived on aid from family members. As a result, the economic environment of middle-income blacks has also deteriorated.[20]

Furthermore, political and economic competition in the United States occurs in an environment defined by the primacy of private earnings. Private earnings largely determine the economic status of non-elderly individuals and families. As economist James Galbraith points out, wage inequality is the foundation of the general structure of inequality. "This is partly because wages and salaries remain such a large fraction of total incomes and also because the distribution of certain other forms of income, such as private pensions, depends directly on each recipient's past history of earnings and hence on the inequality of the wage structure."[21] In addition, the American government plays a decidedly lesser role in mitigating economic insecurity than the role assumed by government in any other democratic nation. Robert

Goodin and his colleagues concluded, based on a ten-year study of individual respondents in the United States, the Netherlands, and Germany, that although the pretax and transfer income inequality was roughly equal among the three countries, the impact of government via taxes and transfers resulted in substantially greater income equality in the Netherlands and Germany than in the United States.[22] American workers compared to those in other OECD countries are also least compensated by unemployment benefits. Based on the ratio between the average unemployment compensation and the average wage for manual workers, individuals in Canada, France, and Germany receive approximately one-half the average wage, versus 0.2 in the United Kingdom and 0.15 in Italy and the United States.[23] In the United States welfare state benefits are at best an austere supplement of the private earnings of the non-elderly. Consequently, the possession of a good job is critical for the acquisition and maintenance of middle- and upper-middle-class lifestyles and for their intergenerational transfer.

Thus, the greater economic difficulties encountered by less-skilled and lower-income Americans over the last quarter century are partly a consequence of the retrenchment in welfare policy. The present era stands in sharp contrast to the era immediately preceding it. The years 1930–70 were a time in which reductions in economic inequality accelerated partly because improvements in private earnings were augmented by more generous social support. Nowadays, the difficulties encountered in the private economy by less-affluent Americans have become even more burdensome due to the mean-spirited atmosphere permeating social welfare policies over the last generation.[24] A central reason for the greater parsimony of social welfare policy has been the growth of racial polarization in electoral politics.

Contrast, for example, the support given to programs that benefit the (predominantly white) middle class, such as Social Security and Medicare. These programs are automatically adjusted for the cost of living. In comparison, the eligibility requirements and benefit levels of the major low-income program—Aid to Families with Dependent Children (AFDC)—are determined annually by individual states. These programs have a disproportionately greater minority clientele. Furthermore, Ronald Reagan's ascension to the presidency brought with it eligibility restrictions for welfare that greatly reduced overall benefits.

The Dimensions of Economic Competition

Clearly, the transition from an economy whose core was in manufacturing industries to one based in services, termed a postindustrial economy, has affected the livelihood of all groups. Nonetheless, it can be argued that it is white males with a high school education or less that have suffered the greatest status anxiety. A key reason for the growing economic insecurity and rising status anxiety of white males is that manufacturing industries have historically provided jobs allowing less-educated men to earn high wages. In the 1950s and 1960s, six million jobs were created in mining, construction, and manufacturing. From 1960 to 1979, slightly more than two million new jobs were created in those industries. Furthermore, the entry of baby boomers into the labor force accentuates the good-jobs deficit for the less skilled, for example, fewer jobs in high-paying industries accessible to less-educated males. Even if the nation's industrial structure had not changed, there would have been less stable, high-paying employment for recent labor force entrants due to this demographic bulge. Consequently, male employment in manufacturing declined by 15 percent (from 30 percent to 26 percent) between 1969 and 1979. The 1980–82 recession only added to the woes of those seeking well-paying employment in manufacturing, as employment declines were concentrated in this sector.[25]

Young men with no more than a high school education are responsible for most of the decline in the middle of the earnings distribution and for the expansion of the bottom. According to the *Economist,* "In 1973 64 percent of high-school–only men aged between 25 and 34 earned more than 20,000 (in 1987 dollars). By 1986, the ratio had dropped to 40 percent."[26]

Real wages declined in the 1980s for those with twelve years of schooling or less, whereas real wages rose for those with sixteen years of schooling or more. Economic returns to schooling surged to extraordinary highs during the 1980s. Consequently, the wage premiums for college graduates rose markedly between the early 1970s and the late 1980s.[27]

It is no surprise then that white male economic insecurity is overladen with status anxiety and impressions of relative deprivation. In comparison to other groups, white males have historically been the ones least affected by barriers (due to custom or segregation) in their choice of careers.[28] Neither women nor black men have faced a comparable increase in the degree of their insecurity. Although young less-educated male workers of all races have faced economic dislocation due to this industrial transition, young less-educated black men have not experienced the rising status anxiety perceived by their white counterparts.

When material rewards are valued because of their social prestige, they convey a positional or status value, independent of their intrinsic or use-based value. Competition for such rewards necessarily involves redistribution because status gains for some entail losses for others.[29] In this context, the advantage of being white is partly a status advantage. This benefit, termed "white skin privilege," has been receiving more attention from both historians and sociologists.[30] White skin privilege is thus a positional good. In other words, one of the benefits of white supremacy is that it confers a status or positional advantage, that is, white skin privilege. Consequently, as white supremacy declines, so does the value of white skin privilege.

Thus white supremacy's demise is responsible for the positional decline of white Americans, in other words the diminution of white skin privilege. Fundamentally, white supremacy insured that the status of whites would always be higher than that of blacks. However, the more intense economic competition of the last generation makes the loss of status due to declining white skin privilege more severe. Overall then, both positional and material competition have intensified as a byproduct of the demise of white supremacy. Hence, racial tensions increased because the demise of white supremacy and the diminution of white skin privilege upset the established racial status quo.

Economic Competition from New Groups

Nowadays educational credentials play a primary role in job allocation. But the supply of educated workers has risen much faster than the demand. In 1952, 2.2 managerial and professional jobs existed for each college graduate; by the early 1970s the ratio had dropped to 1.6.[31] More intense competition fuels economic insecurity, especially as women and minorities have entered occupations that once barred or substantially limited their numbers. Of course, the deteriorating earnings of the non–college-educated population increase the pressure to attend college and graduate. In combination the perception of relative deprivation for younger white males who face more intense competition is intensified.

Racial competition in employment has risen due to the increasing "credentialing" of minorities at a pace faster than the increase in "good jobs." Such competition provides a catalyst for a resurgence of racial conflict. Economic competition heightens discrimination in part because discrimination varies in accordance with employment conditions, worsening when unemployment rises, declining when it falls. Darity and Myers believe the magnitude of discrimination is linked to the employment needs of white males. As jobs traditionally held by white males are eliminated, they secure less attractive jobs at the expense of black males. The magnitude of discrimination therefore varies: intensifying when the dominant group's status is threatened. [32] It is no accident that, as widening earnings differentials grew during an economic downturn, the dismantling of affirmative action policies accelerated. This scenario is, however, inconsistent with the prominent thesis that racial conflict stemming from employment has been attenuated by the segmentation of labor markets, insulating many black and white workers from conflict stemming from competition for jobs.[33]

Consequently, as inequality has climbed over the last generation, so has the competition for good jobs. According to James Galbraith, "Affirmative action was first conceived, around 1965, under conditions of genuinely strong demand and short supply of skilled labor. The minorities and women who benefited from affirmative action were joining a wage structure characterized by declining wage and salary inequality and by rapidly increasing availability of good jobs. Under these conditions political opposition was minimal, for few could feel displaced by the success of those who were being assisted."[34]

However, the relative value of the prizes has increased. Galbraith believes that increasing inequality raises "the premium associated with passing through the most prestigious and prominent gateways."[35] Consequently, affirmative action provides an attractive target, and opposition to it resonates strongly because of the entry of blacks and women into positions that were once a nearly exclusive preserve of white males. For occupations in which whites and blacks compete, the presumption that blacks are unfairly aided by quotas, special programs, and the like contributes to a rise in racial antipathy. The view that black Americans' occupational upgrading is at least partly at the expense of whites is a conclusion supported by a number of investigators.[36] Sociologist Paul Burstein finds, for example, that in terms of group income shares the gap between white men and other groups has narrowed between 1953 and 1978.[37] But affirmative action's symbolic significance is magnified well beyond its actual impact since only about half the private sector noneducation workforce is covered by statutes.[38]

Affirmative action's social and political resonance stems from its role as a microfoundation—a compelling base motivation—for conflict in the workplace while simultaneously displacing anxieties about future economic security. In other words, because of affirmative action, anxieties due to growing economic insecurity are creatively translated into a preoccupation that at times becomes an obsession regarding the gains made by minorities.

Political scientist Paul Peretz has used the term "demand transference" to describe situations in which "people whose financial situation is getting worse for reasons unrelated to inflation, such as a decline in demand for their occupational skills, or a reduction in overall demand due to recession, come to blame their misfortune on inflation rather than on its real cause."[39] Given the declining demand for less-educated and less-skilled workers, "racial transference" heightens racial tensions by providing a focus and scapegoat for anxieties stemming from economic insecurity. Affirmative action thus becomes a foil for anxieties stemming from economic transformations.

Although the end of white supremacy alone creates positional losses, the concurrence of wage stagnation encourages the cause of those material losses to be misinterpreted. Those whose living standards are most threatened are also the ones most prone to fear the diminished positional advantage of being white. These individuals are most often in conflict with blacks for dwindling resources.

Growing Inequality and Political Mobilization

There is little question that difficult economic conditions intensify racial antagonisms. It is, therefore, not surprising that the dominant economic trends of the last generation have fueled a resurgence of racial antagonism. In a nutshell, the transformation of the nation's industrial base has created an economic environment marked by more intense economic competition. As economic competition intensifies, racial polarization increases.

Arguably, occupational displacement from unionized manufacturing employment to nonunionized service employment has sparked conservative political mobilization. Even though American unions are conservative by cross-national standards, industrial unions in the United States have consistently supported equalization and social justice since the New Deal. Economists Richard Freeman and James Medoff have shown that, on balance, industrial unions' wage and employment policies promote greater economic equalization.[40] The role of industrial unions in political coalitions that support progressive causes is also well established. Hence, by shifting employment from union-organized mass production to less organized and unorganized occupations, deindustrialization has undermined a major bulwark of social reform.

The decline of mass production industries especially diminishes the supply of good jobs available to non–college graduates. Although service industries are not uniformly hostile to unionization, the net effect of the absence of strong unions in rapidly growing service occupations is the diminution of union benefits. As the benefits of effective unions are restricted to an ever-smaller proportion of workers, the base of support for such benefits shrinks even more. Thus support for strong unions has become an electoral loser in ever more areas of the country, even for example, in the industrialized Northeast and Midwest, which have historically been their greatest regions of strength.

Political conflict over the distribution of good jobs is shaped by shifting alignments within the party system and strengthens such trends. Difficult economic conditions alone frequently cause rightward shifts in the political agenda. But the electoral volatility of middle- and working-class whites has made the allegiance of these voters especially valuable. Their frequent departure from the Democratic Party is closely attuned to their increasing discomfort with greater intraparty competition with newly emerging constituencies (blacks, women, and Hispanics) and the embrace of civil rights by the national Democratic Party. For middle- and working-class white males a multiplicity of resentments coalesce around the presumption that minorities are unfairly advantaged, that contemporary welfare state programs offer few benefits for whites, and that higher taxes to pay for such benefits, primarily for those unlike oneself, are unacceptable. Moreover, the reliance on regressive public financing sources such as sales and excise taxes inflames already high antitax sentiments and antiminority resentments.

The changes that have been occurring in urban politics, specifically the increased competitiveness of racial and ethnic minorities, also contribute to this perception that minorities garner unfair and unearned advantages. Political machines function by favoring some groups at the expense of others.[41] Disadvantaged groups have historically served as outsiders, bearing the brunt of the burden for the privileges accruing to insiders. Traditionally, those left out were invariably minorities, but increasing rates of political participation, changes in legal statutes, and suburbanization have combined to make minorities a plurality if not an outright majority in a number of cities. Larger minority populations reduce the possibility of maintaining the nonreciprocal relationships between political organizations and minority constituents that once typified American cities.

What is essential in sustaining the antiminority and antiblack thrust of modern "New Right" conservativism, however, is this relative deterioration in the life chances of white males who have historically formed the most privileged race by gender stratum. According to political scientist Joel Krieger, "The prism of decline tends to refract national interest into divided particularistic and sectional interests and to reduce the political/electoral utility to which a governing party can put promises of welfare provision."[42] In essence, economic hard times fuel rising racial polarization and racial antagonisms, thereby undermining major components of the welfare state.

The backlash against affirmative action is a clarion call to those facing uncertain prospects and increasing insecurity. Its message is tailored to those who reasonably expected to enjoy a privileged access to the pool of good jobs and relatively high standards of living. Moreover, since affirmative action programs grew most rapidly in an era of considerable wage stagnation, the false inference that such programs are responsible for stagnant wages gained credibility.

Affirmative action, in essence, was a convenient scapegoat. Like most scapegoats, it contained a kernel of truth: in this case, the perception that some whites have lost jobs to some blacks. Yet affirmative action's political potency as a cause of backlash is a consequence of the intense economic competition of the times. Consequently, affirmative action offers a comforting perception of unfair and unearned advantages to white Americans who find themselves competing with blacks. Grievances attributable to affirmative action can be found in virtually any situation in which racial distinctions exist among individuals and groups who compete for material resources. This applies particularly to the threat posed for the newest and most recent entrants into the labor market. As competition for privilege and status becomes more intense, so does racial conflict.

The result is that the symbolic significance of affirmative action resonates far beyond its actual impact. Fears that surface as resentment to affirmative action incorporate anxieties stemming from several sources: the dynamic effects of labor markets, current economic transformation, and social policy. Affirmative action consequently serves as a useful foil in translating anxieties attributable to economic insecurity, interracial political competition, and continuing apprehensions about minorities into a potent source of conservative political mobilization. Hence, racial equality is perceived, perhaps inevitably, as imposing losses on whites, and especially on those whites whose life chances are diminishing as well. Thus the growing economic inequality of recent years has given affirmative action symbolic significance far greater than its actual impact.

Has Racial Progress Stalled?

There is evidence that progress made by black Americans in a number of professions is not simply being eroded but is actually being reversed. Government civil rights enforcement agencies have become "paper tigers." The Equal Employment Opportunity Commission no longer operates as a law enforcement agency, choosing negotiated settlements with little threat of litigation leading to minimal substantive compliance with equal opportunity statutes. Employment discrimination has become a domain in which the victims have become primarily responsible for dealing with violators.[43] The lack of enforcement has stalled further progress in removing barriers. Meanwhile, the economic progress of black Americans has stalled. Blacks remain overrepresented in relatively menial occupations and in the public sector. Nursing aides and orderlies, hotel maids, taxicab and bus drivers, security guards and janitors are occupations in which black Americans are overrepresented in comparison to what one might expect given their proportion of the American population.[44] The setbacks in racial progress are also apparent in high-paying blue-collar work. The Philadelphia Plan discussed earlier in this chapter was initially successful, as unions recruited black workers into their apprenticeship programs. Black membership in skilled trades rose dramatically from zero percent in the 1960s to approximately 15 percent by 1995. However, blacks are finding it more difficult to work in unionized skill trades, a consequence of both the difficult economy and the preferences of white foremen for white relatives and friends. Consequently, unionized white workers earn roughly 25 percent more than unionized black workers.[45] Similarly while there are plenty of black waiters in New York City, for example, there are not many in mid- to high-priced restaurants. Waiters at the best New York City restaurants earn between $40,000 to $70,000 a year, sometimes even more.[46]

Blacks are strongly underrepresented in such well-paid occupations as engineers, physicians, architects, and lawyers.[47] A survey of the twelve highest grossing law firms in the country revealed that while the number of minority associates has reached 8 percent, only 5 percent of minority lawyers were promoted to partner.[48]

Racial barriers are prevalent in many white-collar occupations. For many mid-level white male managers the inclusion of minorities and women in management is a direct threat to their advancement prospects. They fear their competitive advantage is eroding. Mid-level corporate white male managers thus perceive a loss of opportunity. Actually the odds of reaching the top are roughly the same as they were thirty years ago. But the gender and skin color of their competition has changed. According to a report by the Federal Glass Ceiling Commission, "White men have circled the wagons against challengers whom they view not in terms of their merit but in terms of their color and their sex. In hearings across the country, commission members heard hundreds of top- and mid-level managers, male and female, testify that white men were stymieing the progress of women and minorities."[49]

White male managers in intermediate positions are most threatened by newcomers, and their perspective is typically underestimated by CEOs. According to sociologists Joe Feagin and Melvin Sikes, "The replacement of old white males by new white males in an organization's promotional system provides an important form of reassurance in the face of uncertainty about performance measurement in high-reward, high-prestige positions. . . . Management positions become easily closed to people who are different."[50] Sociologist Rosabeth M. Kanter, in a study of corporate behavior, argues that within corporate hierarchies, affirmative action is most resented by those most vulnerable to competition from women and minorities.[51] Inadvertently, the resistance to hiring minorities for upper-echelon positions works in favor of those few who are included—who are, in the words of one CEO, often stolen, pirated, and seduced to change jobs, and do so frequently. But more generally, corporations' unwritten codes limit minority advancement. Their internal labor markets rely on networks and informal mechanisms. If CEOs and senior management do not show that minority inclusion is a top priority, the actions of mid-level supervisors will prevent minorities from competing for top-level positions.[52]

In order to evaluate disparities in life chances, measures of intergroup equality are necessary. In particular, changes in the magnitudes of group shares provide an indication of changes in the life chances of respective group members. Undoubtedly black Americans have made considerable gains, but the racial gap remains considerable. Starting in the 1950s, it is clear that the relative advantage that white males have had over non-white males and females and white females has declined substantially. Paul Burstein believes that "since the early 1950s, however, nonwhite men and women and white women have all gained relative to white men, whose relative incomes have fallen from 175 percent of parity in 1953 to 156 in 1978."[53] However, the primary counterpart to the losses of white men has been gains by white women.

The persistence of disparate income returns to schooling by race conveys the considerable distance yet to go to reach equality. Black men with high school diplomas earn $786 for every $1,000 earned by white men with high school diplomas. Black men with bachelor's degrees earn $764 for every $1,000 earned by white men with bachelor's degrees.[54] Furthermore, since the mid- to late 1980s highly educated black males have experienced a greater relative income decline than their less-educated counterparts.[55] Current racial income and wealth disparities have multiple causes. However, the reliance on human capital explanations so beloved by mainstream economists and politicians have several clear deficiencies: (1) no matter how black/white groups are matched on human capital characteristics of education and experience blacks do substantially worse in earnings, and (2) black/white income differentials increase at higher education levels. Thus Darity and Myers conclude that "independent of the relative quality black males present to the labor market, processes persist that exclude them from comparable participation with non-black males with similar productivity-linked characteristics. To put it bluntly, discrimination in a comprehensive sense lies at the core of matters, not just at the point of employment but throughout an entire range of stages that affect labor market outcomes."[56]

Numerous indicators suggest that the absolute disparity in income between blacks and whites is not decreasing and that for some subgroups racial income disparity is on the rise. Absolute disparity can be just as important as relative disparity because the existence of a substantial absolute income differential indicates substantial differences in opportunities and quality of life.[57] Such growth in the absolute gap in income is inconsistent with the widely shared premise that inequality between the races is declining. Furthermore, the racial gap is widest when education levels are the greatest.

Another reason for pessimism concerning the current stalling of racial progress is that black Americans remain the most segregated ethnic/racial group in the nation. Their racially segregated residential patterns are not solely an underclass phenomenon. Residential segregation is a common experience for middle-class blacks as well.[58] Feagin and Sikes argue that a significant dimension of modern racism is the racially motivated "blocking of space," whereby blacks venturing into historically white spaces are brought to understand that such sites remain for "whites only," or at minimum it remains up to whites to determine who can be present and who is excluded.[59] Similarly, C. Eric Lincoln believes that race and place have forged distinctive white and black worlds, worlds that have contact, may overlap and collide, but never merge.[60]

For example, enduring residential segregation decisively influences access to employment. The relocation of manufacturing jobs to the suburbs makes them inaccessible to black inner city residents in several ways. Relocation hampers employment for blacks by: (1) increasing their transportation costs due to the greater distance of work from their neighborhoods of residence; (2) increasing the difficulties of acquiring information about job openings; and (3) stigmatizing blacks due to the location of their residences.[61] Thus, the combination of a changing economy and persistent residential racial segregation reduces employment opportunities considerably for many disadvantaged black Americans.

Ultimately then, the evidence available from a variety of source points in much the same direction: there are (1) enduring and even increasing gross racial disparities in numerous occupations, especially in high-level positions; (2) persistent and growing differentials in returns from schooling (increased earnings per an additional year of school) for blacks and whites, especially at the upper end of such distributions; (3) persistent absolute gaps in income and wealth; and (4) reduced employment opportunities for those black Americans in the lower tier of the economic spectrum, as a result of stable residential segregation. Whether in isolation or in combination such evidence clearly suggests that life chances of black and white Americans remain unequal, and that racial inequality will not disappear in the foreseeable future.

Has Discrimination Moved Underground?

The situation many black men in particular confront is one in which the competitive marketplace fails to prevent discrimination because the costs of discrimination can rarely be directly linked to discrete discriminatory acts. Hence, collusion may not be necessary to maintain discrimination. Rather, what may be in operation is analogous to the economic theory of insiders and outsiders used to account for wage increases during periods of persistently high unemployment. Those employed inside a firm are not perfectly interchangeable with outsiders—their experience generates a premium, but this premium allows insiders to resist the hiring of outsiders, whether overtly or covertly.[62]

The adaptation of this model to the problem of racial discrimination is fairly straightforward. Getting hired depends not simply upon the capacity to carry out tasks effectively, but on the sense that other employees will be comfortable with the new hires. Much like integrating neighborhoods or schools, insiders may not resist the employment of a few black male workers, but will strongly resist the employment of substantial numbers. A tipping point is reached whereby increases in the proportion of blacks beyond a certain magnitude dramatically intensify resistance to hiring more. Because profits are rarely attributable to the performance of any single individual but rather result from the interactions of whole divisions, departments, perhaps even the entire firm, policies that create permeable barriers to the employment of outsiders will not be regarded as cutting into profits. This is especially true when such practices are supported by stereotypes regarding the difficulty of blacks (especially black males) in fitting in. The result is that the status quo is not disturbed. Consequently, inherent difficulties in measuring the contribution of individuals to a joint product may impede the elimination of discrimination, thereby reinforcing a racially discriminatory status quo.

Yet stereotypes do not simply allow racial discrimination to survive in the midst of ambiguity, they also allow it to survive in the face of concrete evidence of achievement. At times, the resistance to integration is a consequence of stereotypes that suggest that blacks are not "team players" or "management material." Such perceptions can be used to justify workplace discrimination, and by protecting any individual from responsibility for a discriminatory judgment, make it elusive to pinpoint. The result will be to deny rewards in spite of evidence of clear achievement.

A Post–Affirmative Action Era

Verdicts on the usefulness of race-based preferences reflect different perceptions of whether a level playing field has been achieved and the objectives of public policy fulfilled. Certainly the distance between the races in terms of their perspectives on racial progress remains considerable. According to a 1993 *New York Times*/CBS News poll, 38 percent of whites but only 27 percent of blacks believe current race relations are generally good. Fifty-four percent of whites but only 45 percent of blacks believe race relations are better than twenty-five years ago. Finally, 66 percent of blacks but only 28 percent of whites believe that preferential hiring and promotion of blacks should be used to compensate for past discrimination.[63]

What might counter recent trends favoring increasing racial inequality? There is certainly little reason to believe that competitive markets and recent advances in black political participation will, unaided, narrow the substantial and in some cases increasing racial differentials present in American life. The current trends in the American political economy have intensified economic competition. The parsimonious level of the citizen wage and the limited and declining proportion of public goods available to the population at large sharpen competitive pressures, enhancing the segmentation of life chances by race. Nowhere is this more important than for the 30 percent of black children below the poverty line (by comparison to the 12 percent of white children).[64]

The rollback of affirmative action that began during the Reagan administration is a compelling indicator of the growing opposition to affirmative action. Reagan's attorney general William French Smith, assistant attorney general for civil rights William Bradford Reynolds, and EEOC chairman Clarence Thomas initiated quiet, behind-the-scene maneuvers to undo affirmative action. In 1985, during Reagan's second term, the Justice Department chose to support white firefighters and engineers in Birmingham, Alabama who claimed to have been denied promotions in favor of blacks. In 1986, the U.S. Commission on Civil Rights requested a one-year moratorium in federal programs that set aside contracts for minority businesses.

Reagan's conservative appointments to the Supreme Court made possible the 1989 *Wards Cove v. Atonia* decision in which the Court revised its earlier *Griggs* ruling, holding that employers no longer had to show that business practices that caused disparate impact were essential, only that they were convenient.[65] The Supreme Court in *City of Richmond v. Croson* (1989), ruled against the city of Richmond's plan to set aside 30 percent of contracts for minority-owned companies. The Court termed affirmative action a "highly suspect tool" that must be used with "strict scrutiny."[66]

In the 1995 case of *Adarand Constructors v. Pena,* the Court limited the available justifications for affirmative action programs. The Court ruled five to four "that programs that extend advantages to minorities and women must serve a compelling national interest and must be narrowly tailored to protect as much as possible the rights of white men."[67] In the 1996 case *Hopwood v. Texas* the U.S. Court of Appeals for the Fifth Circuit ended the University of Texas Law School's affirmative action program, a program that used numerical goals to increase the school's admission of underrepresented groups. Guided by the Supreme Court's *Croson* ruling, the judges of the Fifth Circuit concluded that university affirmative action plans were unconstitutional.[68]

Since *Hopwood*, the percentage of black freshmen admitted has declined to 2.7 percent. In comparison, the percentage of black freshmen admitted ranged between 4.1 percent and 5.6 percent over the preceding five years. In 1992, blacks were 8.1 percent of the entering class, but just 0.9 percent afterward. Furthermore, according to University of Texas law professor Doug Laycock these percentages understate the impact of the *Hopwood* Court decision due to the considerable growth of the minority population.[69] Although this case does not establish a national precedent, it reflects the clear trend in court rulings.

In 1996, California voters passed Proposition 209 forbidding the consideration of race, sex, or national origin in hiring or school admission decisions. In 1998, voters in the state of Washington followed California's lead, eliminating preferences in government hiring and school admissions.[70]

However, the Court reversed course in the June 2003 case of *Grutter v. Bollinger* (University of Michigan Law School). The Court ruled that "narrowly tailored race conscious" admission policies as employed by the University of Michigan Law School were permissible. Simultaneously, it rejected the university's position in the parallel *Gratz v. Bollinger* (University of Michigan undergraduate) case. Here the court ruled six to three that the undergraduate admissions policy employed an unacceptably mechanical quota. According to *New York Times* legal correspondent Linda Greenhouse, "The Supreme Court preserved affirmative action in university admissions by a one-vote margin but with a forceful endorsement of the role of racial diversity on campus in achieving a more equal society." According to Justice O'Connor, the law school's "holistic" and "individualized" consideration of race was not only acceptable but also, at least for the next twenty-five years, necessary to achieve a more equal society.[71] This decision clearly goes against the grain of the Court's recent decisions on affirmative action. It is possible that the Court's moderates, especially Justice O'Connor, were unwilling to take their opposition to affirmative action to its logical conclusion and effectively end its use in higher education. Still it may be optimistic to believe that the Michigan law school case will serve as a strong precedent.

Overt racial discrimination has undoubtedly declined, but it is in no danger of disappearing. The current status of race in the United States reflects its continued relevance and suggests the country has a very long way to go before race ceases to be a significant factor in American life. Given the disparities in earnings, total income, and group share broken down by race and sex in the United States, it will take another full century of projecting recent trends before the gap between the races by sex is eliminated, if ever. Hence it is likely that current labor market disadvantages will be transmitted for (at least) several generations to come.[72]

Undoubtedly there are innocent victims of affirmative action or of any other government policies and some beneficiaries who were not personally victimized. Yet on balance the perspective that many white Americans are innocent victims ignores the benefits they receive from residential segregation and employment discrimination, both practices that aid white Americans at the expense of black Americans. Moreover, American society is one in which people are evaluated based on their race every day—with greatest consequences in employment, residence, education, and the criminal justice system. And of course affirmative action opponents often overlook the significant successes of affirmative action, as in the growth of a sizable middle-income black community.

Nonetheless, the implementation of policies to achieve racial equality is perceived, perhaps inevitably, as imposing losses on whites, and especially on whites whose life chances are diminishing as well. The conflict is therefore perhaps unavoidable. Inevitably, affirmative action symbolizes a fundamental cleavage in American society, based upon competing claims upon economic rewards. The limits of what can be attained by minorities with limited power resources are revealed by the impasse that has been reached as opponents of affirmative action have succeeded in redefining the issue such as to appear to support justice and fairness. Political opposition to affirmative action is fueled by a backlash that concentrates anxieties from disparate sources.

Also unsurprising is that the dilemmas of affirmative action confront the interwoven obstacles of race and class. Affirmative action is both a response to the limited and emaciated structure of social provision of the American welfare state and a consequence of it. Ultimately, we are forced to confront the issue, Just how racially divided are we? Are we "a society deeply divided by lines of race, ethnicity, or religion [that] must be organized as a federation of groups"? as Abigail Thernstrom depicts the consequences of affirmative action.[73] Are separate groups the equivalent of separate nations? is the question asked by opponents of affirmative action. Yet those who reject the view that racial divisions are an enduring feature of American life need to confront the considerable evidence that racial barriers persist, and that the equalization of life chances by race has stalled.

Thus, the conservative critique of affirmative action strains credulity in its assumption that key decision makers and institutional structures are now capable of an objectively dispassionate neutrality on racial matters.[74] One can only be skeptical of the proposition that three hundred years of near total commitment to white supremacy could be eradicated by forty years of an all too often lethargic commitment to civil rights. As former deputy attorney general Nicholas Katzenbach and former assistant attorney general Burke Marshall point out, "forbidding the use of affirmative action is to proceed as if discrimination were extinct."[75] Contemporary opponents of affirmative action and other dramatic measures to foster equality share the optimism of nineteenth-century liberals who believed that simply removing legal barriers is sufficient to create a fair race. According to historian George Fredrickson:

> The assumption of antislavery reformers that equal opportunity for nonwhites would result from the substitution of contract for status in the economic realm proved to be utopian. It was based on a conception of progress that underestimated the capacity of the old racial order to adapt to changing economic and legal conditions and failed to foresee how privileged groups within a capitalistic society could accentuate traditional racial divisions and distinctions for their own advantage. . . . The ideology of free labor and free men . . . was much less effective in averting more subtle forms of labor coercion that had the outward appearance of contractual arrangements freely entered into.[76]

However, nineteenth-century liberals could not know what twentieth-century conservatives should: Emancipation did not lead to the abolition of race-based barriers and to equality between the races. Rather, slavery was followed by a century of segregation and intensive racial discrimination. Thus, the race-conservative presumption is both unduly optimistic and questionable in light of the historical legacy of discrimination. Justice Thomas's dissent in the 2003 University of Michigan cases offers a prime illustration of such historical blindness. He quotes Frederick Douglass, referring to what Americans should do with blacks: "The American people have always been anxious to know what they shall do with us. . . . I have had but one answer from the beginning. Do nothing with us! If the apples will not remain on the tree of their own strength, if they are worm-eaten at the core, if they are early ripe and disposed to fall, let them fall. And if the negro cannot stand on his own legs, let him fall also." [77]

A common presumption of race conservatives is that competitive markets necessarily reduce discrimination. But this belief reflects a commitment to free market theology that has never been shown to possess any empirical validity. Competitive pressures do not prevent employers from practicing discrimination nor do they even necessarily discourage it. In actuality the view that economic competition does little to undermine racial discrimination has been verified time and time again in so many contexts that the notion that economic competition undermines discrimination can only be attributed to the deep-rooted power of ideology.

Certainly the significance of race is declining if one takes a long view, over the entire twentieth century for example. Yet any conclusion that race is no longer a substantial factor diminishing the life chances of black Americans and thus that black Americans face a level playing field is hasty and inconsistent with a great deal of evidence. Many fear the prospect that if equality is the goal, special measures will have to continue for a very long time, as is argued by sociologist Christopher Jencks. But what is also true is that a projection of current trends suggests that unless strong measures are taken, which include some kind of assistance for substantial numbers of black Americans, racial inequality will continue for a very, very long time.[78]

2

Racial Politics and Stable Majorities

From the 1930s to the 1950s interparty polarization over racial issues was prevented by the heterogeneous racial attitudes within each party. For much of this period the civil rights policies of each major party were broadly similar: individual congressmen proposed civil rights legislation, both parties as a whole responded tactically, emphasizing or underplaying their commitment to civil rights depending upon their respective perceptions of the electoral consequences.

In the late 1950s there were more liberal northern Republicans than liberal northern Democrats. Republicans were freer to address racial concerns given the South's insignificance in their electoral calculations. They did not confront a chasm on racial issues necessitating straddling hostile constituencies —a situation encouraging as much fudging of the issues as possible—as did liberal northern Democrats. However, the 1958 midterm elections brought to a close an era of bipartisan avoidance of race. The catalyst for this dramatic change was the replacement of eleven Republicans senators by Democrats, all but one racial liberals. There was now a constituency of northern liberal senators large enough to articulate an agenda on racial matters in opposition to that of racially conservative southern senators.

Both parties competed for votes in a climate favoring racial liberalism. Neither party was consistently more favorable toward civil rights, and neither could take black voters for granted. Black voters' defection from the Democrats in 1956 reinforced this quandary. By being willing to vote for Republicans as well as Democrats, black voters forced the parties to compete for their votes. Such tactical flexibility complemented the declining economic inequality of the postwar era. Ultimately, dramatic progress in race relations was rooted in declining economic inequality—improving the life chances of the masses of black Americans—and an increasingly hospitable political climate. The decline in economic inequality was a product of a number of conditions: the decline of sharecropping and the migration of blacks into the industrial workforce; the increasing number of blacks finishing high school and attending college, and their movement into white-collar occupations. This topic will be addressed in detail in Chapter 4. Enhanced political competition for the black vote would be vital in accelerating the pace of racial progress. Unfortunately, the era of vigorous political competition for black votes would be short lived.

In 1964 Barry Goldwater led the Republicans to a disastrous defeat. But from this defeat a foundation for future success was laid. The Republicans' rightward shift hastened the political polarization on civil rights issues. Black Americans emphatically rejected Goldwater Republicanism. Goldwater received a postwar low—just 8 percent of the black vote. Goldwater's campaign marks the beginnings of the almost complete alienation of blacks from the Republican Party. The Goldwater debacle spurred the replacement of racially liberal Republicans by racially liberal Democrats. Meanwhile, more conservative Republicans were beginning to emerge in traditionally liberal states, such as California. Whereas in 1955 two-thirds of racial liberals were Republicans, a decade later less than one-fifth of racial liberals in Congress were Republicans. The racial transformation of the parties reflected mirror images—the Republicans lost racial liberals and gained racial conservatives, the Democrats gained racial liberals and lost racial conservatives. During the 1960s and 1970s, the liberal wing of the Republican Party, sometimes termed Rockefeller Republicans, declined steadily, matched by the demise of the Democrats' southern segregationist bloc and its replacement by racially moderate, albeit conservative, southern senators. These southern Democrats were more liberal on race than were their southern Republican counterparts.[1]

The career of Edward M. Brooke illustrates the Republican transition. In 1966 Brooke was elected to the United States Senate. He was the first black American to be directly elected to the Senate (Reconstruction-era black senators were selected by their state legislatures, in accordance with the rules in existence before the Seventeenth Amendment). Senator Brooke was elected from liberal Massachusetts and maintained a generally liberal voting record. He would serve two terms in the Senate, and was perhaps best known for his opposition to the policies of an increasingly conservative Nixon administration. He voted against the unsuccessful nominations of Clement F. Haynesworth and G. Harrold Carswell and the successful nomination of William H. Rehnquist. The first senator to call publicly for Richard Nixon's resignation, he would be defeated by Paul Tsongas in 1978.

Edward Brooke's Senate career epitomizes the odyssey of the Republican Party. As a liberal Republican he was at odds with an increasingly conservative Republican administration and party. Brooke was elected to the Senate during the relatively brief era of bipartisan racial enlightenment. However, by 1978 conservative Republicans had mounted a serious challenge to incumbent president Gerald Ford, and Ronald Reagan was just two years away from the presidency. With the demise of liberal Republicanism and the greater influence of the "New Right," Republicans became much more antagonistic to the material interests and life chances of black Americans. During the 1980s, racial polarization increased due largely to rightward shifts in the U.S. House and Senate and three Republican presidential victories. The result was a political environment less friendly to the aspirations and needs of most black Americans.

Race and Contemporary Party Politics

During the 1960s, civil rights issues became more salient. As long as internal divisions within the parties outweighed the divisions between them, civil rights issues were submerged. However, as partisan differences about race began to emerge, civil rights moved closer to the forefront of the public debate. As a result, racial polarization over civil rights issues grew rapidly.

In general, partisan competition on race grew only when within-party differences became less salient than between-party differences. From the 1920s to the 1950s, more liberal positions on racial issues by Democrats were thwarted by their powerful segregationist bloc, a group sufficiently strong to exercise a veto over legislation. In the 1930s, southern Democratic senators began to use filibusters to prevent movement on racial issues. In the 1950s, a series of bills to protect civil rights were introduced in Congress. The inability to invoke cloture—restricting debate and ending filibusters—assured their failure. Hence, for a time political polarization over racial issues was stymied by the heterogeneous racial attitudes within each party. In effect, intraparty racial divisions prevented interparty racial divisions. The shift of constituencies that realigned the parties in the 1950s and 1960s made race an issue of partisan competition.

The 1964 Civil Rights Act ratcheted upward the Democratic Party's commitment to civil rights quite decisively. Yet the cost of strengthening ties to liberals—black and white—was weakening those to white southern Democrats. Democrat political support among southern whites has declined steadily since 1944.[2] Ever larger majorities of white southerners have refused to support national Democratic Party candidates in presidential elections since 1964. As a consequence of the growing support of Democratic presidents for civil rights—in truth, a mixture of tepid support by the Kennedy administration and robust support by the Johnson administration—Republicans have had greater opportunities to make inroads into the South. Both Barry Goldwater and Richard Nixon sought to capitalize on white southerners' resentment of civil rights advances. By the 1970s the Democrats—both activists and elites—had become the party of racial liberals, a process that accelerated with the 1964 election. The Democrats became more ideologically consistent as the economic liberalism of the New Deal merged with racial liberalism. This reaction spawned a counterreaction as the Republicans moved toward the other end of the spectrum. They began to espouse limited government intervention more consistently—both in terms of the economy and on racial issues. Such increasing ideological consistency reflected increased partisan polarization. Conservative politicians increasingly came to see the road to electoral success as one built upon racially loaded imagery, reflecting and exploiting the electoral opportunities provided by resurgent racial antagonisms.

Republicans and Democrats, in effect, repositioned themselves on racial issues. Since 1964, the switch in partisan allegiances has led to the supreme irony that Democratic attention to black interests has spurred a countermovement of whites to the Republican Party. Republicans have not advocated a return to the Jim Crow era of segregation. But they have routinely chosen a series of presidential nominees who favored more gradual and at times even a glacial pace of racial progress: (1) Barry Goldwater, who voted against the Civil Rights Act of 1964; (2) the Richard Nixon of 1968, who became a vehement opponent of busing and nominated ardent segregationists Haynesworth and Carswell to the Supreme Court, and was very different from the Richard Nixon of 1960, who competed for votes in a climate favoring racial liberalism, due in large measure to Nelson Rockefeller's candidacy for the nomination that stressed his (Rockefeller's) racial liberalism; (3) Ronald Reagan (about whom much more will be said later); and (4) George Bush, who, in the 1980s, opposed the extension of civil rights laws. Through their actions, Republican presidents and presidential contenders have made their appeal to whites in racial terms clear. This trend continued in 1996 as Bob Dole sought to use opposition to affirmative action to attract the votes of "Reagan Democrats."

In 1992, William Jefferson Clinton, admittedly a moderately conservative Democrat, was elected president. Clinton would become the first Democrat to win a presidential election since Jimmy Carter in 1976. Clinton had the advantage of a three-way race. Without Ross Perot's strong showing (Perot received 19 percent of the vote), Clinton probably would not have been elected. Although it was clear that Clinton, like, Carter was not especially liberal, many Democrats believed that they would finally have a president willing to reverse the conservative and often antiblack policies of the previous generation of Republican presidents.

This belief may have been primarily wishful thinking given Bill Clinton's determination to distinguish himself from "traditional" liberal Democrats. As governor, Clinton was notable for his unwavering support for the death penalty. To drive this point home he had even rushed back to Arkansas while campaigning before the 1992 New Hampshire primary to be present in the state during the execution of a brain-damaged Arkansas prisoner, Ricky Ray Rector. Or consider Clinton's outspoken—or as some would have termed it, opportunistic—denunciation of Sister Souljah, a popular young rap singer of the 1980s whose performances were considered antithetical to "family values."

Yet liberal optimism concerning the Clinton presidency came not only from his election, but also from the influence of his more liberal spouse, Hillary Rodham Clinton, as well as from the 1992 election victories of six moderate-to-liberal women to the United States Senate in the wake of the Clarence Thomas/Anita Hill controversy. There was thus good reason to think that Democrats might be able to reverse a number of the conservative trends that impeded racial progress during the Reagan-Bush era. Almost immediately, however, it became clear that such hopes were unlikely to be met. Ironically, the case that most clearly signaled Clinton's timidity was that of the (at the time) University of Pennsylvania law professor Lani Guinier, whose legal and political writings introduced the idea of majoritarian tyranny to a wider audience. Professor Guinier argued that in certain cases racial (and perhaps, ethnic) minorities face such extraordinary obstacles to having their policy preferences taken seriously that they were victims of "majoritarian tyranny." She argued that several alternative models of voting, such as plural voting, might serve as modest reforms to allow minority preferences to become law. She at no time advocated that minorities be granted fixed proportional representation, as her opponents depicted.

An old friend of the Clintons, Professor Guinier was nominated to be assistant attorney general for civil rights. The day after she was nominated, Clint Bolick, a well-known conservative, described her in a *Wall Street Journal* article as a "quota queen." He and other conservatives produce numerous press releases, reports, and op-ed pieces depicting Guinier as a left-wing extremist determined to subvert democracy. The press, following his lead, described Guinier as a radical who desired a "racial spoils system." The term "quota queen" was used by *Newsweek*, the *Washington Post*, *USA Today*, and the *Chicago Tribune*. The White House insisted that she not respond to the attacks, and finally President Clinton chose to withdraw her nomination before she could be examined by the Senate Judiciary Committee, on the dubious grounds that once he had actually read what she had written, he could no longer support the nomination.[3]

The withdrawal of the Guinier nomination before the nominee received the opportunity to air her views deprived the nation of a chance to hear positions, which are not often addressed within mainstream political discourse. Nor was Guinier's the only nomination hastily withdrawn by Bill Clinton, who was rapidly developing a reputation for political cowardice. The fiascos that surrounded the quick withdrawal of the nominations of Zoe Baird and Kimba Wood to be attorney general were other noteworthy examples. Yet Guinier's case involved political principles, while the Baird and Wood withdrawals were supposedly based on the nominees' personal peccadilloes.

Certainly Clinton's political cowardice compares unfavorably with Lyndon Johnson's willingness to nominate Thurgood Marshall, a far more controversial figure at the time given his role as legal counsel to the NAACP, to the Supreme Court—a lifetime appointment, no less. It compares unfavorably as well to George Bush's more recent willingness to stand by his nomination of Clarence Thomas to the Supreme Court, when that nomination ran into trouble before the Senate.

But perhaps more important than what it revealed of comparative presidential backbone is that the withdrawal of the Guinier nomination suggests that national Democratic leaders now believed, probably accurately, that they could take black voters for granted, that given twelve years of overt and covert hostility during the Reagan and Bush era, blacks and their liberal allies would have nowhere else to go. The apparent validity of this presumption is ironic because Guinier's treatment supports the thesis that she has become identified with—American democracy has become insulated from black interests. Consequently, black political and economic advancement is hampered by "majoritarian tyranny." According to Guinier, "Majority approval is legitimate *only* if we can assume that neither the majority nor the minority has disproportionate power. . . . Majority rule legitimates a voting procedure, if at all, only to the extent the procedure is fair. To be fair, a procedure must be more than just efficient." Hence, a system in which a permanent and homogenous majority consistently exercises disproportionate power is neither stable, accountable, nor reciprocal.[4]

Bill Clinton has had far more support among blacks than among whites. In 1992 he received 39 percent of the white vote, Bush received 40 percent, and Perot received 20 percent. Clinton received 83 percent of the 1992 black vote versus Bush's 10 percent and Perot's 7 percent. In 1996 Clinton received 43 percent of the white vote versus Dole's 46 percent and Perot's 9 percent. In comparison, he won 84 percent of the 1996 black vote to Dole's 12 percent and Perot's 4 percent.[5] In a sense Clinton has been able to use his considerable political skills to convey his empathy with the plight of black Americans, while simultaneously supporting measures that offered harsh social policies and draconian penal policies. Among the examples of draconian measures is his agreement to end welfare, as well as the most dramatic reductions in affirmative action programs since their beginnings. His administration modified or ended seventeen affirmative action programs between 1996 and 1998.[6] To be fair, President Clinton operated in a far different political and social environment than existed during the heyday of racial liberalism. But he also benefited from memories of the intense racial hostility black Americans received during the administrations of his immediate Republican predecessors, Ronald Reagan and George H.W. Bush. Thus if Clinton's presidency has proven to be less satisfactory for black Americans than many had hoped, it has been perceived as a substantial improvement upon the administrations of his immediate Republican predecessors.

Ronald Reagan and Contemporary Republicanism

From 1980 to 1992, a Republican conservative coalition dominated national elections. This coalition was forged through the repeated use of a "southern strategy" that sought to unite whites across class lines while paying scant attention to the interests of the majority of black voters. The success of this strategy reoriented social, political, and economic policies to more effectively insulate the majority from the minority. In creating a majority coalition, Republicans were able to fuse racial issues in a pseudo-populist fashion, which gave race the appearance of neutrality while its actual meaning was easily deciphered by virtually everyone.[7] According to political scientist John Petrocik, "Race conflict [has become] the major new element in the party system agenda."[8]

It is no accident that this consolidation occurred during the presidency of Ronald Reagan. No post–World War II president was more hostile to black interests than Ronald Reagan. Reagan's presidency compiled a record of enmity to the needs and interests of black Americans that would place him squarely in the mainstream of presidents a half century or more earlier. In the twentieth century, only Woodrow Wilson, who oversaw the segregation of Washington, D.C., was directly responsible for a greater level of racial animus. Not many prominent northern Republicans opposed both the Civil Rights Act and the Voting Rights Act, as did Reagan. Reagan clearly signaled his intentions during the 1980 presidential campaign when he told an audience of roughly 10,000 white Americans in Philadelphia, Mississippi, "I believe in states rights." It was no accident that these sentiments were expressed in the area where three civil rights workers—Michael Schwerner, Andrew

Goodman, and James Chaney—were brutally murdered in 1964. In the view of civil rights legend Andrew Young, "Reagan's affirmation of states' rights looks like a code word to me that it's going to be all right to kill niggers when he's President."[9] Reagan signed the twenty-five-year extension of the Voting Rights Act very grudgingly, and favored diminishing its scope. He initially opposed but later hesitantly accepted a federal holiday honoring Martin Luther King, Jr. His administration supported the effort of Bob Jones University to retain tax exemptions despite its racially discriminatory practices. This position was rejected by the Supreme Court by an eight-to-one margin. Reagan advocated ending affirmative action, and he was the first president since Andrew Johnson to veto a civil rights bill. Furthermore, of the 366 judges he appointed to the federal bench (more than half of the federal judiciary at the time), only seven were black.[10]

Although careful to avoid presenting himself as a virulent racist in the George Wallace mode, Reagan made a calculated use of both racial code words and an aggressive advocacy of policies that have done considerable harm to black Americans. According to political scientists Donald Kinder and Lynn Sanders, Reagan proved himself a master of "the new etiquette governing public discussion of race." "The new rules governing public discussion of race require not the abandonment of racism, but rather that appeals to prejudice be undertaken carefully, through indirection and subterfuge. Political debate on matters of race now often takes place in code. Racial code words make appeals to prejudice electorally profitable even when, as in contemporary American society, prejudice is officially off limits."[11]

Reagan's success was based on his capacity to make racial appeals coolly rather than in the hot-tempered mode of a George Wallace, Orville Faubus, or Lester Maddox. Relying on misleading and often deceitful anecdotes about welfare queens and food stamp chiselers, Reagan's image as a conservative but not racially bigoted candidate appealed to millions of white Americans, but very few blacks. Among major-party postwar candidates, only Barry Goldwater received a smaller percentage than the 9 percent Reagan received in 1984. Without standing in front of schools, barring black students, and by employing his legendary affability, Reagan helped to make racism, or at the very least racial policies that severely damaged the life chances of black Americans, eminently respectable. Ronald Reagan was both the most popular president since Franklin D. Roosevelt among white Americans and the most despised among black Americans. Blacks by a three-to-one margin viewed Reagan as a racist.[12]

Yet, perhaps the lowest depths of overt race-baiting in the post–World War II era of presidential campaigning by a major party candidate was undertaken not by Ronald Reagan, but by his vice president and successor,

George Bush. The 1988 Bush campaign successfully used racially loaded imagery in the infamous Willie Horton advertisements. Willie Horton was a black convict, who, while on a weekend furlough, raped a white woman. During the 1988 campaign, an "independent expenditure" group, Americans for Bush, spent over half a million dollars in one month for televisions ads about Willie Horton. A flier for Bush distributed by the state GOP in Maryland showed pictures of Democratic candidate Dukakis and Horton together with the message "Is This Your Pro-Family Team for 1988?" The Illinois State Republican Committee produced a pamphlet that continued the message that "All the murderers and rapists and drug pushers and child molesters in Massachusetts vote for Michael Dukakis." Bush campaign manager Lee Atwater told a group of southern Republicans just prior to the Democratic convention, "there is a story about a fellow named Willie Horton who, for all I know, may end up being Dukakis' running mate." Not long before he died Lee Atwater confessed that the decision to politicize the Willie Horton issue was made at the top echelons of the Bush campaign team. Willie Horton told *Playboy* magazine that a woman who identified herself as an employee of an organization related to the Bush campaign telephoned him and wrote him letters asking that he endorse Dukakis.[13]

According to a Bush campaign aide who helped produce the Horton commercials, "Willie Horton has star quality. Willie's going to be politically furloughed to terrorize again. It's a wonderful mix of liberalism and a big black rapist."[14] The stratagem worked well enough for some pundits to ask if the Democratic ticket consisted of Dukakis and Horton, instead of Dukakis and Bentsen!

True, George H.W. Bush and Lee Atwater's manipulative use of race appears to have been more a reflection of calculated opportunism than of deeply held conviction. But using racially loaded messages opportunistically rather than sincerely hardly constitutes mitigating circumstances. Kinder and Sanders examined survey responses before and after the Horton story became central to the campaign. They conclude that the Horton story helped to activate racial resentments, just as Republican strategists intended. Similarly, Andrew Kohut, Gallup poll director, believes racial intolerance was a substantial reason for whites to vote for Bush.[15]

Antiblack Republican rhetoric has not been limited to presidential candidates. Recently, Trent Lott has been the subject of heightened scrutiny because of comments he made praising Strom Thurmond's 1948 segregationist "states rights" presidential campaign. Lott argued that the nation would have been better off if Thurmond had won the election. At Senator Thurmond's one-hundredth birthday party, he said "I want to say this about my state: When Strom Thurmond ran for president, we voted for him. We're proud of it. And if the rest of the country had followed our lead, we wouldn't have had all these problems over all these years, either."[16]

At one level, the furor is surprising because Lott's views have been, in the words of *New York Times* columnist and Princeton economics professor Paul Krugman, "hidden in plain sight."[17] Senator Lott has been making similar comments throughout his political career. After a speech by Senator Thurmond at a Reagan campaign rally in Jackson, Mississippi, in 1980, then congressman Lott said "you know if we had elected this man thirty years ago, we wouldn't be in the mess we are today."

In 1984 Congressman Lott spoke to a gathering of the Sons of the Confederate Veterans. He followed up this speech with an interview in a magazine named *Southern Partisan*. "I think that a lot of the fundamental principles that Jefferson Davis believed in are very important to people across the country, and they apply to the Republican Party. . . . The Republican agenda from tax policy to foreign policy, from individual rights to neighborhood security are things that Jefferson Davis and his people believed in." At a library dedication in 1998, Lott said, "Sometimes I feel closer to Jefferson Davis than any other man in America." In 1979, Congressman Lott received the Jefferson Davis Medal from the United Daughters of the Confederacy for his role in the successful restoration of Jefferson Davis's American citizenship.

Nor are these merely thoughtless utterings. Lott's politics both before he entered electoral politics and after his election to Congress demonstrates behavior consistent with these views. In 1964, he led the opposition to the desegregation of his fraternity, Sigma Nu, at the University of Mississippi. He was also instrumental in keeping the national fraternity segregated. In 1968 he became a top aide to one of the House's leading segregationists, William Colmer, a vociferous opponent of the 1964 Civil Rights Act and 1965 Voting Rights Act. Congressman Lott voted against the Martin Luther King holiday and the 1982 extension of the Voting Rights Act. More recently, Senator Lott cast the only negative vote against Roger Gregory's nomination as the first black to serve on the Fourth Circuit of the U.S. Court of Appeals.[18] Senator Lott resigned as Senate majority leader in January 2003, after losing the support of the Bush administration.

Former attorney general John Ashcroft, however, has expressed similar views. In a 1998 interview in the same *Southern Partisan* magazine, Ashcroft called Confederates "patriots," arguing that they should not be regarded as having died for "some perverted agenda." Ashcroft helped to derail a federal judgeship for Missouri Supreme Court judge Ronnie White, the first black on the state's supreme court. Ashcroft also accepted an honorary degree and gave the commencement speech at Bob Jones University, an institution renowned for its opposition to interracial dating and marriages.[19]

The views of Lott and Ashcroft like those of Jesse Helms (to be discussed next) typify a party whose electoral success in the post–civil rights era has been built on the embrace of retrograde racial views and the evisceration of moderate Republicanism. When Republicans seek to neutralize the taint of bigotry, they rely heavily on symbolism, such as the parade of minority Republicans at the 2000 Republican national convention, a gathering in which it seemed as if every black Republican in attendance made an appearance on the podium.

Moreover, the successful campaigns of Ronald Reagan and the first George Bush highlight an important trend of the recent political era: unlike the 1950s, when a key to black advancement was the emergence of interparty competition for black votes, during the last generation, a different type of swing voter has become the object of interparty competition. The parties have been more likely to compete for voters with little sympathy for black Americans. Political scientist John Petrocik argued that the exit of white southerners from the Democrats and their willingness to vote for Republicans is the most dramatic shift of any group in the American electorate. According to Petrocik, between the 1950s and 1970s, "Southerners, who represent only about 20 percent of the electorate, contribute almost 39 percent of the change in partisanship that is found in the entire electorate."[20] In effect, the movement of conservative white southerners from the Democratic to the Republican Party made the Republican electoral core more uniform throughout the nation. According to Kinder and Sanders, "American national elections . . . are infected by racial troubles, they are mired in a racial predicament more than a generation in the making. The predicament is over campaign strategy, about how to frame winning appeals to the American public given the persistence of racial resentment."[21] Whereas Democrats resort to silence and evasion to attract conservative whites, Republicans rely upon racial code words. Racial code words are words or phrases that communicate "a well-understood but implicit meaning to part of a public audience while preserving for the speaker deniability of that meaning. . . . Code words are intended as rhetorical winks."[22] One of the more successful examples is Jesse Helms's infamous "white hands" advertisement depicting white hands crumpling a job application while a voice-over claims the job was awarded to a black applicant due to quotas.[23] Helms also claimed that his Democratic opponent, Harvey Gantt, supported quotas favoring blacks. Of course Helms has a well-earned reputation as an old school racial demagogue. In 1950, at the tender age of twenty-eight, Helms termed the University of North Carolina "the University of Negroes and Communists." Helms never supported any civil rights legislation. He conducted a month-long filibuster against a holiday honoring Martin Luther King, Jr. In the 1960s Helms argued that the Klan was as legitimate politically as the civil rights movement, a notion reminiscent of George Wallace's presidential primary campaign. Wallace neither endorsed segregation nor white supremacy in explicit terms. Instead he talked about violations of states rights, about law and order, about protecting property rights. Such allusions allowed Wallace to discuss race without actually mentioning it.[24]

In November 2003, former chairman of the Republican national committee Haley Barbour was elected governor of Mississippi. During the campaign Barbour announced that he would not ask the Council of Conservative Citizens, an anti-Semitic white supremacist organization, to remove his picture from their web site. Barbour argued that although some of the group's views were indefensible, he did not want to tell any group it could not use his picture. The web site displays Confederate flags and has links to articles titled "in defense of racism" and a book that denies the Holocaust. This tactic simultaneously appeals to those supportive of such sentiments while disclaiming responsibility for them on free-speech grounds. During the campaign, Barbour was also accused of using racial codes in linking the gubernatorial race to the separate race for lieutenant governor. Barbour repeatedly linked his Democratic opponent with the black candidate for lieutenant governor.[25] Such adroit maneuvers illustrate the use of racial codes.

The Emergence of a Conservative Majority Coalition

Republican strength in presidential elections from 1968 to 1988 was aided by the converging economic concerns of the party's supporters. Racial antipathy to blacks provided a valuable common denominator for key constituencies necessary to create a Republican majority. The votes most valued are those cast by white conservatives. According to Kinder and Sanders, "The balance in national elections now rests in the hands of what are often referred to as 'Reagan Democrats.'" Ordinarily, merging the agendas of affluent whites with middle- to working-class whites would be difficult. But they share opposition to government interventions that seek to aid black Americans. Policies to insure equal opportunity for blacks are clearly unpopular among whites. And such policies have grown more unpopular over the last twenty years, an era of more difficult economic conditions. According to Kinder and Sanders, "the divide between black and white on those race policies most central to the politics of the times seems if anything greater today than in any other period for which we have data."[26]

The polarization of public opinion on policies relating to race over the last generation parallels the polarization of the political parties on race. Such partisanship in an economic environment defined by slower economic growth and rising economic inequality has helped to widen the racial divide. Persistent, albeit at times submerged, racial antagonisms have been instrumental in the polarization of social and economic policy preferences.

The coalescence of affluent, middle-, and working-class whites into a majority coalition from 1968 to 1988 was based greatly upon their sharing of attitudes that can be termed "conservative populism." We might also term conservative populism the protection of white skin privilege. The less-sophisticated members of the electorate frequently use race as a concrete referent to help structure their political opinions.[27] Conservative populism solidified the alliance between upper-middle- and upper-income groups favoring anti–government-intervention libertarianism with the antipathy to social programs resonating among working- and lower-class white ethnics (who are often in direct competition with minorities for jobs, government benefits, and social services).

Yet the dominance of the majoritarian perspective is understated and perhaps even overshadowed by an emphasis on its role in partisan conflict. Even though conservative populism has disproportionately benefited Republicans, it cannot be reduced to a matter of strict partisanship. Conservative populism has succeeded in a political era marked by a decline in partisanship.

It is fair to say that the appeal of conservative populism stems partly from its autonomy from partisan strife. In essence, political parties are not the exclusive media for the message. Rather, the more intemperate expressions of racially charged sentiments outside the political mainstream allow antiblack conservative populism to provide both an alternative to partisan appeals (for example, one can simultaneously be antiminority and antiestablishment) and a base of support for politicians espousing policies consistent with such sentiments. Many of the target voters are nonpartisan, given that well-educated young Americans are less partisan than are those who are poorly educated.[28] Conservative populism thus facilitates good cop/bad cop tactics by which politicians can use code words tapping into grievances energized by activists outside the mainstream. Partly by the successful use of underlying racial resentments, political conservativism has become sufficiently powerful to be able to frequently define the terms of debate over social policy.

The addition of elite socioeconomic groups has created a new majoritarian coalition devoid of significant countervailing influences. In comparison, the efforts of liberal Democrats to build a coalition from more diverse constituencies—for example, blacks, Hispanics, women, unionized working-class whites, and upper-income liberals—resemble a pastiche composed of inconsistent and often contradictory interests. Such patchwork alliances frustrate efforts to form an alternative dominant political coalition. The problems confronted by Democrats in creating effective coalitions are exacerbated by the need to raise campaign funds from a comparatively smaller financial base than that of Republicans. Few of the issues dear to core Democrats—for example, civil rights, abortion rights, and the environment—are conducive to the task of raising campaign funds. Thus Democrats are typically dependent on a relatively small cadre of elite donors. Admittedly, Democrats have narrowed the more than five-to-one advantage Republicans had in campaign financing in 1981–82 ($39 million–Democrats versus $215 million–Republicans) to a less than two-to-one disparity by 1995–96 ($281 million–Democrats versus $474 million–Republicans). However, Republicans retain an immense advantage in "independent expenditures" (money spent to support or defeat a clearly identified candidate, without cooperation or consultation with the candidate or the candidate's campaign). Whereas $5.4 million was spent to support Democrats and defeat Republicans in 1995–96, $16.2 million was spent to defeat Democrats and support Republicans in 1995–96. Republicans thus retained a three-to-one advantage in independent expenditures. This disparity did not continue in the 2004 election. John Kerry's presidential campaign received more financial support from independent expenditures than did George Bush's.

In several ways, the Democrats' growing dependence on electoral support from diverse groups hampers their ability to craft effective policies that reward their constituencies. First, Democratic coalitions have to be re-created in each electoral campaign, because the diversity of Democratic constituencies works against a spontaneous rapprochement. Second, key issues for their coalition often promote divisiveness, because linkages between race and public policy inevitably imply redistribution. Robert Weissberg argued that the Democratic Party's failure to succeed in being all things to all of its members is responsible for the sizable defections by whites, defections that often spell the difference between victory and defeat.[29] Third, the difficulty of creating an alternative coalition of their own leads Democrats to run as "quasi-Republicans." Democrats often seek to attract Republican voters by adopting thinly veiled or watered-down versions of Republican policies. Arguably Bill Clinton's electoral success in the 1990s shows that Democrats who adopt Republican "lite" policies can win. However, oftentimes the need to appeal to wealthy donors pulls candidates toward positions at variance with the issues of greatest concern to core Democratic constituencies. Finally, as minority interests are counterposed to majority interests, race influences voting by enabling the development of persistent winning coalitions without any significant representation of minority interests.

By comparison, the emergence of a more homogeneous majority coalition has helped Republicans create consistent political messages. As more effective tactics increase their tenure in government, the opposition has been more ineffectual. Hence, the exploitation of racial antagonisms in contemporary political competition has increased the likelihood that majority rule will be tyrannical and that the ruling coalition will be a stable one.

Republican Dominance: An Era of Majoritarian Tyranny?

The greatest damage of racial polarization in recent years is shown not by racially charged rhetoric and political campaigns that use racial code words, but in the changes in national policy that commenced with Ronald Reagan's election, including: (1) trends in macroeconomic policy; (2) the increasing severity of punishment, most dramatically in the revival of the death penalty; and (3) the racial stratification evident in the war on drugs. I will argue that in each case race has played a central role in the development of a strategy that allows Republicans to use cultural conservatism to attract middle- and lower-class whites. Such conservative populism helps solidify a traditional Republican base among less affluent whites (the so-called Reagan Democrats). Moreover, the use of racially loaded messages on crime is especially important in the crafting of a conservative populism. Finally, because economic and racial conservatism are more strongly linked than in earlier eras—due to heightened partisan polarization—political campaigns that emphasize racial conservatism elect politicians committed to economic conservatism. Hence, antiblack conservative populism provides vital support for conservative economic policies that would have difficulty in their own right.

These examples share an important common denominator in another respect—in each case these policies are preferable to alternatives that would benefit illegitimate "others." Such "others" are enough unlike those in the majority to dampen any concern about ever sharing their circumstances. This collective loss of empathy, of a belief that "there but for the grace of God go I" that certain disasters both natural and man-made evoke, does not extend to the rights of the accused, the imprisoned, the poor, and the homeless. According to John Livingston, "those whose interests are protected in the group process no more expect to be poor tomorrow than they expect to be black. The much publicized taxpayer revolt also reflects the absence of compassion of the middle classes for the less affluent and the poor, when they see their relative affluence or their expectations of greater [affluence] to be threatened."[30]

Racial Polarization and Macroeconomic Policy

The Reagan-era policy most harmful to black Americans may actually have been the decision by Paul Volker, chairman of the Federal Reserve Board, to raise interest rates in 1981–82, a decision that, James Galbraith believes, "provoked the most severe recession of the postwar period, with unemployment surging to near 11 percent by the end of 1982."[31] As an independent agency, the Fed is not under the direct control of the president. Arguably, economic policies pursued by the federal government were directly responsible for much of the growth in inequality through the 1980s. Anti-inflationary policies that fight rising prices by inducing economic slack harmed the lower 40 percent of the income distribution while benefiting the top 20 percent. Moreover, wealthiest taxpayers gained most—in 1984 their disposable incomes were roughly one-quarter higher than they would have been without the changes in tax laws.[32]

Racial polarization contributed directly and indirectly to the Reagan-era shift in macroeconomic policy priorities. Changes in macroeconomic policy have increased the income of the affluent while generating budget deficits whose magnitude has paralyzed fiscal policy—effectively ruling out expansions of public services. The combination of majoritarian hostility to rising taxes, the identification of social programs with racial minorities, and budget deficits resulting in part from windfall payoffs to the affluent has set baseline conditions for public policy.

In general, as middle-class whites have moved from cities to suburbs, the influence of cities on domestic policy has withered, while the presence of minorities in cities has grown. As William Julius Wilson argues:

> Beginning in 1980, the federal government drastically decreased its support for basic urban programs. The Reagan and Bush administrations—proponents of the New Federalism, which insisted on localized responses to social problems—sharply cut federal spending on direct aid to cities, including general revenue sharing, urban mass transit, public service jobs and job training, compensatory education, social service block grants, local public works, economic development assistance, and urban development action grants. In 1980 the federal contribution to city budgets was 18 percent; by 1990 it had dropped to 6.4 percent.[33]

Indisputably, rising state and local sales taxes and flat rate income taxes have made the tax burden more regressive. Higher Social Security taxes have added considerably to the burden imposed by regressive taxation in the 1980s on those of low and moderate incomes. For many of these Americans, payments of proportional Social Security taxes are typically higher than their payments of federal income taxes.

Finally, changes in Internal Revenue Service policy have led to poorer Americans being audited more often than far wealthier ones. The IRS audited 1.36 percent of the tax returns filed by those earning less than $25,000 per year in 1999 versus 1.15 percent of returns filed by those making more that $100,000. According to reporter David Cay Johnston, "Since 1988, audit rates for the poor have increased by a third, from 1.03 percent, while falling 90 percent for the wealthiest Americans, from 11.4 percent."[34] The biggest reason is increased scrutiny of the earned income tax credit, at the insistence of Republican policy makers. According to reporter Mary Williams Walsh, "Republicans and Democrats have both supported expanding the tax credit, but as the cost of the program has risen, many Republicans have been vehement in saying the program is riddled with errors and fraud."[35] Republican congressional critics have demanded that the earned income credit receive special attention.[36] In 1999, 44 percent of all audits were of returns applying this tax credit. In April 2003, the IRS announced its intention to increase its scrutiny of those claiming the earned income tax credit, even though the estimated taxes avoided are dwarfed in comparison to tax avoidance and evasion schemes used by more affluent individuals, corporations, and partnership investors. The IRS estimates that the federal government loses $6.5 billion to $10 billion annually as a result of payments to those ineligible for earned income taxes, versus $132 billion to individuals evading and avoiding taxes, $70 billion to offshore accounts, $46 billion to corporations, and $30 billion to partnership investors. The Bush administration has also announced its intention to mount a similarly aggressive effort to prevent ineligible students from receiving free or subsidized school meals.[37]

The decision to increase scrutiny of the earned income tax credit is especially dismaying because, in recent years, the earned income tax credit has done more to reduce rates of childhood poverty than any other government program. The earned income tax credit (EITC) was created in 1975, and has been expanded several times since. In 1996, 8.0 percent of all persons (8.1 percent of blacks) and 14.5 percent of all children (14.8 percent of black children) were lifted out of poverty by the earned income tax program. Is it possible that the reason for the increased scrutiny of this program rests on its disproportionate benefits for minorities, in light of the smaller proportion of poor whites moved out of poverty? Whereas the EITC lifts 5.5 percent of pre-transfer poor whites from poverty, it lifts 14.8 percent of Hispanics and 8.1 percent of blacks who are poor before the effect of government transfers from poverty.[38] Alternatively, it may simply be that Republicans' hostility reflects their indifference to working poor Americans, who are unlikely to vote for Republicans, if they vote at all.

The shift in policy responsibilities from the federal to the state level in itself has meant less progressive financing. Relative decreases in the distribution of federal dollars to state and local governments has meant more regressive state and local taxes are used for purposes that more progressive federal tax revenues once covered. As the incremental growth of more regressive forms of taxation becomes the major source for new revenues at the state and local levels, this regressivity aggravates the hostility to programs for low-income families financed by state and local revenues. Frances Fox Piven and Richard Cloward argue that state government vulnerability to investor pressure is one reason state and local taxes are highly regressive.[39]

State and local governments have been forced to assume responsibilities once shared with the federal government (minus the federal revenue sources). This assumption of responsibility creates additional incentives to cut programs. Such hemorrhaging of state and local budgets by "new federalism" policies is a harbinger of budgetary problems that have become chronic features of economic downturns. The combination of greater state and local responsibilities and intense pressure for tax cuts (forty-three states cut taxes during the 1990s) has resulted in the most severe budget shortfall since World War II.[40]

Consider the changes in one of the benchmarks of the New Deal, the unemployment compensation system. Fewer workers now qualify for unemployment insurance. As recently as the 1975 recession, over three-fourths of those out of work received unemployment benefits. Roughly one-third of the jobless nowadays receive unemployment benefits. To avoid raising the taxes they charge employers, many states have tightened eligibility requirements so that workers must work longer and earn more to qualify. Additionally, the transition from manufacturing to service-sector employment negatively affects eligibility for unemployment benefits. Workers in services (1) earn less and change jobs more often; (2) are less likely to be unionized; and (3) have employers who are more likely to challenge their claims.

Although the affluent have prospered, the living standards of the non-affluent have stagnated or declined. According to the Center on Budget and Policy Priorities, there has been a 28 percent increase in the number of working people whose income fell below the poverty line since 1978. Census Bureau data depict the 32.7 percent income share going to the bottom 60 percent of the population in 1984 as the smallest in recorded history. Furthermore, the Bureau of Labor Statistics reports that the earnings of American production workers in private nonagricultural industries dramatically declined from 1970 to 1989. "Workers who were earning an average of $186.94 a week in 1970 were making just $172.74 in 1980 when inflation is taken into account, and only $166.52 in 1989."[41] Lester Thurow argues that "between 1973 and 1990 America's real per capita GNP rose 28 percent, yet the real hourly wages for nonsupervisory workers (about two thirds of the total work force) fell 12 percent, and real weekly wages fell 18 percent." The underfunding of public goods and infrastructures is particularly damaging to those at or near the poverty level. Rates of infrastructure investment are more than 50 percent lower than during the 1960s.[42]

Contemporary social welfare programs distinguish entitlements aiding those near or above the midpoint of the income distribution from those targeted at the poor—a disparity that evokes the aphorism "Welfare policies for the poor are poor welfare policies." Programs targeted at the poor are the ones that absorbed the bulk of the Reagan-era budget cuts. In the words of Piven and Cloward, "Non-means tested programs such as Social Security and Medicare and a variety of veteran's benefits have been dealt with delicately and cautiously. The brunt of the cuts falls on public service employment, unemployment insurance, Medicaid, public welfare, low-income housing subsidies, and the disability and food stamp programs."[43]

Perhaps most offensive of all is the percentage of children living in poverty. In 1989, when Ronald Reagan left office, 19 percent of all American children and 43 percent of black children lived in families below the poverty line. By 2000, the figures had improved, but still 15.6 percent of all American children and 30.4 percent of black children lived in families below the poverty line.[44]

Social spending cutbacks have been greatest in programs benefiting the poor. The reductions in food stamp benefits during the Reagan era affected twenty million Americans. Seventy percent of the savings resulted from benefit reductions for those below the poverty line. In the early 1980s, 440,000 low-income working families (almost all headed by women) lost Aid to Families With Dependent Children (AFDC) benefits. Medicaid benefits, linked to AFDC, were also reduced. Consequently, nearly a third of all children now living in poverty have no Medicaid coverage. Furthermore, cuts in low-income housing programs have pushed an estimated 300,000 more families into substandard housing. By 1985, Reagan budget cuts reduced social spending by 10 percent.[45]

Roughly half of the reductions in benefits were apportioned to households with average incomes of less than $10,000; approximately 70 percent of benefit reductions went to households with incomes less than $20,000. On the other hand, households with incomes greater than $80,000 received only 1 percent of the reductions. The result has been a dramatic upward redistribution of American income, leading to the most unequal income distribution since the collection of such data began.

Programs preserved from Reagan-era budget cuts have primarily benefited affluent Americans. The demographic characteristics of Medicare beneficiaries are strikingly different from those of the programs utilized by poorer Americans. Medicare recipients are elderly, white, and affluent in contrast to the poorer, darker, and younger beneficiaries of food stamps, welfare, and family support.[46] Republican positions on government spending involve big cuts in the programs that most benefit minorities and the disadvantaged and smaller cuts (and lower taxes) in those favoring majority voters. The biggest government programs from which white Americans have benefited most are the ones that have been most insulated from budget cuts: (1) Social Security, (2) Medicare, (3) Medicaid, and (4) mortgage interest deductions.[47]

Even Medicaid, widely perceived to provide health care for the poor, has been selectively pruned. Today, more of Medicaid pays for health care for the elderly than for children and adults under sixty-five. In comparison, programs that serve primarily poor Americans have been slashed much more. Nonetheless, the substantially smaller government programs from which minorities benefit receive the lion's share of opprobrium. The shrinking of government programs that benefit blacks and other minority groups has a dual impact: it damages both recipients and the employees of the respective agencies, many of whom are members of minority groups themselves.

It is here that Thomas and Mary Edsall's 1992 bestseller, *Chain Reaction,* misses a vital point: the main beneficiaries of traditional Democratic economic policies have been those who disproportionately enjoy a broad range of entitlements, namely the middle class. This point needs to be reiterated continually in light of the popularity of the view (endorsed by the Edsalls among many others) that liberalism's failure rests on its excessive catering to blacks. This is false—the programs of the American welfare state have always been and remain closely attached to the interests of middle-class and middle-income voters.

It cannot be emphasized too much that the programs serving largely minority clients are dwarfed both absolutely and in per capita terms by those serving the majority white middle-class and elderly citizens. Yet such systematic misperceptions are themselves a consequence of the chasm between perception and reality in the racial distribution of government program benefits.

Race, Crime, and Punishment

Government policies dealing with punishment have always been an issue that disproportionately affects the poor. Economic policy choices both influence the criminal justice system and are influenced by it. High rates of incarceration alleviate a potentially serious unemployment problem, especially of young black men.[48] During early industrialization, changes in the opportunities for earning a living forced many into criminal activities. In certain respects, the same is true today.

The rate of incarceration in the United States is the highest of the industrialized nations. In 2002, for the first time in history, more than two million people were incarcerated in U.S. jails and prisons. Roughly 12 percent of black men between the ages of twenty and thirty-four are currently incarcerated, in comparison to 1.6 percent of white men in the same age group. The expense of administering the American criminal justice system has grown so dramatically that in a number of states more money is spent on prisons than on higher education. The nation's inmates cost an average of $22,000 per year. In 1999, $147 billion was spend on criminal justice at all levels of government. This total is more than four times the total in 1982. The costs of the criminal justice system—police, prisons, and courts—increased every year in the 1990s, although crime rates declined.[49]

Young blacks growing up in impoverished circumstances within densely populated pockets of poverty receive powerful messages, messages that deeply circumscribe their life chances and affirm their marginality. For poorly educated young black men, the alternatives to criminal activity often appear unpromising. Penal policy is also a method of regulating labor, in which prisoners assume a status of marginality, one that closely approximates slavery. Prisoners are in effect "socially dead," to use sociologist Orlando Patterson's phrase. They are deprived of their civil rights, becoming nonpersons in the eyes of the law.[50] Some may consider the notion that prisoners suffer a form of social death to be so much hyperbole, yet what else are we to make of the resurrection of such devices as chain gangs and hitching posts, as well as the obvious conflict of interest between humane policy and fiscal frugality given the growing trend of using private companies to provide prison services?

"Social death" does not end even when prisoners are released. The efforts of many former inmates to "go straight" are frustrated by increased restrictions on the type of jobs they can fill. According to Andrew Hacker, "in New York City, an uproar arose when it was discovered that some of its school janitors had served terms in prison. In other cities, people with prison records are barred from becoming taxicab drivers and security guards, even though they are positions suitable for those seeking a fresh start."[51]

In the 1990s ex-felons have been barred from living in public housing and prohibited from jobs in a number of occupations. According to journalist Fox Butterfield, "in New York, there are more than 100 prohibited job categories, including plumbing, real estate, barbering, education, health care, and private security."[52] Drug felony convictions now include prohibitions on receiving student loans, welfare, and food stamps.

The marginality of young black men simultaneously threatens and secures the social order. Young black men receive disproportionate sentences for both ordinary and capital offenses. According to a recent Justice Department study, racial disparities in the juvenile justice system have a snowballing effect. "Blacks and Hispanic youths are treated more severely than white teenagers at every step of the juvenile justice system. . . . Minority youths are more likely than their white counterparts to be arrested, held in jail, sent to juvenile or adult court for trial, convicted and given longer prison terms, leading to a situation in which the impact is magnified with each additional step into the juvenile justice system."[53]

Politicians frequently capitalize on the misdeeds of black youths to win electoral support from those made anxious in part by media images and political campaigns. Finally, criminal convictions permanently bar many young black men from the mainstream of American life. Having a felony criminal conviction makes one ineligible for many desirable occupations, consigning ex-felons to a status of semipermanent "limited" citizenship. A by-product of imprisonment often results in another dimension of "social death," the removal of black men from the electorate. An estimated 1.4 million black men, 13 percent of the total black male population, cannot vote because of their criminal records. Nine states bar felons from voting for the remainder of their lifetimes.[54]

The Racial Politics of Death

Perhaps the most dramatic example of racial inequality in criminal justice policy occurs in the utilization of the ultimate penal measure: the death penalty. For many years blacks received the death penalty for criminal offenses for which whites would not. It was quite common after Reconstruction for blacks found guilty of an interracial rape to receive the death penalty, a penalty they might not in fact survive to receive, as white mobs frequently broke into jails in order to lynch the offending party (in many cases a mere accusation was sufficient for the lynching to occur).

Between 1930 and 1964, 455 men were executed for rape in the United States. Almost all were executed in southern states. Of the 455 executions, 405 were black men, almost all of whom were charged with raping white women.[55] In fact, the arbitrary racially biased utilization of the death penalty was crucial to its being judged unconstitutional.

The Warren Supreme Court strongly discouraged the implementation of the death penalty. During the 1940s, an average of 128 executions were carried out each year; during the 1950s, an average of 72. By the 1960s the pace of executions had dropped considerably. The number of executions was down to twenty-one in 1963, fifteen in 1964, seven in 1965, one in 1966, two in 1967, and then none between 1968 and 1976.[56] The obstacles to the death penalty were at one time anchored by Supreme Court justices Thurgood Marshall, William Brennan, and Harry Blackmun. But no justice today endorses the emphatic rejection of the death penalty as did Justices Marshall and Brennan, who believed that "the death penalty is an affront to a civilized society." Since the resumption of executions in 1976, legislative and political supporters of capital punishment have been more careful to apply it in ways that appear superficially to be more evenhanded. Executions are on the rise: 100 people were executed in the initial twelve years following the resumption of executions in 1976, and 82 were executed in the first 10 months of 1999.[57] But appearances of evenhandedness do not alter the racial inequities that are common in the application of this ultimate penalty.

Racial prejudice strongly permeates the utilization of the death penalty. Blacks are more likely to receive the death penalty, especially when they commit eligible crimes against whites. A comprehensive review undertaken by the Justice Department reveals significant racial disparities in the use of the death penalty in federal cases. "In 75 percent of the cases in which a federal prosecutor sought the death penalty in the last five years, the defendant has been a member of a minority group, and in more than half of the cases, an African-American."[58]

The death penalty is a punishment with an unacceptably high error rate. Since 1976, more than eighty death row inmates have been freed from prison. In spite of this error rate—roughly 15 percent of the total number of executions—the political champions of the death penalty are currently advocating speeding up its application. The Supreme Court, Congress, and many states have made it much more difficult for defendants to have their appeals heard.[59]

Certainly the increased use of the death penalty in recent years cannot plausibly be attributed to increases in crime. Fewer, not more, people are becoming crime victims. The Justice Department reports a steady decline since 1975 in the percent of households that report they have been touched by crime, from one out of three when the National Crime Survey started in 1975 to one out of four in 1988. Additionally, the rate of violent crime declined by one-third between 1992 and 2001.[60]

The most common justification for the death penalty is deterrence. However, there is little justification for this belief. Rather, those states that chose not to enact the death penalty since 1976 have not had higher homicide rates. Of the twelve states without capital punishment, ten have homicide rates below the national average.[61] Homicides rates have been 50 to 100 percent higher in states with the death penalty than in those without it. But in spite of the absence of credible evidence showing a deterrence effect, support for the death penalty has grown stronger. In fact, federal and state judges can attend conferences to consider ways to expedite its implementation with little notice.[62]

The death penalty is a cheap and easy way for politicians—Democrats as well as Republicans—to show their toughness on crime. Elected governors boast about signing execution warrants. Support for the death penalty helped Bill Clinton neutralize the label of being soft on crime during his 1992 presidential campaign.[63] Support for the death penalty permits an expression of racial (as well as gender) antagonisms in a well-understood if not always explicit code. The death penalty symbolizes the portrayal of female or black candidates as weak. The 1990 Democratic primary for governor in Texas illustrates this code. "The death penalty in Texas was a device," said George Shipley, an advisor to Governor Ann Richards, a device, used by male candidates to separate the electorate by gender, to draw strength and weakness comparisons to show that Richards was too weak to be governor.[64] Arguably, her tenure as governor should have neutralized that charge, given that more than fifty people were executed during her gubernatorial term. Nonetheless, George W. Bush attacked Richards during his successful campaign for not executing people more quickly. And quicken the pace he did, as seventy-seven executions occurred during his first term.[65] The image of young blacks on crime rampages has been a common device used in political campaigns. Perhaps just as pernicious as the racialization of the death penalty are the racial disparities that afflict the contemporary war on drugs.

Race, Civil Liberties, and the War on Drugs.
George W. Bush and the War on Drugs

We have witnessed in recent years the "outing" of politicians and public officials, especially but not exclusively those running for national elective office or needing Senate confirmation, regarding their past behavior in the areas of sex, drugs, and other aspects of personal behavior. Gary Hart, Bill Clinton, Clarence Thomas, and John Tower are perhaps the best known of those who have suffered due to questions regarding past improprieties. Although it is undeniable that such media-driven examination of private lives oversteps any useful boundary, a contradiction seems to be emerging again and again. This inconsistency involves the admission of past drug use, typically marijuana but also at times cocaine, by established politicians. Such admissions often involve drug use well in the past, and can reasonably be considered irrelevant to a candidate's current fitness for office. However, the admissions have frequently come from those most committed to the current war on drugs.

During the 2000 presidential campaign, George W. Bush was subjected to such prurient interest. For Bush in particular, the allegations concerning past drug use are quite relevant. As journalist Joe Conason thoughtfully articulated, the debate is long overdue on "why drug abuse among the rich is a 'disease' while among the poor it is a 'crime.' . . . Are the laws that send thousands of people to prison every year for drug possession administered fairly? Is justice served by incarcerating young, nonviolent drug offenders? Should the courts mandate treatment rather than imprisonment for people who make the kind of 'mistake' that the Republican front-runner has now all but admitted?" [66]

Yet unlike the kid-glove treatment often meted out to affluent drug users, those most likely to face arrest, prosecution, and harshly punitive sentencing are young black and Hispanic males. President Bush has been a zealous advocate of harsh drug policies. While running for governor, he opposed Governor Ann Richards suggestion to increase treatment programs, claiming "incarceration is rehabilitation." Hence, he advocates allocating more state funds to prisons than to treatment. Moreover, as governor, Bush "tightened the state's drug-sentencing laws, OK'd the housing of 16-year-olds in adult correctional facilities and slashed funding for inmate substance-abuse programs."[67] The result is that 13 percent of those incarcerated in state prisons are in jail in Texas. Of course, George W. Bush's stance is entirely consistent with the war on drugs as practiced in this country over the last thirty years. Those most negatively affected by the war on drugs have clearly been young black and Hispanic males. They suffer from racial profiling, longer sentences, and higher rates of incarceration.

In another long series of ironies, recent episodes of gun violence have brought attention to the dramatic contrast between the federal government's obsession with drugs and its relaxed attitude toward gun control. Consider, for example, that in 1981 President Reagan, at the urging of the National Rifle Association (NRA), announced that the ATF (Bureau of Alcohol, Tobacco, and Firearms, the federal agency charged with overseeing compliance with gun regulation) was to be abolished. Although he later reconsidered and withdrew this plan, the agency has been repeatedly hamstrung. Representative John Dingell, a Michigan Democrat who is a member of the National Rifle Association's board of directors, arranged for the gun industry to be exempt from the Consumer Product Safety Commission. Dingell termed firearms agents a "jackbooted group of fascists who are perhaps as large a danger to American society as I could pick today."[68] ATF director John W. McGaw justifies the lenient treatment of gun dealers by calling gun trafficking a "victimless" crime, even though half of the crimes in which guns were used that have been successfully traced by the ATF were to just 389 dealers. One can only wonder if the racial characteristics of crack users and gun users were reversed, would the federal government continue its antidrug campaign? While the Drug Enforcement Agency (DEA) budget (adjusted for inflation) has climbed from slightly over $200 million to $1.4 billion in the last twenty-five years, the ATF has gone from the same slightly more than $200 million to approximately $500 million. The only way this makes sense is if one believes the NRA slogan, "guns don't kill people, people do," while drugs similarly must destroy lives without the intervention of their users. The NRA's influence is certainly a major factor in the relaxed attitudes toward guns.

Or consider the contrast between the treatment of drunk drivers and drug users. It is estimated that 22,000 Americans annually die due to drunk drivers, while drug-related deaths kill an estimated 21,000. Drunk drivers are most often white males. When arrested, they are most often charged with misdemeanors. When convicted they receive fines, suspensions of their licenses, and community service. Drug offenders are, in comparison, disproportionately low income, and black or Hispanic.[69]

It is to no one's surprise that the war on drugs provides a clear example of political agendas that produce comprehensive racial disparities. The zeal to prosecute drug cases and the often unrepresentative symbols used to promote antidrug policies encourage harsh penalties, while enhancing enormously the political value (to candidates and elected officials) of appearing to be tough on crime. Media images of the drug crisis employ stereotypes emphasizing the ethnic and racial differences between those responsible for drug use and the "innocent" majority. Although drugs are widely used in middle- and upper-middle-class neighborhoods, most police action occurs in poor black sections.[70] A study by the Sentencing Project in Washington, D.C., found one in four black men between twenty and twenty-nine years of age to be under the jurisdiction of the corrections system, most commonly due to drug convictions. "Drug use cuts across racial lines, but drug enforcement focuses on the inner cities and blacks," said Mark Mauer, the Sentencing Project's assistant director.[71] And let us not forget that it was a New York detective unit whose primary mission was to search for illegal drugs that cost unarmed Amadou Diallo his life. Diallo was guilty of the crime of standing in the vestibule of his apartment building while being struck by nineteen bullets.

The disparity in sentencing policies for cocaine versus crack (a cocaine derivative) has become a topic of controversy. Unsurprisingly, far harsher sentences are being handed out for possession of crack, used primarily by minorities, than for possession of cocaine, used by many white Americans. This disparity was originally based on the faulty premise that crack cocaine was fifty times as addictive as powder cocaine. Federal sentences were devised to produce a 100-to-1 disparity between crack cocaine and powder cocaine. Consequently, 500 grams of powder cocaine would produce a mandatory five-year sentence, while five grams of crack cocaine produced the same mandatory five-year sentence. Unsurprisingly, blacks constituted 30 percent of powder cocaine defendants in fiscal year 2000, but they composed 84 percent of crack cocaine defendants. Although surveys of drug use suggest that more whites than blacks use crack, the war on drugs concentrates on poor urban neighborhoods. As a result, more blacks are sentenced to prison. Such disparities provide a telling example of the racial disparities in drug policy. A recent study by Humans Right Watch depicts the existence of immense racial disparities in America's prison population. Nearly twice as many black Americans are being imprisoned as white Americans, even though there are five times more white drug users than black ones. In 1996, 62.7 percent of drug offenders sent to prison were black, while 36 percent were white.[72]

The differential treatment of crack versus cocaine is a prime cause of current racial disparities in imprisonment. Whereas 8.3 percent of 25- to 29-year-old black men are inmates, only 0.8 percent of white men in the same age group are inmates. Certainly there are those who believe that such disparities are justified by the greater propensity of crack users to resort to violent crime. Harvard Law Professor Randall Kennedy has argued that the racial disparities in sentencing may well be the result of reasonable judgments made by legislators to address a serious problem, and that harsher sentences for crack have the often ignored benefit of increased safety for black communities victimized by crack offenders.

Yet the passage of time has clearly shown that the furor over crack was excessive, and that crack did not become the epidemic many proponents of differential sentencing had prophesied. Eric Sterling, who helped to draft several laws meant to respond to the drug crisis while serving as a lawyer for the House Judiciary Committee, has stated "that there was a level of hysteria that led to a total breakdown of the legislative process." The disparity continues because as James Alan Fox, dean of the College of Criminal Justice at Northeastern University, puts it, "For politicians the drug debate is driven by the three R's—retribution, revenge, retaliation—and that leads to the fourth R, re-election."[73]

The drug war undermines support for civil liberties and civil rights, support that is often tenuous even in the best of times. Legal scholars and civil libertarians point to disturbing signs that the drug war is eroding constitutional guarantees and altering the shape of American society. Journalist Joseph Treaster questions whether "a bifurcated legal system is emerging, one track for drug enforcement, another for other criminal matters. Several recent court rulings have affected the Sixth Amendment right to legal representation and made it more difficult for suspected drug dealers to defend themselves."[74] But changes in legal procedures for the handling of drug cases are leaching onto the handling of nondrug criminal cases. Suspects' property are being seized before trial, the requirements for searches and seizure are being eased, and the relaxation of the rules of evidence for drug cases is spreading to cases that have nothing to do with drugs.

Yet another indication of the way the drug war infects seemingly unrelated areas of the criminal justice system is shown by the recent revelations that racial profiling—the practice of singling out minority drivers on the nations highways—was initiated in 1986 by the DEA. In fact, "8 out of every 10 automobile searches carried out by state troopers on the New Jersey Turnpike in the last decade were conducted on vehicles driven by blacks and Hispanics," according to internal records of the State of New Jersey.[75] The DEA and the Department of Transportation have financed and taught an array of drug interdiction programs that emphasize the ethnic and racial characteristics of narcotics organization and teach local police ways to single out cars and drivers who are smuggling. According to University of Toledo law professor David Harris, the DEA has "conveyed similar messages across the country . . . [leading to] discrimination in states as diverse as Maryland, Texas, New Jersey, Illinois, Michigan and New Mexico. . . . The DEA has been the great evangelizer for racial profiling on the highways." Harris believes the success of racial profiling achieved in airports led the DEA to teach it to local police departments to use on streets and highways. An investigation conducted by New Jersey deputy attorney general Debra Stone concludes that "in the patrol cars and on the state's highways, racial profiling exists as part of the culture."[76]

The war on drugs has shifted the burden of proof in cases of property forfeiture based on suspicions of drug use. One study reveals that 80 percent of those whose property was seized by the federal government were never charged with a crime. According to Eric Sterling, who helped write the law while serving as legal counsel on a congressional committee, "the innocent-until-proven guilty concept is gone out the window." Under the government's seizure procedures, the police can seize cash and belongings: (1) if an individual fits the profile of a drug runner, a profile strongly weighted against minorities; or (2) if an individual is in possession of cash tainted by drugs, something that is true of nearly all U.S. currency; or (3) if an individual has property used in the commission of a crime, even if the individual was not involved. In order to recover seized assets, one must hire a lawyer and sue the federal government. Cases commonly take months or years and may not succeed. "The government need only show probable cause for a seizure, a standard no greater than what is needed to get a search warrant. The lower standard means that the government can take a home without any more evidence than it normally needs to take a look inside."[77]

Many direct participants in the criminal justice system—judges, defense attorneys, and prosecutors—have come around to the view that this out-of-control war on drugs has spawned sufficient unintended and unforeseen consequences to bring the entire federal court system into jeopardy. The increasing number of drug cases (up 270 percent in the last decade) has meant a near elimination of civil proceedings in some districts, denying justice to some poor plaintiffs. More than one authority believes the current war on drugs does serious damage to the quality of justice meted out by the system. According to Judge William Schwarzer, director of the Federal Judicial Center, "As a solid, efficient and stable institution, the federal courts are in jeopardy. . . . The popular political apparatus cries for harsher and harsher attacks for people involved with drugs and for more involvement of the courts. We get this blind emotional commitment without looking at the facts and assume any war that the U.S. gets into it will automatically win. . . . The courts are not a place to fight a war." According to James Neuhard, chief public defender for Michigan and a member of the American Bar Association's Task Force on the Crisis in the Court System, the war on drugs is comparable to McCarthyism, and similarly results in more injustice. "We have gone from probable cause to believe that you are guilty to reasonable suspicion that you are not innocent. . . . Court dockets are choked; probation officers, marshals and public defenders are overwhelmed; and the balance of power in the courtroom has shifted substantially to the prosecution, impairing the quality of justice that is meted out. Federal courts, historically a crucible for major social issues, now resemble assembly lines, raising serious questions about the integrity of the system."[78] There are more people imprisoned for drug offenses in the United States—about 400,000—than are imprisoned for all crimes in England, France, Germany, and Japan combined.[79]

Certainly, policies involving crime and punishment are a response to the public's perception of vulnerability to increasing crime. Yet the reliance on draconian measures also suggests that the heightened sense of vulnerability is not tempered by any concern that the rights diminished offer important protections that supporters of current policies, or those close to them, might themselves need. These popular perceptions and the way they are politically exploited are also inconsistent with the evidence on the racial backgrounds of crime victims and assailants. In 1997, for example, 85 percent of white murder victims were killed by whites, and 94 percent of black murder victims were killed by blacks.[80] As the great majority of serious crimes involve assailants and victims of the same race, the stereotypes are highly misleading. The resulting erosion of civil liberties has led to the reversal of the rights enjoyed by the entire citizenry. According to Steve Wisotsky, professor of law at Nova University in Fort Lauderdale, "The American people are simply less free than they were 10 years ago. Some people know it, and the scary part to me is that some people say that's the price you have to pay. We're at war."[81] "The root problem is that government, and I guess society in general, does not recognize the fact that the resources that go into protecting constitutional rights ought to be equal to those that go into prosecuting crimes," said Robert B. Remar, who is representing the American Civil Liberties Union in a federal lawsuit challenging the adequacy of indigent defense systems throughout Georgia.[82]

The Rehnquist Court and a Conservative Judicial Majority

An increasingly conservative Supreme Court, the most conservative since 1937, has been a key factor in the conservative shift in public policy. The replacement of racial liberals and moderates with conservatives sparked a decisive shift in the Court's orientation, particularly since William Rehnquist replaced Warren Burger as chief justice. The conservative shift in desegregation cases, for example, is highlighted by the case of the *Board of Education of Oklahoma City v. Dowell.* The court found resegregation based on private choices permissable.[83] The rightward shift in voting rights is highlighted by *Shaw v. Reno* (1993), wherein the Court's conservative majority in a five-to-four ruling overturned redistricting in North Carolina favorable to minorities. According to historian J. Morgan Kousser, *Shaw v. Reno* and its successors constitute a counterrevolution, one that effectively "turned the intent of the Fourteenth and Fifteenth Amendments on their head and deliberately distorted history and language in an effort to stamp out the embers of the 2nd Reconstruction." "Shaw and [the] succeeding cases seemed to threaten to ban governmental distinctions between people, with the effect of facilitating discrimination against the very "discrete and insular" minorities that the Reconstruction Amendments were passed to protect and of insuring that one interest—the heretofore least powerful interest—would not be equally represented in bargaining over changes in political structures and processes."[84]

The status of affirmative action was discussed in Chapter 1, so there is no need to revisit it here. But it was in the pivotal *Adarand v. Pena* case that Justice Clarence Thomas issued the memorable phrase "government cannot make us equal," in support of the majority position striking down an affirmative action program. Justice Thomas's remarks echoed those of Justice Henry Billings Brown in *Plessy v. Ferguson* (1896): "If one race be inferior to the other socially, the Constitution of the United States cannot put them upon the same plane."[85] Justice Thomas has also expressed serious reservations about the wisdom of the *Brown* ruling and the pro-integrationist course of action that followed it.

The Rehnquist Court has become a vital member of a dominant national

Republican coalition, consistently favoring the interests of Republican constituencies at the expense of their opponents. The *Hopwood* decision by the Fifth Circuit Court of Appeals also reflects the growing conservatism of the entire federal judiciary. Inasmuch as Republicans have held the presidency for all but eight years since 1980 and as their representation in Congress has increased as well, the judiciary has grown increasingly conservative. Since Reagan, Republican administrations have given priority to creating conservative majorities on appellate courts. President Clinton, by contrast, did not give a high priority to appointing liberals. On the thirteen federal appeals courts, for example, Republicans have a majority in seven, Democrats in just two. These courts, directly below the Supreme Court, are considered to be crucial barometers of the prevailing judicial winds because the Supreme Court decides fewer cases than ever and also because most cases that come before federal appeals courts are decided by three-judge panels.[86]

The direction of the court reflects a rejection of the Warren Court's legacy. Rather than protecting the disadvantaged, a common theme of the Warren Court's rulings, the Rehnquist Court's majority has become a part of the Republican majority coalition. Their decisions have followed a consistent pattern—one shared by the executive and legislative branches—of a redirection in government policy that favors the interests of those constituencies found regularly on the winning side and is detrimental to those found regularly among the losers. Republican constituencies have been the clear winners of changes in federal spending priorities; Democratic constituencies—the poor, big city residents, consumers of social services targeted to the poor and near poor—the clear losers. Thus, the 1980s gave rise to a polarized consolidation of economic and political haves and economic and political have-nots. The general maxim has been: those who have suffered the most are the electoral losers—the poor, the near poor, urbanites, and racial minorities. Ultimately, the decline in the net redistributive impact of government programs in the last twenty-five years parallels the increasing stability of the majority and minority political coalitions. According to political scientist Walter Dean Burnham:

> The gross boundary between the top and bottom halves of the nation on this long term trend line broadly etches the difference between those parts of the country which have acute and obvious urban decay problems and those which do not; between those parts of the country which are absolutely or relatively losing population, and those which are not; between those parts of the country whose surplus energy "taxes" in an age of expensiveness are high and those whose are not; between those parts of the country where blacks and unions are relatively well organized, and those where they are not.[87]

Macroeconomic policies responsible for a record trade deficit, declining social welfare spending, and an increasingly regressive tax structure have led to a dramatic increase in wealth inequality in the United States. A major reason such policies are acceptable to many Americans is the ideologically potent but inaccurate conflation of the poor with racial minorities. Parsimonious social and draconian criminal justice policies also help bond social and economic conservatives whose economic interests diverge while sharpening racial polarization. In other words, conservative antiminority populism helps sell conservative economic policies to people who might otherwise view such policies with suspicion. A by-product of focusing economic and social grievances on problems attributable to racial minorities is to characterize young black men as a class of potential Willie Hortons.

Declining redistribution in the public sector and growing inequality in the private sector are perhaps the clearest indicators of the declining political influence of America's have-nots. These trends provide very strong circumstantial evidence to support the thesis that the growing overlap between political and economic haves and political and economic have-nots has produced a political and economic climate that can credibly be described as majoritarian tyranny.

The Presidential Election of 2000

It may never be possible to fully answer whether disparate racial treatment on Election Day changed the outcome of the presidential election of 2000. But in addition to the Election Day snafus recounted in the introduction, the actions of Katherine Harris, the Florida secretary of state, fatally hindered an accurate recount. As reported in the *New York Times,* "Over the 36 days it took to settle the Florida election, Ms. Harris made a series of crucial decisions, and each one without exception, helped Mr. Bush and hurt Mr. Gore. She told county canvassing boards they lacked the discretion to conduct manual recounts—recounts Mr. Gore desperately wanted. She enforced strict counting deadlines, just as Mr. Bush wanted, and then, contradicting an earlier directive from her office, she advised counties to apply a liberal standard for counting absentee ballots, a move that helped Mr. Bush pick up hundreds of critical votes."[88] The rowdy demonstrations by protestors in Miami-Dade County provide another example of the egregious conduct that prevented an accurate recount in Florida. Although ultimately irrelevant due to the Supreme Court ruling disallowing the recount, the decision by the local canvassing board to stop counting ballots may well have been influenced by these protests. It turns out that a number of these demonstrators were subsidized by the Republican Party and included employees of such prominent

Republicans as Tom Delay, the House majority whip, and Senate majority leader Trent Lott.[89]

The sizable racial differences in the rates by which ballots were voided was a consequence of decisions to void ballots, especially in majority-black voting districts, that ignored clear evidence of the intent of the voter. One cause of this disparity is that higher proportions of black voters live in counties that used the now notorious punch card machines. Fewer blacks than whites live in counties using optical scan readers, which alert voters of an error. Of the twenty precincts with the highest voided ballot rates, nineteen were in Duval County in northern Florida. According to Anthony Salvanto, a researcher at the University of California at Irvine, perhaps 1,700 Miami-Dade County voters' presidential ballots were invalidated because they incorrectly punched the chad beneath that of their chosen candidate. In many cases their mistake was due to a misalignment of punch card ballots and voting machines. With the proper alignment, Vice President Al Gore would have gained 316 more votes in Dade County alone.[90]

Vice President Gore also lost a significant number of votes in counties that voted for George W. Bush due to questionable rulings by local canvassing boards. These boards threw out more than 1,700 votes in which the intention of the voter could be easily discerned. Many ballots were voided because voters selected either Bush or Gore, and then wrote in the candidate's name. These ballots were read by counting machines as double votes, and were thereby discarded by canvassing boards. These ballots clearly indicated the intent of the voter, and if the canvassing boards counted those votes, George W. Bush's margin of victory would have fallen by 366 votes, two-thirds of the official margin of 537 votes.[91]

A recount conducted in Orange County, Florida, shows that Al Gore would have gained 203 votes if a hand recount had occurred. Voting machines rejected 799 ballots for having either no votes or multiple votes. This county used paper ballots that were to be marked with special pens. The most common reason for rejection of ballots was due to voters using unapproved pens, that is, not the pens provided in the voting booth. Consequently machines did not detect votes on ballots that were filled in with black ink. While adhering to this rigid principle in counting votes cast on election day, the county counted absentee ballots (which generally favored Republicans) on machines that were much more sensitive to the voters choice. There were also hundreds of ballots that were discounted because they were marked in the wrong places. The candidates' names were circled or a bubble marked "PRES" was filled in, rather than the approved procedure of coloring in an arrow that pointed to the correct name.[92]

More recently, a post-election study conducted by the National Opinion

Research Center (NORC) at the University of Chicago came to the conclusion that the Supreme Court did not cost Al Gore the election. Rather, a recount of the ballots in the counties the Gore campaign requested would have narrowed but not prevented Bush's victory, depending on the criteria used. But that resolves only one kind of irregularity, and confirms the flaws in the Gore post-election strategy to examine four Democratic counties rather than push for a recount of the entire state. What if a full recount of the entire state had been ordered? Examining a broader group of 175,010 rejected ballots shows that the results might very well have resulted in a Gore victory. According to the NORC analysis, the cumulative effect of counting correctly marked paper ballots and poorly marked paper ballots and disqualified but fully punched punch card ballots would have given Gore another 554 votes and thus the election.[93]

Examining 2,490 ballots from Americans living overseas that were counted as legal votes after election day, the *New York Times* found 680 to be questionable. The ballots possessed a variety of flaws: some lacked postmarks, others were postmarked after the election, others lacked witness signatures, or were mailed from towns and cities within the United States, and in some cases were cast by voters who had already voted. These ballots should not have been counted, yet they were accepted in counties that favored Bush. Clearly the Bush campaign aggressively pushed to count these votes, and the Gore campaign conceded because many of these ballots were cast by members of the armed forces.[94] In truth, since the election was a statistical dead heat, small changes in the interpretation of valid ballots could have changed the winner.

This issue of ballot spoilage had a serious disparate impact on minorities. According to the House Committee on Government Reform, "voters in low-income, high-minority congressional districts throughout the country were three times more likely to have their votes for president discarded than those in more affluent, low-minority districts, and were twenty times more likely to have their votes for Congress go uncounted." A study by Harvard University's Civil Rights Project "found a strong relationship between ballot spoilage and a sizeable black population; specifically as the black population in a county increases, the spoiled ballot rate correspondingly increases. . . . In Florida, racial disparities in ballot spoilage across counties persisted even when comparing counties with identical income, education, and other factors."[95]

It is certainly reasonable to ask whether these events further confirm an overall trend, of a conservative Republican coalition, one including both elected officials and Supreme Court justices, using questionable methods to assure their preferred outcome.

The Stable-Majority Problem

The question of what distinguishes democracy from highway robbery has long been a classic theme of political theory. As Robert Lowell put it, "If two highwaymen meet a belated traveler on a dark road and propose to relieve him of his watch and wallet, it would clearly be an abuse of terms to say that in the assemblage on that lonely spot there was a public opinion in favor of a redistribution of property. . . . The absurdity in such a case of speaking about the duty of the minority to submit to the verdict of public opinion is self-evident."[96] A staple of conservative classical political thought is the notion that there is no essential distinction to be made between democracy and majoritarian highway robbery. Democracy equals the rule of the mob; it is merely a majoritarian tyranny. According to Macauley, "the first use which the people will make of universal suffrage will be to plunder every man in the kingdom who has a good coat on his back and a good roof over his head. . . . Working class suffrage would bring about the end of literature, science, commerce and that a few half-naked fishermen would divide with the owls and foxes the ruins of the greatest European cities." Similar apprehensions concerning democracy have been found among more liberal democratic theorists. For example, "during the debate over the 1832 Reform Bill in England (which increased the franchise to 3.1% of the total population) John Stuart Mill foresaw the prospect of a revolution that would 'exterminate every person in Britain and Ireland who has 500 a year.'"[97]

I have laid out a case in this chapter that such concerns are neither antiquarian nor simply theoretical but pose an issue relevant to contemporary American politics. Political theorists have long acknowledged that majoritarian tyranny is at least theoretically possible. Political scientist Dennis Mueller believes that "what is required for redistribution to take place under majority rule is that the members of the winning coalition be clearly identifiable, so that the winning proposal can discriminate in their favor."[98] Stable political coalitions are especially susceptible to degenerating into tyrannies of majorities over minorities. By stable I refer not to the stability of political regimes, but to the permanence of the constituencies within coalitions. Is it sufficient that winners and losers will remain constant over extended periods of time?

James Madison was one of the early modern political theorists to recognize that absent strong restraints, those in political power will use it tyrannically. The Madisonian compromise between majority power and minority rights rests most of all on constitutional inhibitions, upon the belief that if constitutional limitations on excessive power are to be effective through the separation of powers, they must be partially countervailing. For Madison it was essential that those in power have distinct and discordant interests. The interests of the politically powerful must be inharmonious, separating rather than joining them. Madison's assumption that a large republic will produce so many factions as to counterbalance each other is itself an act of faith.[99] But he recognized that in the absence of some "social checks" constitutional checks would be insufficient.[100] According to Sam Bowles and Herb Gintis, "the Madisonian accommodation relied upon the heterogeneous economic and social situation of the major producing class (farmers, wage workers, and artisans), upon the strategic exclusion of some groups (such as blacks and women), as well as on racial, ethnic, religious, and regional antagonism to forestall the threat to the structure of privilege proposed by the extension of the suffrage."[101]

Madison and John Stuart Mill (another noted pluralist) each believed that a balance among rival classes or factions was required to prevent majoritarian tyranny. More contemporary pluralists, however, argue that the invariably transitory nature of democratic majorities insures their ineffectiveness.[102] According to Dennis Mueller, "Implicit in the arguments supporting majority rule we see the assumption that no stable majority coalition forms to tyrannize."[103] Inconstant majorities provide the essential protection against exploitation of minorities. Flexible alliances mean majorities are continually reformed from disparate groups. Crosscutting political cleavages thereby moderate passions. In general then, the pluralist expectation that majority rule would not result in majoritarian tyranny rests upon empirical rather than philosophical criteria. *Thus, the possibility of majoritarian tyranny cannot be ruled out a priori.*

Many believe the existence of constitutional safeguards is sufficient to protect legitimate minority rights, rebutting the possibility of majoritarian tyranny. But the adequacy of constitutional protections rests squarely upon the shoulders of its judicial interpreters. Traditionally, such interpreters have opted for the most minimal interpretations of such protections possible, especially when the rights of unpopular minorities are involved. As political scientist Robert Dahl properly notes, "there is not a single case in the history of this nation where the Supreme Court has struck down national legislation designed to curtail, rather than to expand the key perquisite to popular equality and popular sovereignty."[104] Judicial protection, then, does not protect minority interests, certainly not racial minorities. According to political scientist Joel Krieger, "during the Reagan years the ability of victims of discrimination to sue the state has been reduced by the Supreme Court's use of doctrines of sovereign, judicial, and prosecutorial immunity and by a set of more restrictive criteria for determining standing. Decisions concerning the right to bring cases involving both educational and employment policy have indicated that the court is generally unwilling to provide group remedies for group wrongs."[105] For most of American history judicial protection of civil rights guaranteed indifference, if not hostility. In fact, since the selection of judicial interpreters is done by winners of elections, notions of constitutional rights in time strongly resemble the sentiments of the appointers. If majorities are stable, perceptions of constitutional rights held by judicial interpreters will eventually assume a majoritarian flavor. Sensitivity to losing minorities will not be a strong consideration in the criteria for appointments, and may even serve to disqualify potential appointees, as occurred during the Reagan administration. Those who believe constitutional safeguards are invariably sufficient must also keep in mind the view expressed by Chief Justice of the United States Supreme Court Charles Evan Hughes: the constitution is what the justices say it is. Or consider the view of current Chief Justice William Rehnquist, who, while clerking for Justice Robert Jackson in 1952, wrote a memo favoring maintaining segregated schools. Rehnquist argued in this memo that the view "that a majority may not deprive a minority of its constitutional rights . . . while . . . sound in theory, in the long run it is the majority who will determine what the constitutional rights of the minority are." Rehnquist went on to argue in his memo that *Plessy v. Ferguson* correctly interpreted the constitution and should be "reaffirmed."[106]

Ultimately, the strongest protection of minority rights rests neither on constitutional proscriptions nor paternalistic good intentions but rather upon a healthy awareness of self-interest and realistic expectations that a significant degree of cycling will occur into and out of majority coalitions. For constitutional and judicial protections to be adequate, some among those currently on the side of the winners must expect that in the foreseeable future they may find themselves among the losers and have need of firmly established and respected rights to protect their own interests. Shifting coalitions are therefore an essential component of liberal democracies. Thus the uncertainty of current winners that they will remain in the majority provides the most valuable safeguard for minority rights. However, when the stability of political coalitions is such that the alignment of opponents is largely predictable, majoritarian exploitation becomes plausible. Stable or consistent political outcomes increase distributional inequities.

It may be suggested that this scenario is unrealistic and static—that the dynamics of electoral competition prevent such rigidity. It is here that the impact of racially oriented voting comes into play, as dissimilarities between the interests of the majority of white voters and those of many black voters forestall cycling. Instead, current patterns of racial voting make possible increasingly predictable winners and losers, providing a catalyst for majoritarian tyranny. Moreover, coalitional rigidity reduces empathy—it becomes ever more difficult for those in the political majority to see themselves as likely to be in the political minority. Compelling evidence of such a loss of empathy can be drawn from numerous developments in contemporary social policy that are mean-spirited in their treatment of those unfortunate enough to fall within their client populations.[107]

Ironically, the framers of the Constitution intended to create a system that would constrain the power of majorities. But their creation has evolved into one that protects the interests of the majority over and against those of minorities. According to Robert Dahl:

> There is this strong bias against minorities in the political system the framers helped to create. Because they succeeded in designing a system that makes it easier for privileged minorities to prevent changes they dislike than for majorities to bring about the changes they want, it is strongly tilted in favor of the status quo and against reform. In their effort to protect basic rights, what the framers did in effect was to hand out extra chips in the game of politics to people who are already advantaged, while they handicapped the disadvantaged who would like to change the status quo.[108]

A Shifting Tide: Toward a Stable Majority

Looking backward on the program defined by the ideological proponents of Reaganism at the beginning of the 1980s suggests the limits of their success. Their antistatist rhetoric reflected their desire to reshape the relationship between state and market by scaling back government intrusion on market relations. According to political scientist Ira Katznelson:

> A striking feature of the 1980 campaign is that it explicitly and directly placed issues of social policy at the heart of the competition for votes. Fundamental questions about what may be called the social democratic agenda were politicized in a way they had not been since the Truman years. . . . This agenda has been concerned with the following: 1) the capacity of government to regulate, plan for and modify the private economy; 2) the choices government makes in creating macroeconomic policies to deal with unemployment and inflation; and 3) the scope and character of welfare state programs, including social insurance, such as social security and nonmarket transfers of money, including food stamps and welfare payments.[109]

The scorecard indicates the Reaganites were partially successful. Where the targets reflected efforts to apply a blunderbuss of philosophical libertarianism to the American political economy, the intense resistance indicated that conservative radicalism had overreached. However, attacks more narrowly focused—targeting those on the fringes or outside the majoritarian coalition—were far more successful.

Political scientists Martin Shefter and Benjamin Ginsberg have defined the following as essential characteristics of the formation of a durable regime in American national politics:

> First, if a regime is to endure its leaders must succeed in defining the central issues of national politics—that is, the content of the nation's political agenda. Second, to be stable a regime must forge a support coalition that controls more in the way of politically relevant resources than the coalition supporting its opponents. A third characteristic of a stable regime is its ability to develop a legitimating ideology that plausibly presents the interests of its supporters as general or common interests. Fourth, a stable regime must inherit or construct governmental institutions and processes that enable it to enact policies beneficial to its supporters. Fifth and finally, to remain in power a regime must foster prosperity, and finance the flow of public benefits to its supporters without slowing the growth of the national economy.[110]

Racial politics may not be *the* defining issue in national politics, but few issues on the domestic agenda are not directly affected by it, particularly since severe and chronic federal budget deficits have made policy alternatives part of a zero-sum game. Whether the budget shortfall was an accident or an intentional design to reduce the role of government in America by reducing fiscal revenues, in effect "starving the beast" (as some believe), may never be definitively established, but the effects are the same, and the widespread indifference to the damage done is eased greatly by the perception that program cuts are limited to the "undeserving poor," that is, blacks and other racial minorities.

Employing a legitimating ideology that leavens antiblack conservative populism with libertarianism, Reagan's tax and budget cuts have created potentially durable linkages between privately employed upper-middle-class professionals and middle-class whites as dependably national Republicans. Furthermore, by relegating more of the burden for social provision to state and local governments, they have succeeded in forcing services to be paid for with regressive funding sources, thus insuring their unpopularity even among their beneficiaries. The Reagan program can be considered successful in all but Shefter and Ginsberg's final criterion—to foster prosperity and finance the flow of benefits to supporters without slowing the growth of the national economy—and the causes and consequences of a failure to foster economic growth and prosperity are often too diffuse for blame to be easily apportioned.

The "consumption" binge of the 1980s illuminates the sizable payoffs generated by redistributional policies favoring affluent entrepreneurs and professionals.[111] "Most of the Reagan decade, to put it mildly, was a heyday for unearned income as rents, dividends, capital gains and interest gained relative to wages and salaries as a source of wealth and economic inequality."[112]

Racial conflict has been essential in creating a stable majority coalition, one that has succeeded in arresting and perhaps even reversing what Joel Krieger has described as "the historic tendency for citizenship rights to expand from civil rights (securing individual freedoms) to political rights (participation in the governmental exercise of power) to social rights (provisions for need which reduce the natural pattern of social inequality in a capitalist society)."[113]

Windfall gains for the rich, deterioration of the well-being of many with modest incomes, collapse of the living conditions of the poor—these are the contours of the political economy of the 1980–92 era. To some these are seeds for a neo-populist revolt of have-littles and have-nots. Although the convergence of economic and political haves and economic and political have-nots appears to open the way to a resurgence of class politics, it is more realistic to believe that ongoing racial cleavages and antagonisms will continue to frustrate efforts to merge disadvantaged constituencies. For example, neither of the organizations that have been even modestly successful in this endeavor—industrial unions and the Democratic Party—is in any position to fulfill such objectives any longer. A more detailed exploration of these issues will be undertaken in Chapter 5.

The most recent era of political competition has been one in which electoral winners and losers have become more consistent. The dominant coalition in American politics since the late 1960s has been more conservative and homogeneous, meaning there has been less and less reason for politicians to devise appeals that cross racial lines. Such winning coalitions have been both covertly and at times overtly based on appeals to race and racial sentiments, as in the 1988 presidential election.

Conservatives have become dominant in the judicial branch, and if at times less dominant in Congress, they more often than not hold the upper hand given the large contingent of southern conservatives (whether Democrats or Republicans) and the pivotal influence of swing voters. The key swing constituencies (white southern conservatives and northern white ethnics who may be nominally Democratic but who have often voted Republican in national elections) have a disproportionately large influence on political calculations.[114] Politicians desirous of winning elections pay most attention to these voting blocs.

The dominant national coalition mirrors the attitude of these swing voters on a number of key issues, but especially in their racial resentments and antitax conservatism. Moreover, there is simply no branch of the national government in which the interests of non-conservatives are sufficiently powerful to provide an effective counterweight to those of the majority.

So even if the notion of dominant coalitions is expanded to include congressional coalitions, only a slight adjustment is required in this thesis. Conservatives on both sides of the aisle hold the balance of power steadily in the Senate and not infrequently in the House, despite the prominence of Democratic liberals.[115] When considering the effects of the (long-term) Republican dominance of the presidency, the gradual but nonetheless considerable translation of control of the presidency into conservative judicial majorities, and the perhaps more tenuous but frequently right-oriented coalitions that are strongest in the Congress, it is apparent that there is no branch of the national government in which non-conservative economic, political, and social interest groups are as strong as or stronger than competing conservative interest groups. Not since the 1960s has the federal government been an important advocate of race relations progress. According to historian James Patterson, "neither Congress nor the Clinton administration did much to combat segregation in schools or housing."[116] Nor I might add did the Supreme Court. According to Harvard University's Civil Rights project, the growing balkanization of school districts is a consequence of the Supreme Court's 1974 *Milliken v. Bradley* decision, which barred desegregation across city-suburban boundaries.[117]

Classical democratic theorists believed the populace would either be sufficiently homogeneous to prevent divisions in interests from becoming pervasive or that cycling would prevent rigidities from becoming stable. Arguably, majority rule works well when consensus is great and the opinions of the majority and minority are close, but in the view of political scientist Arend Lipjhart, as the distance between groups grows, the significance of political decisions does as well.[118]

During the present era the question of whether racial polarization is transforming the indisputably desirable ideal of political equality into an empty formalism is unavoidable. Race has come to define predictable axes of political power and economic redistribution. Under such circumstances competitive democracy has diminished the political influence of black Americans.

Clinton's victories (and Gore's popular vote majority) necessitate modification of the view that Republicans have an "electoral lock" on the presidency. Yet Clinton's victories have not altered the underlying electoral calculus, a calculus based on catering to racially resentful white swing voters. The most ambitious component of his first-term agenda—universal health care—was stymied by a Congress closely attuned to the preferences of a stable majority, complacently comfortable with employer-provided health insurance. After the failure of his ambitious health care proposal, President

Clinton became substantially more conservative, allegedly compromising with Republicans, but in actuality handing them victory after victory, most notably in the 1996 welfare bill, which ended fifty years of social protection for American children.

True, the economic prosperity of the late 1990s made the connection between hard times and racial resentment less relevant. But better economic conditions did not dampen the drive to end welfare. Certainly one factor for the obsessive political commitment to end welfare by Republican conservatives has been the intense political polarization of the 1980s and 1990s, which has created a Republican Party devoid of black supporters in the midst of an economic expansion that has reduced welfare rolls by a disproportionately greater number of whites. In 1996, 3 percent of Republicans identified themselves as black and 2 percent as Hispanic. By 2004 only 2 percent of Republicans were black, while 12 percent were Hispanic (of any race). As white welfare recipients have left in larger numbers, the political support for welfare has softened even further.[119] Although growing prosperity may bring with it a lessening of economic inequality and once again a turn toward more socially progressive policies, it would be premature at this point to come to such a conclusion. This topic will be addressed more fully in the final chapter. First, however, we will further explore the historical relationship between changes in economic inequality and the race relations climate, by turning the clock back and examining the post-Reconstruction era.

3

The Decline of Racial Democratization

During the late nineteenth century rising economic inequality fostered greater political inequality. By the end of the century blacks were politically isolated and marginalized, a state of affairs that continued until the 1930s. This combination of rising economic inequality and growing political isolation created a hostile racial climate and contributed to a reversal of democratization. To put it simply, the white southern elite used white supremacy to repress southern blacks and exclude them from political participation in order to reestablish and maintain an oligarchy.

The abolition of slavery and the incorporation of former slaves as citizens extended the franchise to a large, propertyless working class, and raised hopes that the contradictions in the American version of popular sovereignty might be resolved once and for all. Racial tensions eased and institutionalized racial prejudice softened in many northern communities.[1]

Between 1865 and 1885, fourteen states passed civil rights laws barring discrimination in public places. The integration of schools and public accommodations and the enfranchisement of blacks supplanted the Jim Crow segregation of the antebellum era. Racially integrated residential areas were common. Predominantly white electorates voted for black candidates to the state legislature and the county board of commissioners in Illinois.[2] True, the antebellum color line persisted in employment, but the small number of black residents and the lack of competition between blacks and European immigrants made more amicable race relations possible during these years.

Closing the Door on Progress

The late nineteenth century experienced a resurgence of white supremacy, in essence degrading the legal, political, and economic conditions of life of black Americans. Fundamentally, white supremacy has meant that the status of black Americans is distinctly inferior to that of white Americans, legally, economically, socially, and politically. The legal inferiority of black Americans corresponded to the beliefs of most white Americans that whites were naturally superior. White supremacy thereby provided a status floor for white Americans above the ceiling for black Americans. Sociologist C. Eric Lincoln argued that "as the color of privilege in America, anybody who is white is automatically presumed to warrant certain prerogatives, privileges, and preferences over anybody who is black."[3] White definitions of proper behavior determined the range of allowable behavior for blacks. Blacks had to come to terms with an exercise of power by white southerners that was literally without restraint. Ultimately, this meant segregation was not to be challenged in any significant way.[4] Racial antagonisms intensified in the North as well. As black migration to the North increased after 1890, the black population became more visible. The black population may have surpassed a hypothetical tipping point, sparking a disproportionate increase in racial discord. The combination of growing racism throughout American society and greater economic competition with European immigrants led to greater racial hostility in many northern communities.

The disfranchisement of southern blacks and their small numbers outside the South relegated black Americans to a politically marginal existence. The federal government promoted black powerlessness by ignoring their grievances. Such behavior transmitted the message that the failure of black collective action was preordained.[5]

White Supremacy in the Army

The treatment of the first black cadets to attend West Point, the United States Military Academy, portrays the power of white supremacy. In 1870 James Webster Smith would be the first black appointed to West Point. Smith was treated unconscionably from the moment of his arrival. Those opposed to Smith's admission gained promises from every member of his class that he would not be helped or supported in any way. The silent treatment was only one facet of the persistent harassment and abuse Smith faced. No one intervened to protect him, and although President Ulysses S. Grant supported his admission, he did nothing to restrain his son, Fred Grant, from being a ringleader in Cadet Smith's persecution. Fred Grant actually said that no black would ever graduate from West Point. After much turmoil, Smith would leave West Point after failing a philosophy exam under suspicious circumstances. The exam was privately administered (unusual in itself) and the professor had previously publicly announced that blacks were not capable of learning philosophy. Smith died of tuberculosis at the age of twenty-six, shortly after his expulsion.[6]

Henry O. Flipper, one of three blacks enrolling in 1872, would become, in 1876, the first black to graduate from West Point. Shortly after receiving his commission, Flipper would be charged by his commanding officer with embezzling approximately four thousand dollars and, simultaneously, of conduct unbecoming an officer (essentially for lying to cover up discrepancies in the accounts). He was acquitted of embezzlement, but convicted on the conduct unbecoming charge. Flipper contested his dismissal and tried unsuccessfully to clear his name during the remainder of his life.[7] Perhaps the best known of the black cadet pioneers was Johnson Whittaker, who entered West Point in 1876. Shortly thereafter, three men wearing masks, generally believed to be cadets, entered Whitaker's room without permission, slashed his face and hands with a razor and left him bleeding, unconscious, and bound to his bed. Whittaker was court martialed and expelled as administrators accused him of faking the assault in order to bring dishonor upon West Point. Although his court martial was overturned by President Chester A. Arthur, Whittaker was never commissioned as an officer.[8] Between 1870 and 1889, twelve blacks (out of twenty-two receiving appointments) passed the entrance exam for admission to the U.S. military academy. Of these twelve, three graduated: Henry Flipper, John Alexander (in 1887), and Charles Young (in 1889).[9] The army retired Col. Charles Young, the highest ranking black officer in World War I, to avoid promoting him to general. It was not until 1949 that the first black graduated from the Naval Academy.[10] No blacks were even eligible to join the Marines until 1942. As late as 1949, the Marines had one black officer in their total officer contingent of 8,200.[11]

These examples vividly portray the hostile racial environment of the late nineteenth and early twentieth centuries. The mistreatment of black cadets reflected fundamental premises of white supremacy. The ostracism of the young black cadets indicates that they violated an important racial taboo: it was unthinkable that blacks should have the opportunity to succeed in positions where they might actually give orders to whites. White America had determined that blacks were a subordinate caste.

The intense harassment of black cadets also serves as a reminder of the symbiotic relationship between military service and freedom. During the Revolutionary War, thousands of slaves won their freedom by joining the army (either British or American). The removal of the slaves who had fought with the British afterward seriously depleted the southern labor force, leading George Washington to demand (unsuccessfully) compensation. The offer of freedom would be repeated by the British during the War of 1812.

Military Service, Freedom, and Citizenship

Perhaps the most clear-cut and stirring examples of the bond between military service, freedom, and citizenship occurred during the Civil War. The freeing of slaves and their enlistment in the Union Army were vital and necessary elements in the eventual Union victory. Military service played a critical role in the expansion of the suffrage. In the words of General William Tecumseh Sherman, "when the fight is over, the hand that drops the musket cannot be denied the ballot." Sherman's view was shared by prominent minister Henry Ward Beecher, who argued "blacks had earned the franchise through their heroic military service and their unswerving fidelity to the union."[12]

During Reconstruction, some Republicans advocated the full integration of the military.[13] However, Congress chose to create six Army regiments of black troops instead, exemplifying the ambiguities of Reconstruction. On the one hand there were some Republicans, admittedly a minority, who sincerely advocated the full integration of the new citizens into American life, something only possible if Reconstruction heralded a social revolution. But the more powerful adversaries of full integration desired to create a status quo in which white supremacy (and planter hegemony) could be firmly reestablished.

The incongruity of blacks fighting for democracy in World Wars I and II for a country that denied them the full rights of citizenship has long been grist for the mill of anti-American propaganda, and eventually became an embarrassment to national political leaders. The threat by A. Philip Randolph to lead a march on Washington against racial segregation moved President Franklin D. Roosevelt to issue Executive Order 8802 banning discrimination in federal government agencies (an order that was never carried out). It took a threat of political retaliation on the eve of a presidential campaign for President Harry S. Truman to issue Executive Order 9381 in July 1948, forbidding racial segregation in the armed services. Black veterans helped to spearhead post–World War II civil rights activism, often refusing to accept segregation after having fought against the doctrines of racial supremacy.

The mistreatment of Cadets Smith, Flipper, and Whittaker also reflected the prominent place of the military in the pantheon of national heroes. Nowadays media attention and hero worship are focused on celebrities, typically entertainers and athletes. Jesse Ventura and Arnold Schwarzenegger are only the most recent cases of celebrities moving from entertainment to the statehouse. But for much of the nineteenth century, before the development of mass media and modern communications that we nowadays take for granted, military leaders were routinely the nation's supreme heroes. Military service was a common route to a political career. Among nineteenth-century presidents, only John Quincy Adams, Martin van Buren, and Grover Cleveland did not have some form of military service.[14] Generals commonly ran for and won political office. In the nineteenth century eight generals were elected president: Andrew Jackson, William Henry Harrison, Zachary Taylor, Franklin Pierce, Ulysses S. Grant, Rutherford Hayes, James Garfield, and Benjamin Harrison.[15] Generals George B. McClellan, Winfield Scott, and John C. Frémont ran unsuccessfully as major party presidential candidates. Given the prestige and status bestowed on military leaders, successful black military officers might have shaken the very foundations of white supremacy.

White Supremacy in the Law

As the rights of black Americans were being restricted, the words of Chief Justice Roger Taney's infamous *Dred Scott* decision resonated. In the 1857 *Dred Scott* decision the Supreme Court decided that Scott's residence in a free state did not make him a free man. Rather, he remained a slave. Second, according to Taney, the Missouri Compromise was unconstitutional; Congress could not prohibit slavery within a territory. Third, no black person had any rights under the Constitution nor the right to sue in federal court, because blacks were not citizens of the United States.[16]

Taney died in 1864, but the Supreme Court continued to play a major role in the debasement of black Americans by extinguishing their citizenship rights. In the Slaughterhouse cases in 1872 and the Civil Rights cases in 1883, the Court restricted the domain of federal protection. By narrowly interpreting the Fourteenth Amendment, the Court reinterpreted its principles so as to dilute its safeguards against discrimination. In the Slaughterhouse cases, the Court restricted the scope of the Thirteenth and Fourteenth Amendments. According to the Court, "if the authors of the Fourteenth Amendment had wanted to grant the federal government the power to be a 'perpetual censor upon all the legislation of the States,' they would have made it clear that they were bringing about such a revolution."[17] Not long after, the Court determined that the 1875 Civil Rights Act did not provide protection against actions by private parties. The Court's eight-to-one majority found civil rights to be primarily a state matter, and the Fourteenth and Fifteenth Amendments to offer protection only against governmental discrimination.[18] Justice Joseph Bradley proclaimed an end to what he regarded as the federal government's paternal protection of freedmen: "When a man has emerged from slavery, and by aid of beneficent legislation has shaken off the inseparable concomitants of that state, there must be some stage in the progress of his elevation when he takes the rank of a mere citizen, and ceases to be the special favorite of the law, and when his rights as a citizen or a man are to be protected in the ordinary modes by which other men's rights are protected."[19]

Plessy v. Ferguson (1896) is generally regarded as the Supreme Court's affirmation of racial segregation. Homer Plessy was arrested in June 1892 for violating a Louisiana law that called for "equal but separate accommodations" for the white and colored races on all passenger railways within the state. Plessy's arrest was part of an intentional challenge to the law by New Orleans blacks, designed to prod the U.S. Supreme Court into declaring segregation laws unconstitutional.

Speaking for the Court, Justice Henry Billings Brown argued "the framers of the Fourteenth Amendment could not have intended to abolish distinctions based upon color." Accordingly, the social difference between the races had a foundation "in the nature of things." Since the Louisiana law mandated not merely separate, but rather "separate but equal," facilities, the underlying fallacy of Plessy's argument, according to Brown, was the "assumption that the enforced separation of the two races stamps the colored race with a badge of inferiority. If this be so, it is not by reason of anything found in the act, but solely because the colored race chooses to put that construction upon it." In other words, a white person was prohibited from sitting in a black car, thus whites and blacks were treated equally under the law. Furthermore, according to Justice Brown, Plessy's argument assumed that "social prejudices may be overcome by legislation, and that equal rights cannot be secured to the negro except by an enforced commingling of the two races."[20] This decision gave impetus to a growing wave of segregation laws.

White Supremacy in the White House

Post-Reconstruction presidents and presidential candidates repeatedly echoed these judicial views. Democratic presidential candidate Williams Jennings Bryan supported disfranchisement, arguing that civilization has a right to preserve itself. Progressive stalwart Theodore Roosevelt prodded the Republicans into adopting a more rigid racial stance.[21] Following the criticism of his luncheon invitation to Booker T. Washington, he reduced the patronage available to black Americans, including the number of black federal officeholders, emphasized his belief in black racial inferiority, and refused to allow southern blacks to be seated at the 1912 Progressive Party convention. His successor, William Howard Taft, opposed voting rights for blacks by arguing that they were "political children, not having the mental status of manhood."[22]

Taft was succeeded by Woodrow Wilson, the first southerner to be elected president since the Civil War. Wilson's credentials as an ardent segregationist were established long before his arrival in Washington. Wilson blocked the enrollment of blacks at Princeton University while serving as that institution's president. According to Desmond King, "Wilson's election marked a sharper accent upon the segregationist propensity in Washington."[23] During his tenure in Washington, racial segregation gained momentum in federal offices and agencies, provoking the NAACP to break openly with the president, arguing that "public segregation of civil servants in government employ necessarily involving personal insult and humiliation has for the first time in history been made the policy of the United States government."[24] But segregation was not simply a presidential initiative. Once Democrats gained control of Congress in 1913, Congress took the lead in promoting and protecting segregation. Numerous bills were introduced to enforce segregation in federal employment.[25] One sure way to strengthen segregation was to decentralize federal programs, thereby diminishing federal control of local practices. For southern Democrats, states rights and local control were always core issues of concern.

Wilson's successor, Warren Harding, notwithstanding his reputation for personal warmth and geniality, openly stressed the "fundamental, eternal, and inescapable differences" between blacks and whites as the basis underlying his pledge to "stand uncompromisingly against every suggestion of social equality. . . . Racial amalgamation there cannot be."[26] Herbert Hoover, the last president of the era spanning Reconstruction's end to the New Deal's beginning, encouraged the formation of white-only Republican organizations in the South. Nor were such sentiments merely those of elite figures; they were widely shared among white Americans. In 1939, 69 percent thought blacks less intelligent than whites. As late as 1944, the National Opinion Research Center (NORC) found 80 percent of southerners and 47 percent of northerners supported racial discrimination in the labor market.[27]

The Significance of Reverse Democratization

Although Reconstruction's aftermath was marked by a prolonged deterioration of the racial climate, it began with the bright promise of a new dawn in race relations. Arguably, the end of the Civil War marked a dramatic shift toward the expansion of democracy to the South. But the tentative beginnings of a new order reflected the uncertainties that pervaded southern Reconstruction.[28]

Reconstruction, at least at first glance, presaged a potential revolution, providing unprecedented opportunities for blacks to make inroads into the political structure of southern states. So why did the "bright promise of Reconstruction" result in a deteriorating racial climate? Perhaps the answer should be in the form of an alternative question: Why should it not have? After all, it is by no means unusual for advances in democratization to be followed by retrogression. Significant democratic reversals have occurred in more than a handful of societies. Well into the twentieth century, Marx's prognosis that democracy would prove to be indigestible for ruling elites seemed quite plausible. For predemocratic ruling elites, mass democratization—the extension of the franchise to the masses—has typically represented a Hobson's choice: unavoidable but unwelcome.

Several historical-comparative studies of democratization offer a number of insights that suggest why Reconstruction failed to improve the racial climate:

1. As political scientist Stein Rokkan argued, a formative influence upon the decline of popular sovereignty is a style of rule inherited from an earlier era—in this case, the plutocracy of a planter elite that was defeated but not destroyed.[29]
2. Suffrage extension was a result of the partly opportunistic calculations of elites (in this case, leaders of the Republican Party) that democratization would give them the chance to compete in the South. Thus, enfranchising new groups provided a new set of allies against common enemies. Northern Republicans viewed racial democratization as an opportunity to build support in a region in which they were widely unpopular. Bluntly, Republicans needed black votes, because without them Democrats would surely rule the South. And since blacks now counted as full persons for congressional representation, rather than being limited to the pre-emancipation three-fifths rule, the enlarged southern electorate might return control of the national government to the Democrats for the foreseeable future.[30]
3. The rapid pace of democratization was profoundly destabilizing. According to historian George Fredrickson, "The enfranchisement of southern blacks by the Reconstruction Acts of 1867 inaugurated what may have been the most radical experiment in political democracy attempted anywhere in the nineteenth century."[31]
4. Yet, the maintenance of a fully democratic political order clashed with the aims of indigenous elites—in this case, southern plantation owners—to reestablish their dominance.
5. Furthermore, although democratization would alter the postbellum balance of power, it left northern politics largely unchanged. Because blacks resided almost entirely in the South following the Civil War and northern political leaders (in keeping with the preferences of their electorate) were committed to keeping them there, there was

no political constituency in the North to be wooed by supporting southern democratization. Northerners were unwilling to extend full citizenship to their own black residents. Only in the New England states were blacks allowed to vote. It is true that several midwestern states did extend voting rights to blacks during this era, but the limited size of the northern black population—slightly more than one percent of the total population in New York, Chicago, and Boston, up to a maximum of 3.7 percent in Philadelphia, in 1880—limited the significance of enfranchisement.[32] Furthermore, proposals to enfranchise blacks were defeated in fifteen northern states between 1863 and 1870.[33]

Students of democratization have emphasized that the incorporation of new groups occurs based on opportunities provided for alliances with already established and enfranchised ones.[34] Thus, the extension of voting rights to ex-slaves came by way of the needs of the national Republicans for a southern constituency. Blacks were granted voting rights in southern states only because of the electoral needs of northern Republicans. Creating an electoral base for Republican politicians in the South meant requiring southern states to extend voting rights to blacks as the price of readmission to the Union. The readmission of southern states to the Union, without the support of blacks, would have insured Democratic rule both in the South and, quite probably, nationally.

Furthermore, in gaining the right to vote, blacks were on the threshold of a political revolution that could not help but have profound economic consequences, consequences that threatened the restoration of planter dominance. First and foremost, how would the southern economy be reshaped? The limited support by Unionists for full southern democratization during Reconstruction waned very quickly. Northerners rapidly grew weary of the "negro problem" and turned their attention elsewhere, most importantly to the issues of the industrialization and economic development of the North and the West. The rapid decline in the appetite and interest of the northern public for reforming southern racial practices suggests that emancipation had never been intended to start a social revolution, but rather was a strategic measure to hasten the war's end. During the war only a few of the Radical Republicans were prepared to endorse black enfranchisement.[35] Moreover, white southerners' intransigence, and their deep commitment to use coercion and intimidation to oppose Reconstruction, offered the prospect of a permanent military and political occupation.

As emancipation proved to be a component of an incomplete revolution, its ambiguities became even more visible. Perhaps the most important consideration was that blacks were free but not independent within the confines of a plantation society. This meant the uncertainty of their status awaited future clarification. In other words, was abolition an end or merely a beginning? According to historian Eric Foner, "Should the freedmen be viewed as individuals ready to take their place as citizens and participants in the competitive marketplace, or did their unique historical experience oblige the federal government to take special action on their behalf?"[36]

A key factor in the process leading to eventual democratic reversal was the emergence of a relatively intact Democratic Party from the Civil War, able to critique and oppose Republican Reconstruction policies. No small amount of credit for this must go to President Lincoln's successor, Andrew Johnson, whose initial Reconstruction plan allowed much of the southern political elite to rapidly regain their former prominence. Most important, the hope of the Radicals to establish a more extensive Reconstruction was perceived to jeopardize Republican control of the national government. The Democratic Party's intact survival eased the tasks of reasserting the agenda of the traditionally dominant class of landowners. From a theoretical perspective, the influence of a cohesive opposition implacably committed to restoration of a conservative status quo was a powerful brake upon social transformation.[37]

Among the conclusions to be drawn from this exegesis are: First, democratic transitions are never established upon on a clean slate. In this case, democracy would have to overcome a powerful antebellum tradition of planter domination of the southern political economy. Second, democratization usually occurs because elites are forced to expand the citizenry in order to maintain their rule. Third, the speed of racial democratization during Reconstruction made it especially ominous, raising the prospect that a revolutionary transformation of the social order was in the offing. Fourth, democratization was unsustainable because it directly clashed with the interests of the most powerful elements of southern society, who were implacably committed to its overthrow. Fifth, the democratic transition failed because racial democratization was not a vital issue for any substantial northern constituencies, not its political and economic elite nor the northern public. Ultimately, Reconstruction failed because citizenship rights of black Americans carried far more risks of continued entanglement in southern affairs than any potential reward.

Labor Repression in the Late Nineteenth-Century South

Perhaps the most important work of comparative sociology of the last half century is Barrington Moore's *The Social Origins of Dictatorship and Democracy*. His magisterial analysis offers an illuminating guide to the failure of democracy in the post-Reconstruction South. Moore believes the decline of landlord authority is a central feature of democratic development. Consequently, the elimination of agriculture as the predominant economic activity of a society is the basis of indigenous democracy. This step facilitates the destruction of the political hegemony of the landed elite and the conversion of the peasantry into substantial farmers producing for the market. Accordingly, if landlords and peasants make successful adaptations to industrialization, resistance to democracy will be weakened. On the other hand, if landowning elites are left behind, they will obstruct social change.[38]

I will use Moore's framework to illustrate how racial democratization in the South was stymied and reversed. In general, class coalitions in the American South were formed within a post–Civil War reconsolidation of agricultural relations of production that somewhat resembled the reactions to economic and social crisis of landowner elites in Germany and Eastern Europe.[39] In other words, to return hegemony to the landowners necessitated reversing the political consequences of democracy and halting the erosion of their economic base. Landlord reaction was a major, albeit not the only, component of the anti-democracy movement.

The consequences of freedom were potentially revolutionary, at the very least sufficient to inspire a reactionary mobilization. Much of the inspiration was due to the rapid enfranchisement of blacks, an event that occurred much more rapidly than had the gradual enfranchisement of white males in the early years of the republic. Rapid enfranchisement was an ominous development, because political freedom for former slaves threatened the resumption of production and the restoration of order, which were of more concern to powerful interests in both the North and the South than were the rights and well-being of freedmen. Rapid enfranchisement was also dangerous because it meant there was little time to adapt—to devise some means to insure continued planter dominance, such as modifying election rules or political institutions, as might have happened given a more gradual pace.

Perhaps the most important obstacle to a thoroughgoing Reconstruction occurred right at the start in the decision by the federal government not to distribute planters' holdings to former slaves. This decision assured that freedmen would continue to labor for others—the others most likely being their former masters within the confines of a plantation economy. Hence, freedmen would labor on terms that assured their inferiority. Equally relevant, the failure to confiscate and redistribute land assured that plantation owners would retain a leading role in the southern political economy.[40] Rather, confiscation of southern land threatened to open the door to a process whose end was uncertain. Land reform might not stop with plantation owners. What, for example, prevented confiscatory schemes from spreading northward? This unwillingness to redistribute land to freedmen was so important that it casts doubt on the revolutionary potential of the Reconstruction experiment altogether.[41]

But simply retaining control of their land did not insure planter dominance. Plantation systems require a dependable labor supply. Landowners urgently needed to control the freedom of labor to move, in effect to immobilize farm labor, at the very least until the end of each harvest season. Southern plantation owners found themselves in a dire predicament because their laborers were no longer legally bound. The immediate postwar years were a time of frequent movement by blacks. Much of this movement was local in character in order to re-create family ties torn by slavery. Others moved simply to take advantage of a freedom they had been denied by their condition as slaves. Additionally, blacks were no longer docile. On numerous occasions they showed a readiness to defend their interests, whether this meant using collective action to control the product of their labor or asserting their right to self-protection. As citizens they formed militias in association with the Union Leagues (Reconstruction-era Republican organizations), which mobilized black votes throughout the countryside, stimulating the growth of southern Republicanism.[42]

Sharecropping and Labor Repression

Was sharecropping a repressive system of labor control? If so, then the fundamental relevance of the comparative argument made by Barrington Moore that landlord persistence stymies democratization via labor repression is confirmed. We will see in this section that sharecropping does qualify as a repressive system of labor control, at least under certain definitions of market relations.

Of course, sharecropping was not merely an instrument of landowners to control black freedmen, but represented an adaptation to specific conditions of the late nineteenth-century South, in particular the nature of a plantation-based economy plagued by chronic shortages of credit and frequent declines in the price of the major cash crop, cotton. The spread of credit rationing made post-harvest payments an attractive option for planters.[43]

At the same time, the spread of sharecropping also reflected the resistance of the freedmen to labor on terms resembling the gang system of the slave plantation. Initially, sharecropping was in certain respects a progressive step— it meant loosening the control of landowners and hence the bonds of freedmen's dependence. Although some landowners tried to maintain centralized production by organizing laborers into units of multiple families, many freedmen sought to form small-scale collective contracts. A common countermove by landowners was to subcontract production to one individual with discretion over hiring, sustenance, and control. According to economist Gerald Jaynes, the use of subcontracts "was a natural strategy for employers who had no experience or desire to indulge in the distasteful labor of hiring and managing on a day to day basis, laborers whom they viewed as unruly and insolent."[44] In general, sharecropping thereby resolved some of the difficulties many planters had in managing free workers.

Some analysts, most notably economists Gavin Wright and Jaynes, believe less consideration should be given to the repression and control of labor in sharecropping and more to its utility as a solution to key problems of the post-emancipation agricultural economy. They depict sharecropping as an institutional adaptation to employers' lack of information concerning the intensity of laborers' effort. In other words, as Jaynes argues, given employment systems based upon collective rather than individual assignments, how do employers evaluate the respective efforts of their labor force? Sharecropping offered a feasible solution by effectively displacing the problem of labor discipline to foremen and heads of families (often the same person).[45] Family hiring also reduced the difficulties of mobile labor, a mobility formerly unknown to newly freed blacks. Hence, sharecropping was at minimum a semi-voluntary evolution to an equilibrium, one that offered valuable benefits to both landlords and sharecroppers. Sharecropping (1) minimized the need for money in an economy plagued by cash shortages; (2) delegated supervision of labor to croppers, thus allowing family heads to organize and supervise most of the work; (3) reassigned a considerable degree of the risk of enterprise from landowners to croppers; and finally (4) effectively managed the transition of a workforce accustomed to close supervision under slavery to the more indirect restraints characteristic of a market economy.

These factors all imply that suggestions of labor repression are overblown and that sharecropping was more of a practical adaptation to conditions in which planters were cash poor and unable to regulate the intensity of the effort of workers possessing limited skills or motivation. But if this were true there should have been little need for the extensive range of extraeconomic coercion mechanisms. Hence, although it may be true that sharecropping originated as a market solution to difficult circumstances, sharecroppers soon found themselves under additional and clearly repressive restraints.

Consider for example the spread of laws that insured that for those laborers who received wages, their claims to pay were made second to the landlord's claims to rent, and at times were subordinate to the claims of merchants and cotton factors with liens on crops as well. Among other indicators of the deteriorating status of freedmen concurrent with the growth of sharecropping were the introduction of the black codes (which regulated the behavior of only blacks in such areas as which occupations they could enter and under what terms they would labor), the convict-lease system, the introduction of forms of (often debt-based) peonage, and the eventual expansion of segregation. As the repression of southern blacks intensified over time, the consolidation of landlord authority over their labor power grew as well.

How much extraeconomic coercion was involved in sharecropping? In Wright's highly influential view, the economic deficiencies faced by croppers were primarily the result of economic underdevelopment and the isolation of the southern labor market, an isolation stemming from poor and costly transportation, as well as high rates of illiteracy among workers.[46] Hence high transitional costs associated with labor migration—especially high information and search costs—prevented blacks from moving to areas outside the South where higher-paying employment was plentiful. Wright further argues that blacks were locked into agricultural labor due to their lack of experience in local industries, for instance, textiles. This inexperience meant they had steeper learning curves than more experienced white workers. But the problem with this perspective is that failure in textile mills was not limited to black workers. Inasmuch as some of the same mills that failed using black labor had failed previously using white labor undercuts this portion of Wright's argument.[47] Hence, it was not only blacks who failed outside agriculture.

Employing an economic institutionalist perspective one might argue that racial exclusion was a part of the economic transaction that allowed white families to send their family members, especially females, into mills without worrying about possible contact with blacks, especially black men. Racial exclusion thereby facilitated the utilization of more malleable and cheaper women and children in the textile industry.

For sure, white supremacy would become both more intensive and extensive as sharecropping spread. White workers excluded blacks from certain occupations. Employment barriers thus undermined the status of blacks. Whites' refusal to work with blacks narrowed the job opportunities for blacks and reduced their bargaining ability. Blacks' dependence upon sharecropping grew, as did their isolation from employment outside its confines.

Furthermore, the exclusion of blacks from industrial work served the interests of industrialists because it meant that the existence of a large black labor surplus limited the ability of white workers to demand higher wages and successfully form unions. The cheaper pools of white labor available in the South due to the exclusion of blacks stimulated the growth of a low-wage industrial economy. For example, North Carolina textile manufacturers had considerable discretion in their decisions determining wage rates due to the abundant supply of labor and the absence of high-wage competition. This latitude gave them a substantial competitive advantage over their northern counterparts.[48] And notwithstanding the growing exclusion of blacks from many industrial occupations, industrialists retained the option to use blacks as strikebreakers to undercut militant white labor. The use of blacks as strikebreakers was a catalyst for several prominent race riots during this era.

Finally, the narrowing economic opportunities available to black Americans fit into a pattern of growing racial discrimination during the late nineteenth and early twentieth centuries, a pattern that was multi-institutional and multidimensional. The dense and increasing web of racial exclusion throughout American society, both northern and southern, suggests the growing integration of economic markets and political power. Yet, Wright's analysis, at the very least, suggests that racial exclusion might be explained by economic factors in isolation from political and social forces. But controlling the ability of blacks to act as independent economic agents was an essential component of sharecropping. If blacks, for example, could have successfully competed in industrial settings, white supremacy would have been jeopardized. Thus the barriers erected to prevent blacks from leaving sharecropping were an example of the commitment of southern landowners to maintain their power, a power whose influence was felt throughout every domain of the southern political economy and society.

Hence, the practical meaning of black freedom was limited by the paucity of available alternatives, a range that was diminishing over time. The onerous burden imposed on black freedmen is also revealed by the durability of landlords' control over their sharecroppers. As late as the 1960s sharecroppers were being evicted from their plots for registering to vote. For example, Fannie Lou Hamer, a Mississippi sharecropper and leader of the Mississippi Freedom Democratic Party, was told that she must either renounce her application to register as a voter or be evicted.[49]

To summarize the above argument: (1) the poverty of exit options suggests the status of croppers lacked some of the norms frequently associated with free wage laborers; (2) their alternatives were clearly suppressed on noneconomic grounds—their race; and (3) planters exercised a considerable degree of paternalism, controlling the lives of their ostensibly hired hands. Hence the coercive elements of sharecropping went beyond what we might consider the conventional legal boundaries of landless agricultural labor. Ultimately black workers lacked credible alternatives—and were therefore free neither within sharecropping nor outside of it. According to economist Jay Mandle:

> the ubiquity of the planters' control over the lives of estate residents clearly exceeded that of industrial managerial prerogatives over a firm's labor force. Residence on the plantation meant that the range of behavior over which plant-

ers could claim authority was exceedingly wide. Schooling, housing, and religion, as well as credit extension, are areas of worker activity under which capitalist industrial relations are not normally subject to direct managerial control, but under plantation conditions were subject to such authority.[50]

Although such limitations on autonomy during nonworking hours were not unknown for presumably free laborers living in closely supervised environments, such as in company towns, that limitation speaks to the bondage of purportedly free laborers, rather than to any freedom of blacks employed under labor contracts. Thus sharecroppers were subjected to restrictions that may be considered economic, but were considerably at variance with the prevailing conventions of free labor.[51]

That ostensibly free white laborers outside of sharecropping were not always free of noneconomic limitations either testifies to the increasingly inequitable environment faced by poor- and working-class late-nineteenth-century Americans of all races. Just as freedom tends to be infectious, so is bondage. Hence, textile mill owners created a pass system that prevented millworkers from being hired by an employer without the consent of the prior employer.[52] Company stores were a regular feature of the textile industry, making it a near equivalent to the plantation.

Ultimately, the coercion to which sharecroppers were frequently subjected suggests that there was enough labor repression embedded within sharecropping to qualify as a labor-repressive regime as defined in the beginning of this section. The establishment of sharecropping as a stable system of labor control was partly dependent upon the manifestly inferior political status of sharecroppers.

Immobility also fostered sharecropper dependence. True enough, sharecropping did not tie particular individuals to particular plantations, but it was a major factor in creating and sustaining a political and economic environment that anchored poor blacks and whites within a low-wage southern economy. Sharecroppers were less than free wage laborers, as that term is commonly understood; and the reasons for their unfreedom were partly political. White paramilitary organizations used terror to undermine blacks both politically and economically. So even if, as Wright argues, the isolation of the southern labor market was an essential cause of black economic dependency, it is striking that none of the influential forces in late nineteenth-century southern politics were willing to rely on the market alone, but rather insisted upon supplementing market subordination with political disabilities.

But my major emphasis is elsewhere. It is that, first of all, the impoverishment of black southerners was a structural aspect of sharecropping—based in a concentration of land ownership from which croppers were largely excluded and the growth of tenant farming.[53] Second, the political and economic deterioration of the status of black Americans was converging and spreading, fostering an onrushing tide of political inegalitarianism and economic inequality felt in virtually every sphere of life.

The burden of southern landowners' discriminatory behavior was strengthened rather than offset by their industrial counterparts. Discrimination in the industrialized economy occurred primarily by the exclusion of blacks from particular occupations and trades, rather than through discriminatory wage differentials. Although competitive pressures promoted equality in the market for unskilled labor—a market open to blacks and whites—for skilled labor, racial privilege and exclusion remained the rule. Over time this phenomenon would spawn the formation of a dual economy—one in which black and white workers occupied different jobs at different wage rates. With the exception of a small number of urban artisan trades, white supremacy commonly meant that southern employment was divided between jobs reserved to whites versus those reserved to blacks. Factory work was most often reserved to whites while domestic service was monopolized by blacks. The overlap in unskilled and low-skilled manual labor prevented a sizeable racial wage gap.[54]

In time large numbers of rural whites moved into occupations in which blacks were already employed. As timber workers, coal miners, and longshoremen, blacks and poor whites actually performed similar tasks at similarly low rates of pay. According to historian George Fredrickson, "the basic or characteristic pattern in the South for the half century after emancipation was one of economic segmentation rather than competition or cooperation between white and black workers."[55]

In general, industrial development in the South replicated the pattern of inequality already established in southern agriculture. Railroads owned by northern capitalists regularly set higher freight rates in the South, compensating for the often fierce competition among northern railway lines to the detriment of southern farmers. Freight rates were also set to discourage movement of finished goods north. The nation's largest steelmaker, U.S. Steel, purposely set prices at its Birmingham steel works higher than the competitive price to protect its northern factories, a policy followed by other major steel producers.[56]

Northern producers used their economic power to expand their competitive advantage over southern producers, to the detriment of southern industrialization. By actively discouraging new industries, southern manufacturers sought to prevent competition for labor and rising wages. Thus, southern industries were able to exploit the supply of cheap labor generated by the "southern system of politics and race relations." As a result, low wages necessitated the employment of every family member, thereby increasing the size of the available labor pool, resulting in an additional drag on wages.[57] This series of adaptations by southern industry to the cheap labor environment of the southern economy was extremely detrimental to industrial and economic progress. Such systematic "development of underdevelopment" intensified the long-term technological stagnation of the southern economy. Ultimately southern industrialization reinforced the economic dependency of southern labor.

In sum, sharecropping, cheap labor, and Jim Crow segregation assured the economic domination of landowners over sharecroppers (black and white) and the political domination of landowners over tenants. The South's already high level of inequality became even more inequitable with the extension of sharecropping.[58]

Consequently, whether sharecropping is perceived as an extraeconomic system of exploitation—based upon the application of political coercion through legal and extra legal forms of coercion—or alternatively as a hybrid market institution produced by the combined influence of economic and political factors, what is undeniable is that the degradation of southern agricultural labor—both black and white—fostered similar conditions of life. Such homogeneity created a serious threat to planter hegemony. The threat that poor white farmers and black sharecroppers might form a political alliance capable of contesting planter rule was a real one. In order to insure that the economic domination landlords were well on their way to establishing would not be frustrated at the ballot box, black American's voting rights had to be extinguished. The proclaimed desire of white conservatives to prevent blacks from casting deciding or swing votes both enabled one-party Democratic rule and disenfranchised large numbers of poor whites.

In general, such widespread use of extraeconomic coercion is consistent with repressive systems of labor control even within market-based institutions, a repression not diminished by its market rationality. According to historian Eric Foner, this "seamless web of oppression was one whose interwoven economic, political, and social strands all reinforced one another."[59] The reciprocal economic dependency and political inequality that blacks in particular but sharecroppers in general lived and labored under suggests that sharecropping, as an adaptation to distinct conditions of the late nineteenth-century southern economy facilitated unequal political relations between landlords and tenants, in effect a political subordination of tenants to landlords attuned to their relations of economic domination.

Sharecropping played a significant role in the reconsolidation of landlord control and of white supremacy: (1) it functioned as a system of social control; (2) it reinforced the characteristics of rural life that in themselves restricted the possibilities available to blacks—sporadic communication, over-whelming poverty, and vulnerability to oppression; (3) it depended both upon systematic forms of subordination—such as exclusion from certain kinds of employment, racial wage differentials, and school segregation—as well as more hazardous forms of subordination, such as punishment for petty and at times bizarre offenses. Otherwise petty and arbitrary crimes helped to trans-mit the meaning of white supremacy from one generation to the next, thereby establishing the relative status of blacks and whites.

Racial subordination permitted virtually any white to design individually tailored boundaries of appropriate behavior through personal instructions, administered with sudden brutality. Failure to learn could cause "a loss of employment, foreclosure, loss of credit or credibility, intimidation, personal assault, jail time, a 'bad name' or any combination of these. Repeated failure to learn meant long-term incarceration or permanent exile. Peremptory chal-lenge meant death."[60]

Hence, sharecropping's inequities were derived from market forces, but not based solely upon them. It is thus not unreasonable to view sharecrop-ping as a system of labor control that can be termed labor repressive. The bonds of sharecroppers were systemic rather than individual—reflecting the absence of options to exit from sharecropping itself. Consequently, Barrington Moore's model of democratization does apply to the late nineteenth-century southern reversal of democracy, a reversal due, in large measure, to the re-surgent power of landowning planters.

The Reversal of Democratization

Sharecropping played an integral role in an emerging order that catered to the interests of planters and merchants. But economic privilege could not be sustained without political reinforcement. Without political control, the ex-tensive democratization promoted by emancipation and the early Reconstruc-tion and the chaotic economic and financial conditions of the postwar South might have overturned or at least restrained landlord domination.

Reconstruction governments had imposed a heavy tax burden, which plant-ers were eager to reduce. Furthermore, the converging material interests of poor blacks and whites threatened to foment a collective mobilization of the lower classes. White farmers like black ones faced immiserization. Hence, the movement to reverse democratization was a prime economic and politi-cal necessity.

The solution was to undermine democracy. Reversing democratization enabled the reconsolidation of a southern oligarchy, culminating in a regime supportive of planters' class interests and harmful to both lower-class whites and blacks. Without suffrage restriction and eventually Jim Crow segregation, arguably the contours of both southern and national politics would have been dramatically different. Sharecroppers—white and black—shared common relations of production. By 1900 a majority of sharecroppers were white. If blacks had not been ostracized, the ability of white southern populists to reciprocate violence with violence might have, in time, nullified extralegal repression as a guarantor of the racial state. It is certainly plausible, although not necessarily probable, that without suffrage restriction and Jim Crow segregation, white and black agricultural laborers might well have led the South onto a very different path for national politics and twentieth-century American history.

Planters were clearly prominent in the coalition favoring democratic reversal. According to Foner, the South's antidemocratic advocates were not merely a narrow constituency of planters, but encompassed a broad coalition of Democrats, Whigs, Confederate veterans, and advocates of modernization.

> Redeemer constitutions reduced the salaries of state officials, limited the length of legislative sessions, slashed state and local property taxes, curtailed the government's authority to incur financial obligations, and repudiated Reconstruction state debts. Public aid to railroads and other corporations was prohibited and several states abolished their central boards of education. . . . The tax system was made increasingly regressive: raising sales, poll and consumption taxes, restricting tax exemptions to items such as machinery and implements utilized on plantations.[61]

White southerners came to rely on the dual mechanisms of economic control through the system of sharecropping and political control based in an unrepresentative franchise. Those who dissented publicly were frequently targets of both legal and extralegal harassment and intimidation. The significance of violent repression was magnified by the fact that southern vigilantes enjoyed the tacit and active assent of state authorities. State support solidified white supremacists' power from the late 1890s to the 1960s.

In perhaps the definitive study of the southern suffrage restriction movement, historian J. Morgan Kousser has argued that disenfranchisement was primarily the work of those who stood to gain most from the nonrepresentation of the lower classes. Socioeconomically privileged Democrats, usually from the Black Belt, were the most avid proponents of disenfranchisement and they articulated "consciously elitist theories about suffrage and wrote these theories into law in a successful effort to reform the polity."[62]

The actions of the suffrage restriction movement fit political scientist Juan Linz's comparative analysis of the breakdown of democratic regimes. Linz argued that declines in cohesion are often a consequence of efforts to remove issues of conflict from partisan politics by transforming them into legal or technical issues.[63] In this case restrictionists used recurrent registration (meaning the necessity to register separately for elections for different levels of government), multiple boxes for the depositing of ballots, secret ballots, literacy tests, property tests, clauses requiring an understanding of the Constitution, grandfather clauses, and poll taxes. The Australian ballot, a technique that listed all candidates for each office on a single sheet of paper, was especially effective in disfranchising many illiterate and near illiterates of both races. The purpose of all of these innovations was to assure the Democrats' dominance of their respective states.

The restrictions generally came in a series of waves, peaking between 1888–93 and 1898–1902. The years 1888–93 were when the Republican Party in the South might have gained strength due to the Lodge Fair Election Bill, a measure the South had good reason to fear, and 1898–1902 marked the decline of the Populists. The Lodge "Force Bill" was designed to enforce fairness in federal elections by using federal election supervisors in areas where elections had been tainted by fraud and widespread denials of voting rights. If passed, all-white Democratic supremacy would have been jeopardized and a second Reconstruction would have perhaps been made feasible.[64] It passed the House and was stymied only by a filibuster in the Senate. But the failure to pass this bill brought a close to federal intervention in southern politics.

By 1903, legislative restrictions on the suffrage were in place in every southern state.[65] Dramatic reductions in turnout and the political strength of opposition parties soon followed. Almost immediately black voting declined. Black disenfranchisement, racial segregation, and lynch terror were used to establish an apartheid-like regime in the American South. White southern Democrats benefited systematically from overrepresentation in congressional (and electoral college) seats as the total population of their states increased the size of southern congressional delegations relative to the actual number of voters.[66]

Furthermore, black disfranchisement signaled the beginnings of an era of setbacks in electoral participation that affected many whites as well. The new rules governing suffrage hampered uneducated and illiterate whites unable to read and mark voting ballots correctly, as well as those too poor to pay a poll tax. The establishment of disenfranchisement provisions meant southern elites could insist not only that blacks were not political citizens, but even whites did not have an inviolable right to vote. According to political scientists Earl and Merle Black, "As a democracy of white and black males gave way to a 'broadly based oligarchy' of white males, southern politics shifted from active competition to mandatory tranquility."[67]

The bulwark of this southern oligarchy was the political power held by plantation owners. Because of the exclusion of blacks from the franchise, election districts with large black populations overrepresented small numbers of whites. Moreover, state legislatures were not reapportioned as population shifted to industrial and commercial centers in urban areas. Hence, relatively few southern white voters residing in areas with large black populations maintained political control, in a manner reminiscent of the three-fifths rule during slavery.[68] Consequently, the essence of popular sovereignty—the capacity to make meaningful choices—did not apply for a substantial number of citizens.

Nationalizing Democratic Reversal

Mass democracy relies on the belief that the franchise is a right rather than a privilege, in other words a growing acceptance of the ideology of popularity sovereignty.[69] Reversals in democratization, on the other hand, entail the converse—a growing popularity of the view that the franchise is a privilege rather than a right. As J.J. McMahan, a southern conservative, succinctly put it, "the right to vote was 'a privilege to be bestowed by the state only upon citizens who had a vested interest in it. Book education . . . is no indication of judgment, of character, or of patriotism.' The only true test is property in land."[70]

It is not uncommon for great surges in democratization to be followed by counterreactions. In other words, in the aftermath of the Reconstruction-era advances in democratization, elites frequently sought methods to undermine the saliency of democratic participation. The motivation of unreconstructed white southerners was simple and direct—because to do otherwise and accept the racial democratization of southern politics would endanger not just the one-sided distribution of political power, but also the one-sided distribution of economic power. Without reversing democratization, the political economy of sharecropping would have been difficult to sustain.

The southern ruling elite was an oligarchy grounded in white supremacy, and white supremacy depended on the repression and exclusion of blacks from political participation. Black disenfranchisement was essential for the consolidation of political power by reactionary southern Democrats. Thus, the reverse democratization of suffrage restriction left southern democracy woefully incomplete. Given a political system of one-party rule, based on mechanisms of white-only primary elections, southern Democrats effectively transformed general elections into a series of rituals. Thus, the disenfranchisement of blacks led directly to the reduction of popular sovereignty for the white southern working class as well.

According to historian Mike Davis, the establishment of a one-party system constituted a reverse (Andrew) Jacksonian revolution.[71] From diminished lower-class participation to the essentials of southern politics in the one-party era was a relatively short leap: a politics of limited taxation, limited spending, and resistance to change in the racial status quo. Southern Democrats formed a cohesive coalition committed to a southern political economy that maintained the status quo in labor standards, labor relations, work relief, racial issues, and agriculture. On these matters, southerners voted in solidarity and quite often with Republicans.[72]

Yet the unease of economic elites with democracy in the late nineteenth century was not simply a southern phenomenon. Sentiments similar to those of the southern antidemocratization forces were widespread in the North. In fact, criticism of universal manhood suffrage was widespread in Northeastern cities. A not inconsiderable element in the diminishing resistance to the southern antidemocratic agitation was the prominence of antislavery activists in the immigration-restriction movement. In the North, reversals of democratization were less dramatic, but by no means inconsequential.

The dramatic increases in immigration from 1870 onward energized a movement to restrict the franchise in the North. The concurrence of immigrants, political machines, and corruption that often characterized American cities, provided inviting targets for attack. Reformers wanted restrictions on the franchise based on education and property. According to Charles Francis Adams, Jr. (grandson of John Quincy Adams), "Universal suffrage can only mean in plain English, . . . the government of ignorance and vice:—it means a European, and especially Celtic proletariat on the Atlantic Coast; an African proletariat on the shores of the Gulf, and a Chinese proletariat on the Pacific."[73] Restrictionists argued that immigrant voters were prone to ignorance, vice, and corruption. They were the beneficiaries of fraudulent naturalization mills, whereby "professional perjurers and political manipulators transformed thousands of immigrants into citizens in the weeks before elections."[74] Northern states also adopted literacy tests. By the mid-1920s, thirteen northern and western states disfranchised illiterate citizens.[75] Laws requiring urban-only registration, lengthy residency requirements, the phase-out of alien suffrage, disqualification of paupers, and secret ballots propelled a contracting franchise in the North. According to historian Alexander Keyssar:

> By the beginning of World War I, the ebullient, democratic political culture of the mid-19th century had given way to a more constrained and segmented political order. Throughout the nation, large slices of the middle and upper classes, as well as portions of the working class, had ceased to believe in universal suffrage, and had acted on their beliefs. In the South, blacks and many poor whites had been evicted wholesale from electoral politics. In the North and West, exclusions were on a smaller scale, but still

numerous: depending on the state or city in which he lived, a man could be kept from the polls because he was an alien, a pauper, a lumberman, an anarchist, did not pay taxes or own property, could not read or write, had moved from one state to another in the past year, had recently moved from one neighborhood to another, did not possess his naturalization papers, was unable to register on the third or fourth Tuesday before an election, could not prove that he had canceled a prior registration, had been convicted of a felony, or been born in China or on an Indian reservation.[76]

Many northern reformers shared J.J. McMahan's view that only shareholders and taxpaying owners of property should have the right to vote.[77] Yet northern and southern restrictions were not comparable. Southern restrictions were more comprehensive and more violent. For one thing, not all northern reformers supported restrictionism. Northern restrictionists were also thwarted by powerful ethnic political machines. Ultimately, there would be no equivalent to white racism or planter hegemony to fuel the antisuffrage drive in the North. Eventually, reformers turned from directly attacking immigrant suffrage to more realistic and moderate alternatives, such as diminishing the weight of representation in urban areas in which most immigrants congregated.

Nonetheless, efforts to undermine northerners' voting rights echoed albeit less vigorously the establishment of Jim Crow in the South. In each case the purpose was to protect elite hegemony. Through southern suffrage restriction and less dramatic but nonetheless significant declines in democratic participation in some but not all areas of the North, millions of Americans were less able to exercise a meaningful right to vote before the New Deal. Barriers diminishing mass participation in various portions of the United States especially reduced the meaning of voting for working-class and other low-income voters.[78] Rotten boroughs—regions in which elites controlled politics via a limited franchise and shrunken electorate—were most common in the South, but not uncommon in the North as well.

A Shifting Tide: Reversing Democratization

I have argued in this chapter that rising political and economic inequality was greatly responsible for the deteriorating racial climate of the late nineteenth century. The expansion of sharecropping made an immense contribution to greater economic inequality. To protect a strongly inegalitarian economic order, southern elites promoted suffrage restriction. In essence, the most vigorous late nineteenth-century efforts to restrict the franchise were a product of the economic inequality produced by sharecropping and resulted in long-term declines in mass electoral support in the United States.

These political and economic trends favoring greater inequality were interdependent. Without the antidemocratization movements, the extreme landlord domination typified by sharecropping would have been difficult to sustain. Landlords needed to use the political system to regain and secure their hegemony. In other words, they needed to disenfranchise blacks in order to consolidate a web of economic dependency.

The attention paid by prominent economic historians, most notably Gavin Wright, to the isolation of the southern labor market as a central feature of the late nineteenth-century southern political economy is not to be slighted, but it is just as important not to slight an essential maxim: markets never exist in a vacuum. Particular market relationships favor certain political alternatives and discourage others. The influence of these political forces then reverberates onto markets. Thus, the isolation of the southern labor market reinforced the decline of black citizenship.

Ultimately landlord control of civil society in the late nineteenth-century American South depended both upon their strong hold over local government and a truce with the national state. The Compromise of 1876 can be seen as a rapprochement of northern industrialists and southern planters. This rapprochement, termed by some a "gentlemen's agreement," was a reflection of the converging interests of dominant concerns.[79] By the end of the century the federal government, primarily by noninterference in southern affairs, gave its assent to the restoration of white supremacy. Reconstruction's end brought with it broad state neutrality on the part of the national government and noninterference in the affairs of the South. Such noninterference reflected a harmonization of interests between southern landlords and northern industrialists, reminiscent of the conservative late nineteenth-century German rye and iron coalition that, by Barrington Moore's argument, formed the prototype for labor-repressive regimes.

This combination of reactionary politics joined to a retrograde economy, in the words of writer John Egerton, made the South into a land ruled by ancient and immobilizing "isms." . . ."medievalism in agriculture and industry, fundamentalism in religion, traditionalism in academia, racism in the laws and customs of white supremacy."[80]

However, southern black economic dependency and political impotence was a function of the irrelevance of southern blacks to the labor needs of northern industry. Once the flow of European immigration was disrupted, first by war and then by a drastic tightening of immigration, the needs of northern industry for unskilled labor begin to be felt within the southern plantation belt. Almost immediately the stable balance by which the excess supply of labor helped to maintain labor force docility begin to erode. In the next chapter we will see that migration of blacks out of the South began to weaken the foundation of white supremacy a generation before its actual disintegration.

4

Resurgent Democratization and the End of White Supremacy

From the 1930s to the early 1970s, declining economic inequality due to black migration out of the South, the decline of sharecropping, and the movement of blacks into industrial occupations nourished the political empowerment of black Americans. Black empowerment, a product of such positive developments as growing black political mobilization and increasing competition for black votes, strengthened demands for racial equality. Hence, broad trends favoring growing economic and political equality created a hospitable environment for progress in race relations.

In Chapter 3, I used Barrington Moore's analysis as a guide to understanding the democratic reversal of the late nineteenth century. In this chapter the argument is framed by a more recent comparative analysis, that of Dietrich Rueschemeyer, Evelyne Huber Stephens, and John Stephens in their *Capitalist Development and Democracy*.[1] They emphasize the critical role of industrialization in strengthening those strata favoring democratization by (1) increasing the size of the subordinate (prodemocracy) group; (2) simultaneously undermining the basis of their dependency; and (3) aiding the growth of resources that promote organization and erode dependency.

Accordingly, industrialization facilitated racial democratization by gradually dissolving the chains relegating blacks to a dependent status. The slow erosion of black economic dependency was a vital step in the groundswell of increasing economic equality that marks the initial phase of this period (1930 to the mid-1950s). Perhaps the core element in this eroding dependency was the migration of blacks out of a lower-paying agriculture sector and into a higher-paying industrial one. Going north also meant that blacks were exiting a labor system that verged on feudalism (in terms of the latitude despotic plantation owners enjoyed), and entering a region in which they were not just workers but also citizens.

As is often the case with profound social changes, the first steps are barely visible. The dramatic breakthroughs of the 1950s and 1960s were set in motion several decades earlier. Important long-term, albeit barely noticeable, improvements in the educational attainment of black Americans were evident by the end of the nineteenth century. Rising black educational attainment continued throughout the first half of the twentieth century, leading to a substantial narrowing in the racial literacy gap. Between 1910 and 1950, the racial literacy gap declined from 25 percent to approximately 8 percent.[2] Moreover, the continued industrial development of both the North and South allowed literate and educated blacks to move out of agriculture and into industrial, professional, clerical, and sales occupations in both regions. Such occupational upgrading, most often accompanied by relocation to urban areas, fostered greater autonomy.

Greater economic and political independence helped to undermine the dependency of sharecropping. Ultimately the southern racial caste system would not survive the demise of its economic foundation. Greater economic independence encouraged aspirations for political power. Black political influence grew commensurate with the growing number of blacks in the North. Black migration was a product of both the pull of growing opportunities in northern industry as well as a concerted push stemming from the mechanization of southern agriculture and the decline of the plantation economy. Consequently, political pressures and calculations that had long marginalized black Americans now began to work to their advantage. Beginning in the 1930s, a series of small steps paved the way for a powerful post–World War II movement.

These enormous changes had inauspicious beginnings. Economic inequality rose substantially in the decades following the Civil War and remained high through much of the early twentieth century. But the Great Depression inaugurated a period of declining inequality, a trend that would persist through most of the next forty years. During World War II, the combination of low unemployment and wage controls accelerated the declining inequality of the Depression decade.

From 1900 to 1940, the ratio of black/white earnings inequality fell only 3 percent, with black men earning roughly half as much (48 percent) as white men. In the postwar era, the pace of economic improvement of black Americans accelerated. Substantial economic advances in the private economy diminished black/white inequality. By 1980, the earnings gap would narrow another 13 percent, with black men now earning 61 percent as much as white men. These gains resulted from a combination of factors including the rapid entry of blacks into the industrial working class beginning in the late 1940s, and the growing black presence in white universities and white-collar professions in the 1960s and 1970s.[3]

These indications of a dramatic upsurge in economic equality are confirmed by other data that measure the decline in inequality occurring between 1940 and 1970. Black families made impressive gains, as per capita black income rose fourfold from 1939 to 1964.[4] From 1945 until 1969, the gap between black and white (adjusted) median family income narrowed substantially. A major cause of the narrowing gap in family income was declining black unemployment. During the 1960s economic expansion, black unemployment fell 2 points for every 1-point drop in white unemployment. According to Frank Levy, "Low black unemployment was strong medicine for black incomes."[5] Certainly through much of the post–World War II era, diminishing unemployment rates and a growing GNP led to increasing living standards for all Americans.[6] For black men, tight labor markets, gradually eroding discrimination, and increasing educational attainment were collectively responsible for their considerable economic progress.

Yet another catalyst for economic equality was the 1960s profusion of Great Society programs. Federal spending on human resources encompassing education, training, employment, social services, health, Social Security, Medicare, income security, and veteran benefits doubled from $32 billion to $66 billion from fiscal year 1962 to 1969. Poverty among black families fell from 39 percent in 1960 to 15 percent in 1980.[7] Ultimately the combination of economic growth and expanding public programs dramatically reduced income inequality.

The surge in economic equality spurred greater political equality. As black Americans moved north, they would form a significant political constituency, one whose importance grew with each passing decade. As black political leverage increased, so did the federal government's positive, albeit grudging, responses. This combination of increasing economic and political equality set the stage for dramatic progress in race relations.

Thus, from World War II until the mid-1970s the economic standing of black men improved considerably. The substantial gains of this era were a product of several forces: (1) the movement of black Americans out of geographic regions and economic sectors in which low wages prevailed and into geographic regions and economic sectors in which higher wages were available; (2) the tight labor markets of the 1960s; (3) declining discrimination and the influence of affirmative action policies during the 1960s and 1970s; and (4) a diminishing education gap between blacks and whites.[8]

Ironically, the funding allocated to social welfare programs contributed to a backlash against antipoverty efforts, forming a part of the growing resistance to further progress. In particular, the use of regressive Social Security payroll taxes spurred opposition to the Great Society. It was not insignificant that increasing expenditures for social programs were accompanied by a decline in the proportion of federal revenues garnered from the corporate income tax (dropping from 23 to 17 percent) and an increase in the share provided by individual income and Social Security taxes (increasing from 60 to 70 percent).[9] Since the 1970s the substantial gains in the economic standing of black men have been replaced by a mixture of fragmented gains and declines.

Cracks in the Edifice

By the 1930s the structural conditions that underlay segregation were beginning to weaken. However, the end of white supremacy would require the mobilization of a movement committed to gaining equal rights. Mobilization for civil rights was a product of changing structural circumstances. The activism of this era provides a strong contrast to the 1900–30 era in which black Americans were, by and large, politically impotent. The black political movement with the largest mass base—Marcus Garvey's United Negro Improvement Association (UNIA)—established branches in thirty-eight states. Garvey believed that black Americans could succeed only through their own endeavors. The UNIA sought black improvement through the colonization of American blacks in Africa. Garvey's separatism was rejected by supporters of integration, including W.E.B. Dubois, James Weldon Johnson, and A. Philip Randolph. Yet Garvey's separatist agenda fit the status of black Americans as outsiders. The UNIA epitomized the marginal status of black Americans, who essentially remained on the fringes of northern society. His support also reflected the deep pessimism prevalent among blacks during these years, when the prospects for integration seemed hopeless.[10]

The protection of white supremacy was the foundation and raison d'être of the South's one-party system. However, small cracks in the edifice of white supremacy can be traced to the beginnings of the Great Migration of blacks out of the South and into northern cities. At first, however, the most notable improvements were symbolic: (1) the heavyweight championships of Jack Johnson and Joe Louis; (2) a growing acceptance of jazz and the Harlem Renaissance; (3) the attention paid to the trials and convictions of the "Scottsborough boys"; and (4) the election of black congressmen in New York and Chicago. Certainly, the ideology of white supremacy was flexible enough to "explain" noteworthy black accomplishments—often by means of innate physiological advantages of a primitive race, "primordial equipment necessary to predatory survival," according to sociologist C. Eric Lincoln.[11] Of course symbolic advances did not entail the material advance of the great majority of black Americans.

The 1930s opened the door to an era of gradually rising expectations for black Americans. Rising expectations were a product of three factors: (1) the continuing decline of the plantation economy, a decline that accelerated in the late 1930s and continued through the 1950s; (2) the emergence of black enclaves in the North large enough to initiate party competition for their votes. Even if it would take another generation for the racial transformation of the country to begin in earnest, by the late 1930s the racial status quo was beginning to unravel; and (3) the impact of New Deal policies, which undermined the control of traditional southern elites over property, labor, credit, and local government. In reducing the dependency of laborers, tenants, and debtors, the New Deal echoed the surviving remnants of economic populism among southern whites.[12]

Initially, however, it appeared that the status of black Americans would continue to stagnate, and stagnate only because it could fall no lower. In 1928 W.E.B. Dubois, observing the failure of both Al Smith and Herbert Hoover—the Democratic and Republican presidential nominees, respectively—to address such key issues for blacks as disenfranchisement, discrimination, segregation, economic inequality, and racial violence, remarked, "it does not matter a tinker's damn which of these gentlemen succeed."[13] Herbert Hoover was only one of many Republicans who favored driving blacks out of the party in order to strengthen its (white) southern support. It took no great leap of imagination to foresee the extermination of black political power. As historian C. Vann Woodward suggests in his classic, *The Strange Career of Jim Crow,* the South was on the road to apartheid.[14]

Hoover's antiblack posture helped considerably in the 1928 presidential election. Republicans made significant inroads into a number of southern states, as Hoover won the popular vote in Texas, Florida, North Carolina, Tennessee, and Virginia. These victories were a strong indication of a resurgent two-party politics, at least outside the deep South. Nor was Hoover punished by blacks in the 1932 presidential election. Blacks remained the most loyal Republican constituency, and in some instances their support rose from its 1928 level.

Even in northern cities with a strong concentration of black voters, black political relationships with the white political establishment were firmly subordinate, reflecting little more than "bread crumbs" from the table of white politicians, rather than tangible payments to reciprocate for substantive political contributions. Urban political machines often chose a token black to function as the machine's representative in the black community. Their primary purpose was to turn out the vote for Republican candidates. Black leaders were largely dependent upon their relations with white patrons, not upon the possession of independent sources of power.[15]

Political dependency reflected the race's marginal status—the number of registered blacks North and South were less than 5 percent of the national electorate. This marginality consigned black politicians to an existence as tokens. Northern blacks were generally unable to exercise an influence in any way proportionate to their numbers. Hence, dependency, marginality, and tokenism contributed to a self-sustaining vicious cycle of powerlessness.

The Great Depression set in motion a spiraling downturn in black living conditions. Those who resided in the rural South were most vulnerable to the collapse of cotton prices, down 70 percent between 1929 and 1933. Black unemployment increased dramatically in cities, as whites began to take jobs that had traditionally been reserved for blacks. Racial antagonisms rose as white terrorist organizations such as the Black Shirts coerced blacks into relinquishing jobs to whites. Lynchings, which had declined in the late 1920s, began to increase as well.[16]

Hence, on the eve of the New Deal although the masses of blacks might not have been slaves, they were hardly free. Their situation bore broad similarity to that of free blacks before the Civil War—their options were broadly circumscribed by dependence and the creation of a distinctive, marginal status for black freemen.[17] Although blacks were not necessarily subject to the authority of particular white individuals, they were undeniably subjects of white American society.

A New Beginning

In spite of these ominous indications, the 1930s would show noticeable improvements in a number of areas.

Supreme Court Decisions

The Supreme Court during the Roosevelt era made important decisions in cases with important civil rights issues at stake. These decisions included cases involving blacks' exclusion from juries, the right to picket to protest discrimination in employment, unequal treatment on interstate transportation, disenfranchisement, restrictive racial covenants, and discrimination in graduate education. The Court narrowed the scope of permissible discrimination by federalizing the Bill of Rights and expanding the boundaries of state action. The Court also began to regularly accept civil rights cases and decide them in favor of black litigants. Before 1931, 43 percent of its decisions favored civil rights; from 1931 to 1955, 91 percent of the decisions favored civil rights.[18] The changing attitude of the Court toward civil rights litigation was just one example of the changes occurring in the Court's attitude toward an interventionist federal agenda. In the early 1930s, the Court struck down federal regulation of labor relations in such diverse areas as child labor, retirement and pensions, minimum wages, and maximum hours.[19] Generally, the Hughes Supreme Court rejected the central tenets of the New Deal.

But Roosevelt's post-1937 Court consisted of justices who had occupied high federal positions and believed in the federal government's value. In the late 1930s, the Court's attitude toward New Deal policy shifted, and it began to uphold federal power to regulate employment. Blacks would gain direct and indirect benefits from the Court's affirmation of New Deal social and economic policies. In particular, the growing support for federal economic intervention fostered more active opposition to discrimination. According to Lucas Powe, between 1937 and 1952 "the Court was sustaining anything a president did. The Justices were part of the national Democratic party, sustaining actions of the national Democratic Party."[20]

The Court began to look askance at regulations designed to limit black voting. In 1939 the Court overturned an Oklahoma law employing discriminatory registration procedures. In 1944 the Court ruled (in *Smith v. Allwright*) the white primary unconstitutional. In 1949, it disallowed Alabama's use of an "understanding" test, ruling it arbitrarily denied blacks the right to vote.

The Supreme Court's shift can be attributed to a changing political environment, in no small measure based upon the president's determination to shift the Court's behavior in a more liberal direction. The Court's movement was also a function of Roosevelt's eight appointees to the court who brought, on balance, a more progressive attitude to civil rights issues. Whereas the Supreme Court under Charles Evans Hughes was dominated by conservative business lawyers whose views were forged during the long retreat from racial justice of the post-Reconstruction era, Roosevelt's younger appointees were more attuned to an egalitarian reformist agenda, of which one element (although not its main thrust) was civil rights. Furthermore, several Roosevelt appointees were New Dealers who were experienced politicians—for example, Hugo Black, Frank Murphy, Robert Jackson, and Stanley Reed—well aware of the importance of civil rights for winning the black vote for Democrats.

Growing Influence of the NAACP

The National Association for the Advancement of Colored People (NAACP) had been the most influential civil rights organization from its beginnings in 1909. But in the 1930s it began to experience more success than ever before.

The upward trend in the NAACP's influence predates the New Deal. In 1930, the NAACP participated, albeit as a minor player, in the successful campaign to block the nomination of John J. Parker to the Supreme Court. Parker was an outspoken advocate of disenfranchisement of blacks, stating that "the Negro as a class does not desire to enter politics. . . . We recognize the fact that he has not yet reached the stage in his development when he can share the burdens and responsibilities of government."[21] Although black opposition was not decisive, participation in the campaign stimulated NAACP activism. By 1930, the NAACP had developed an arsenal of tactics that emphasized investigations, publicity, lobbying, and organized protests that were in synch with the vulnerable pressure points of the administration to a much greater degree than in the past.

In the mid-1930s the NAACP's legal team of Charles H. Houston and Thurgood Marshall began to attack the constitutionality of segregation. Their initial successes came by testing the application of "separate but equal." A significant early victory came when Houston and Marshall won the case of *Murray v. Maryland*, overturning the University of Maryland's rejection of the application of Donald Murray to the university's law school. In the late 1930s Marshall won several more cases attacking the pay inequities between black and white teachers in the state of Maryland. Building upon this success, the NAACP began to pursue pay inequity cases in other states.[22]

Furthermore, the NAACP legal team began to actively recruit cases dealing with school segregation, voting rights, and mistreatment of blacks charged with crimes. Houston recruited Lloyd Gaines to apply to the University of Missouri law school, viewing this case as critical to a successful nationwide school desegregation effort. In 1938 the Supreme Court ruled that the University of Missouri had to admit Gaines to its law school. In the majority were Roosevelt's six appointees. The *Gaines* case had national significance because of the Supreme Court's ruling. Missouri tried to subvert the Court's ruling by hastily constructing a black law school at Lincoln University. This stratagem was rejected by the Missouri State Supreme Court. In an unusual footnote to his case, Lloyd Gaines never actually attended law school. His disappearance in March 1939 has never been solved.

The Supreme Court not only encouraged activism, it was itself influenced by the activism of the NAACP, which brought the bulk of these cases before the Court. The Supreme Court's acceptance of the legal arguments favoring desegregation initiated a trend fraught with both symbolic and substantive meaning because its rulings established nationwide precedents. The NAACP's legal strategists and the Supreme Court began to construct a relationship based upon a greater commitment to desegregation. Thus, the successful outcome of cases encouraged greater assertiveness among blacks, promoted membership in the organization, and spurred the initiation of new lawsuits. Mobilization and action bred success, which propelled further action and greater mobilization. Such public activism for black rights propelled the NAACP's growth from less than 100,000 members in 1930 to 420,000 by 1946.[23]

New Deal Activism

Clearly race issues were not a priority in the New Deal at its outset. Still, a new atmosphere began to emerge on civil rights due to the actions of a number of New Dealers occupying powerful positions in the executive branch. Harry Hopkins and Harold Ickes were perhaps the most notable of the white New Dealers who gave civil rights issues serious consideration. And if Franklin D. Roosevelt was disinclined to pay special attention to racial issues, First Lady Eleanor Roosevelt was not. Mrs. Roosevelt lent her considerable prestige to the civil rights cause. By 1935 New Deal relief programs began to upgrade the education, health, and living standards of millions of black Americans.

More than 100 blacks were appointed to posts in Roosevelt's administration. This substantial presence made possible the formation of an informal working group known as the Black Cabinet, led by Mary Bethune Cookman. The Black Cabinet spurred greater awareness in the federal government of the needs of black citizens, especially after 1935. Race relations advisers in the federal government pressed for blacks in policy-making positions, for racial equality in the relief and recovery programs, and for greater administration sensitivity on all civil rights issues. At the very least, according to historian Harvard Sitkoff, "the Black Cabinet signified an interest shown by no other administration within memory."[24] The existence of the Black Cabinet brought attention to civil rights, initially by increasing awareness within the government of civil rights issues.

Growing Influence of the Black Vote

The benefits of the New Deal altered the loyalty of blacks to the Republican Party. Blacks had remained loyal to the party of Lincoln in the 1932 elections. They began to move to the Democrats in the 1934 congressional elections. For the first time a majority of blacks voted for Democrats. In 1936, the first blacks were seated as delegates at a national Democratic Party convention. Later that year, 76 percent of northern blacks voted for Roosevelt, a larger shift than that of any other bloc.

More than 400,000 blacks migrated out of the South during the Depression, mostly to such key industrial states as Illinois, Michigan, Missouri,

New York, New Jersey, Ohio, Pennsylvania, and California. Democrats began to woo voters in black neighborhoods, while Democratic urban machines sought to attract black leaders. The New Deal brought out a larger black vote. Black Americans' growing presence in northern states with more electoral votes than the entire South was pivotal. By the late 1930s northern Democrats had begun to rely upon black voters. This support spurred the formation of a liberal white perspective on racial matters.

Blacks in the urban South were not entirely oblivious to the changing tide either. More blacks voted in 1940 in the eleven ex-Confederate states than in any prior twentieth-century election. These newly enfranchised blacks came almost entirely from urban areas. Mass meetings and campaigns for voter registration in southern cities began to be visible.

The number of blacks in elective and appointive offices began to rise. With the emergence of black Democratic politicians and their inclusion in patronage, black support for the Democrats grew. But as northern blacks began to support the party in large numbers, the "American dilemma" was becoming a "Democratic dilemma."[25] The increasing significance of the black vote also energized Republican efforts to win blacks back to the party of Lincoln.

Industrial Unionism

The emergence of industrial unionism will be examined in detail in Chapter 5. But it deserves mention here because the dramatic growth of the Congress of Industrial Organizations (CIO) in the 1930s and early 1940s was both an indicator of as well as a factor in the changing tide under way in race relations. The personal sensitivities of CIO recruiters to racial oppression were magnified by their recognition that black workers were indispensable to industrial unions. Without the strong participation of black industrial workers there would not have been a meaningful industrial union movement.

Southern Counterreaction

Another sign of changing times was the fierce counterreaction from southern conservatives to efforts of the Roosevelt administration to gain black votes in the North. By 1940, a majority of congressmen from states below the Mason-Dixon line had joined the opposition to the New Deal. Opposition to the New Deal hastened the disintegration of southern progressivism. The challenge of race forced white southerners to make a choice. Most chose racism and economic reaction.

Southern conservatives were quite sensitive to the declining importance of the South to the Democratic Party, shown by the decline in the region's percentage of the party's vote in the electoral college from 90 percent in 1920 to 26 percent in 1932 and 23 percent in 1936. Roosevelt also brought a majority of non-southern Democrats into Congress. From 1896 to 1930, two-thirds of the Democrats elected to Congress came from southern and border states. However, during Roosevelt's administration they were less than half of the Democratic congressional delegation. According to Nicol Rae, "By changing the context of the party alignment from one based on region, ethnicity, and culture to one based on class, the New Deal isolated the southern Democrats decisively from their national brethren and made them an aberrant reactionary element (and ultimately a dispensable element) in an otherwise 'center-left' electoral coalition."[26] It was conceivable, although unlikely, that New Deal legislation might be passed without southern support. According to Senator "Cotton Ed" Smith in explaining his walkout from the 1936 national party convention, "The doors of the white man's party have been thrown open to snare the Negro vote in the North."[27]

The Color Line in the Welfare State

Notwithstanding these positive signs, the New Deal was far from an era of unqualified advancement for black Americans. Major New Deal programs frequently extended racial discrimination. The original Agricultural Adjustment Act did little if anything to improve the condition of black Americans, while the National Industrial Recovery Act (NIRA) legitimated lower southern wage rates and excluded most blacks from coverage by NIRA provisions. The NIRA precipitated a widespread pattern of racial disadvantage: the code set the minimum wage in the South—where the workforce in an industry was heavily black—far below that in the North—where the workforce was predominantly white. When the wages set by the code were high, blacks were fired and displaced by whites, or employers ignored the code and paid blacks a lower wage. Filing a complaint to protest discrimination might lead to termination because of the preponderance of employers on compliance boards.

A similar pattern emerged at the Federal Emergency Relief Administration (FERA), an agency designed to deal with immediate relief needs by dispensing funds to states for unemployment relief. But since the administration of FERA relief efforts was conducted by state and local officials, their views on racial equality generally held sway. Hence the FERA sanctioned racial discrimination including (1) lower wages for blacks, (2) hiring blacks only when there were no more whites to be hired, and (3) employing blacks only as unskilled laborers.[28]

The exclusion of agricultural workers and domestic servants from Social

Security insured that roughly 60 percent of blacks would not be covered and thereby be ineligible for Social Security benefits. Such workers were relegated to more marginal social programs where local authorities controlled benefit levels and eligibility criteria. The Civilian Conservation Corp (CCC), the Public Works Administration (PWA), and the Works Progress Administration (WPA) all discriminated in favor of white workers at the expense of blacks. Blacks were typically beneficiaries of relief, not workers entitled to rights. The concentration of blacks on federal relief was thus a result of the combined impact of private labor market discrimination and government policies that, political scientist Michael Brown argues, "extended the color line into the welfare state. . . .Whites were coercively substituting relief for jobs." The outcome was a racially bifurcated welfare state.[29]

The integration of mothers' pensions into the Aid to Dependent Children (ADC) program was accomplished only by acceding to southern congressmen's insistence that local welfare authorities should determine who would receive benefits. Consequently the first ADC benefits went primarily to white widowed women with children. Over time a number of states in both the South and the North altered eligibility requirements to prevent black women from receiving benefits. Such obstacles as seasonal employment policies that excluded welfare recipients during cotton-picking season and surprise visits by social workers in order to eliminate recipients found to be living with a man made possible the continuation of racial barriers. According to the Jackson, Mississippi, *Daily News*, "The average Mississippian can't imagine himself chipping in to pay pensions for able-bodied Negroes to sit around in idleness on front galleries, supporting all their kinfolks on pensions, while cotton crops are crying for workers to get them out of the grass."[30] In 1939, the Social Security Act was amended to make married women eligible for old age and survivor's benefits. This action elevated widows above other single mothers. The 1939 amendments discriminated in favor of dependents of widows and against the dependents of divorced women and illegitimate children.

Racial exclusion was the price for the passage of social welfare legislation. Insisting upon local administration of major New Deal Programs, southern congressmen were determined to protect white supremacy against erosion. New Deal Congresses were dominated by powerful southern Democratic committee chairmen. In the first New Deal Congress, two-thirds of the thirty most important committees of both houses were chaired by southerners. These beneficiaries of white primaries, property qualifications, and poll taxes could kill reform legislation.

These chairmen collaborated with powerful interest groups to establish guidelines inimical to black interests. Although perhaps most egregious in its delicate treatment of white southerners who insisted on controlling welfare relief, New Deal legislation safeguarded racial boundaries throughout the nation in unemployment insurance and housing programs as well.[31]

The strongest white supporters of civil rights within the administration chose not to directly confront powerful southern segregationists. Rather, they believed that broad-based economic and social reforms were the best strategy for black advancement. Hence, as sociologist Jill Quadagno has argued, the direct, intentional effects of New Deal programs did more to cement the color line than to weaken it. Accordingly, the New Deal reinforced rather than diminished the racial divide among workers. Furthermore, reinforcing the racial divide among wage earners created problems that would have to be resolved if the legacy of a racially segmented social welfare structure was to be overcome.[32]

Ultimately then, in the 1930s neither the White House nor the Democratic Party was prepared to make the type of commitment to civil rights that would allow a direct confrontation with white supremacy. Many of the administration's most influential figures were racial conservatives, especially the leaders of the traditionally powerful departments—State, Treasury, War, and the Navy. In general, calculations based on electoral strategy reinforced conservative sentiments in favor of upholding the racial status quo.

Consequently, the emerging coalition of civil rights organizations, labor unions, and liberals failed to accomplish any of its key objectives on racial matters, whether they involved securing a federal anti-lynching law, ending disfranchisement, or seriously challenging segregation. In general, expedient political calculations took precedence over moral outrage, and the president was unwilling to jeopardize his relationship with southern congressmen. These congressmen, influential southerners born into a segregated world, masters of a political system that excluded blacks from voting, were well aware of the significance of lynching (and of course disenfranchisement) literally and symbolically to the maintenance of white supremacy. According to historian Nancy Weiss, "The New Deal did help suffering blacks in important ways. But it too rarely escaped the racism typical of American society in the 1930s, and discrimination plagued most of its best-intentioned programs. Some New Deal programs were responsible for making the situation of blacks in the 1930s even worse; and some programs that aided blacks in the short run may have contributed in the long run to the relegation of blacks to an economically marginal ghetto existence."[33]

Nonetheless, the New Deal era provided a period of cautious optimism and encouragement to racial progress. Clearly, as northern blacks began to vote for Roosevelt in increasing numbers, their presence as an important constituency for northern Democrats provided a tangible incentive to alter the racial status quo. The New Deal effectively heightened both the interest and the presence of black Americans in electoral politics. The continued migration of blacks to urban areas in the North gave the Democrats a real constituency to be wooed, one no longer pacified by the paternalistic tokenism of the preceding era.

The Postwar Emergence of a Civil Rights Agenda

Until 1940, Roosevelt had only marginally diverged from the long-established presidential tradition that combined indifference and hostility on racial matters. Roosevelt's economic policy was at times pushed leftward, thanks to the possibility that Huey Long might run for president, a threat ended by his assassination in 1935. When policy involved race, Roosevelt consistently sided with southern senators and congressmen, whose support was vital to the passage of his legislative program. These representatives, elected from a one-party region during an era when seniority determined committee chairmanships, held the power to block essential New Deal legislation. The administration valued southern support more highly than black support for almost its entirety.

Political calculations that minimized the status of blacks as citizens restricted their participation in major New Deal programs. Blacks were underrepresented on relief rolls throughout the South, especially in rural areas. Even in the North, they were frequently excluded from relief through strict state residency requirements, which stipulated as many as three to five years of residency to qualify for relief. Such requirements were especially onerous for the poorest Americans, both black and white, who moved more frequently in their search for work. Stringent residency requirements and pauper disqualification clauses also screened the electorate of white and black undesirables. Pauper disqualification requirements penalized relief recipients by disqualifying them from voting. Enforcement of such clauses did decline during the Depression.

From 1937 to 1946 over 150 civil rights bills were introduced in Congress emphasizing three areas: lynching, the poll tax, and fair employment practices. But Roosevelt refused to take a public stand on any of these issues, and he even disavowed his earlier support for anti-lynching legislation.[34]

Yet considerations based upon a political strategy that had long worked against the interests of black Americans began to turn in their favor by the 1940 presidential election. The 1940s saw the emergence of civil rights upon the national political agenda. Republicans began to perceive the black vote as a strategic necessity if they were to return to power. At the presidential convention of 1940, Republican spokesmen supported anti-lynching legislation and the protection of voting rights. Nominee Wendell Wilkie, seeking black support, pledged to end discrimination in the armed forces and in Washington, D.C. The Wilkie campaign kept up the pressure through the fall, highlighting civil rights differences between the two parties. Moreover, the conservative resurgence in 1938 increased the political leverage of the now core New Deal constituencies of liberals, labor, and blacks. To counter the newly attractive Republican positions on civil rights, Roosevelt announced a series of intermediate steps to combat discrimination in the military.[35]

A proposed march on Washington, scheduled for July 1941, would mark a new beginning in the relationship between black Americans and the Democratic Party. Responding to pressure from civil rights and labor organizations (led by A. Philip Randolph, president of the Brotherhood of Sleeping Car Porters), and the prospects of an embarrassing march on Washington by supporters of desegregation, Roosevelt issued an executive order targeted at racial discrimination. Executive Order 8802 made discrimination in government employment illegal and created an (unpaid) Fair Employment Practices Commission (FEPC) to insure nondiscrimination in the defense sector. This order was only a small victory, and was won only after months of resistance from the president. Mindful of the resistance from powerful conservative constituencies, Roosevelt made his executive order relatively toothless, covering only the federal government and defense contractors and lacking any sanctions for noncompliance. Furthermore, Congress would prevent enforcement of the provisions of Roosevelt's executive order until the end of World War II. However, Executive Order 8802 was symbolically important as the first federal action since Reconstruction whose intent was to reduce discrimination. Roosevelt's Executive Order 9346 gave FEPC jurisdiction over all federal employment. Although largely symbolic, these orders set a precedent for President Truman's postwar pro–civil rights agenda.[36]

Congressional support for civil rights began to rise as well. Members of Congress introduced bills to give Executive Order 8802 legal backing and to extend the prohibition against discrimination to private employers and labor unions. The 1940s also saw the political defeats of a number of diehard segregationists, most notably Senator "Cotton Ed" Smith of South Carolina.

The Supreme Court

During the 1940s a series of Supreme Court rulings began to dismantle the constitutional protection of segregation. In *Smith v. Allwright*, 1944, the Court ruled that all-white primaries were unconstitutional. In *Morgan v. Virginia*, 1946, the Court banned segregated seating on interstate buses. The Court found segregation impermissible in publicly supported higher education in two cases decided in 1950, *Sweatt v. Painter* and *McLaurin v. Oklahoma*.

Sweatt v. Painter was a dramatic breakthrough in the attack on segregation. Victorious NAACP lawyers believed this decision set school segregation on the road to extinction. Conservative Chief Justice Fred Vinson wrote the majority opinion that Jim Crow schools were unlikely to ever be equal to long standing state schools. In a speech at Fisk University, Thurgood Marshall argued, "Despite the fact that the Separate-But-Equal doctrine was not technically overruled by these decisions, the force and significance of the languages certainly robs the doctrine of most of its validity. . . . We now have the tools to destroy all governmentally imposed racial segregation."[37] With *Sweatt*, the momentum favoring racial integration was clearly accelerating. The Baltimore *Afro-American*'s headline announcing the Sweatt decision expressed a view that was rapidly gaining strength among supporters of integration: "End of Jim Crow in Sight."[38]

By 1950 each branch of the federal government had demonstrated some degree of commitment to the fight against racial segregation. At first civil rights was an issue of strong public concern only to blacks, Jews, and southern whites. Public opinion remained strongly opposed to equal-employment-opportunity legislation. More than half of those surveyed in the late 1930s and 1940s believed that whites should be preferred over blacks for employment. Support for the principle of equal employment opportunity, as measured in public opinion surveys, grew substantially over time—42 percent in 1944 to 47 percent in 1946 to 83 percent in 1963, and to 95 percent in 1972. However, support for the enactment of laws to enforce equal employment grew at a considerably slower pace.[39]

The postwar era brought more attention to civil rights. The southern black electorate grew from 50,000 in 1932 to 750,000 by 1948. White sensitivity to the changing tide is the most likely explanation of the resulting backlash, foreshadowing the 1950s' and 1960s' counterreaction. Racial atrocities spiked in 1946 and 1947. Black veterans played an important role in postwar civil rights activism. They refused to accept segregation after having fought the evils of racial supremacy abroad. Some paid a very high price for their principles. For example, Isaac Woodward, after being discharged on February 12, 1946, exchanged words with a white bus driver, which led to his being arrested and beaten. A billy club was jammed into his eye sockets, gouging out his eyes.

Black veteran James Stephenson defended his mother from assault by a white store clerk. His action sparked a confrontation in which the state safety commissioner and a unit of the highway patrol led an assault on an all-black neighborhood of Columbia, Tennessee. They proceeded to shoot up businesses, destroy property, and loot and ransack homes. July and August 1946 saw the lynching of a dozen black men in the deep South.[40]

Harry S Truman: Passenger or Engineer?

Responding to stories about the wave of racial violence, President Truman appointed an advisory commission to recommend legislation addressing the inequities in the citizenship rights of black Americans. The responsibilities of the Committee on Civil Rights were to investigate the status of civil rights and to propose legislative remedies. The commission's report "To Secure These Rights," recommended creation of a permanent civil rights commission and a Fair Employment Practices Commission, and passage of legislation to prohibit lynching, the poll tax, and discrimination in interstate transportation.

Harry Truman became the first president to address an NAACP convention. In February 1948, he sent a civil rights message to Congress requesting a federal anti-lynching law. Truman went further, issuing executive orders establishing a fair employment board within the Civil Service Commission, and initiating the desegregation of the armed forces.

There is understandable disagreement as to whether the racial liberalism that Truman prominently displayed during the 1948 presidential election campaign reflected deep personal commitment or political calculation. Truman and his advisors realized that visible support for civil rights would be vital for his political survival and reelection. Truman's actions were undoubtedly a testament to the growing importance of black voters to the Democrats. A key political objective was to prevent Henry Wallace from attracting black (and Jewish) support for his third-party campaign. Wallace appealed primarily to northern liberals and blacks. Moreover, Truman's major party opponent, Republican Thomas Dewey, was considered a racial moderate. Furthermore, Truman vacillated during the campaign, especially once it became clear that the defection of Southern Dixiecrats might cost him the election.

In John Egerton's words, Truman "was as least as much a passenger as he was an engineer on the train of postwar events."[41] Yet, even if Truman's racial beliefs were not distinctly liberal, as many believe, political considerations would no longer allow "Rooseveltian benign neglect" to suffice. The political spectrum was shifting. New attitudes were beginning to influence national politics. Dewey, Truman, and Progressive Party candidate Henry Wallace were competing in a political spectrum dominated by racial moderates and progressives.

Minneapolis Mayor Hubert Humphrey's racial liberalism helped to make him a rising political star. The 1948 Democratic National Convention adopted a strong civil rights platform with Humphrey leading the way, arguing that it was time for the Democratic Party to "get out of the shadow of states rights and walk forthrightly into the bright sunshine of human rights."[42] Black attorney George Vaughan spoke before the nominating convention urging

Mississippi's exclusion from the convention. Truman's qualified advocacy of civil rights was only one among a growing number of positive signs of the importance of civil rights for the national Democratic Party.

Credit for the change in the party's platform on race must be apportioned among the following: the NAACP, A. Philip Randolph and other labor-based civil rights activists, the newly formed Americans for Democratic Action, the threat of Henry Wallace's campaign, and even the Republican Party (whose platform called for an end to segregation in the armed forces and abolition of the poll tax). The net result was that Democrats could no longer afford to neglect civil rights in order to placate Dixie.[43] The response of segregationists was immediate. Meeting in Birmingham, Governor Strom Thurmond of South Carolina was selected as the States Rights candidate for president and went on to win Louisiana, South Carolina, Alabama, and Mississippi.

Congress was slower to adapt to the awakening of civil rights as a national issue during the immediate postwar years. Truman's civil rights bill and other measures on his agenda were blocked by the Senate. In large measure congressional action was stymied by filibustering southern senators. They forestalled passage of civil rights legislation until 1957. Arguably, congressional inaction reflected a public perception that issues of racial discrimination and segregation were not decisive for large segments of the public. In other words, it would require greater support for civil rights in the executive and judicial branches of the national government, as well as in other areas of society, to energize Congress to seriously attempt to pass civil rights legislation.

Growing Political Momentum

On May 17, 1954, the Supreme Court in the case of *Brown v. the Board of Education* struck down school segregation as unconstitutional, by a vote of eight to zero. This decision overturned seventy-five years of federal support for discrimination, including the long-established precedent of *Plessy vs. Ferguson* set in 1896. It has become fashionable to view the *Brown* decision ambivalently, especially since the commitment to end school desegregation remains unfulfilled a half century later. A second decision on the Brown case known as *Brown II* undermined the substance of *Brown I* by enabling delay. Desegregation was delayed for an undetermined time: it was to occur "with all deliberate speed." White resistance to desegregation became "endlessly imaginative," according to historian James Patterson. Law professor Lucas Powe believes that thanks to *Brown II*, "Brown issued a great principle but in results yielded little except minimal desegregation in the border states, a bit in the rural areas of the periphery, and nothing except defiance in Virginia, Florida, and the deep South."[44]

Patterson, on the other hand, believes that the Court went as far as it possibly could, that it had no choice but to accept gradual implementation because it lacked the power to compel compliance. With *Brown*, the Court not only withdrew its support for segregation in education, it also helped to stimulate civil rights activism and a corresponding countermobilization of segregationists.

A symbolic aspect of the *Brown* decision was that the Court was now perceived to be firmly on the side of civil rights progress. According to Patterson, an essential truth about *Brown* is that a number of postwar developments—the rising expectations of blacks, the slow erosion of white convictions about racial segregation, the Cold War, and the damage Jim Crow did to America's quest for leadership—influenced the Court to promote the liberalization of American racial practices.

The 1950s would offer a mixed bag of gradual progress, continued and at times stiffened resistance, and considerable backsliding. Southern black registration continued to surge. One million southern blacks were registered by 1952. Racial terrorism also surged: forty black homes were bombed in 1951 and 1952.[45] Northern Democrats responded to the growing racial polarization by trying to straddle the widening chasm between northern liberals and southern conservatives. Adlai Stevenson, the Democratic presidential candidate in 1952 and 1956, sought to appease the South, and through conciliation keep white southerners in the party. Although the 1952 Democratic platform (passed during Stevenson's first campaign) was not greatly different from that of 1948, Stevenson's 1956 platform made favorable mention of states rights, and barely mentioned the *Brown* decision. President Dwight Eisenhower's commitment to enforce *Brown* was tepid as well, evident in his public statement that the hearts of men could not be changed by laws or court decisions. Stevenson went even further, refusing to employ federal troops to enforce court orders, arguing that such a policy would be disastrous.

Defending White Supremacy

The *Brown* decision also marked the initiation of a pitched battle to defend white supremacy, led by southern politicians. Southern officials increasingly challenged civil rights activism and prosegregation activity increased greatly through the late 1950s and early 1960s. In the aftermath of *Brown* and the Montgomery bus boycott, segregationist organizations grew rapidly. The White Citizens Council was formed in July of 1954, just two months after the *Brown* decision. Its goal was to maintain segregation, peaceably if possible, violently if necessary. Increasing polarization meant there no longer was any room for the "liberal segregationist." Mississippi created a State Sovereignty Commission with the aim of protecting the state against invasive federal authority. The commission's purpose was to collect information on suspected supporters of racial integration. Information on 87,000 people was collected and civil rights organizations were infiltrated by state agents.

In 1956, a Southern Manifesto was published that opposed integration on the grounds that it subverted the American Constitution. It termed the *Brown* decision "a clear abuse of judicial powers that was being exploited by outside agitators." The Supreme Court, it said, "undertook to exercise their naked judicial power and substituted their personal political and social ideas for the established law of the land."[46] The overwhelming majority of southern congressmen (101 of 128) signed the manifesto. Senate majority leader Lyndon Johnson and House Speaker Sam Rayburn were not asked to sign. In the Senate, only Tennessee's Gore and Kefauver refused. In the House, those who abstained included sixteen from Texas, three from Tennessee, and three from North Carolina.[47] The Court's decision was termed national suicide, and southern state legislatures sought to prevent its ruling from being enforced by closing public schools.

In June 1956, Alabama attorney general John Patterson raised the stakes for activists by acquiring a court order banning most NAACP activities within Alabama, including fund-raising, dues collection, and solicitation of new members. When the NAACP refused to turn its membership and contribution lists over to Patterson, the judge levied a $100,000 contempt fine. Arkansas and Florida also sought NAACP membership lists. Virginia went after the NAACP Legal Defense Fund. The net result was to put the NAACP and its legal defense fund on the defensive (and make it nonoperational in Alabama until the mid-1960s).

White southern reactions to the *Brown* decision also included economic coercion and physical violence. News came to light in 1958 that the Internal Revenue Service was harassing black and white southerners who opposed segregation. A 47-year-old NAACP leader in Mississippi was ordered to explain why he should not be reclassified 1-A by his local draft board. More ominously, the White Citizens Council circulated a list of names that became unofficially known as a death list. At least one of the individuals named was murdered. Nor did federal judges have immunity from retaliation. The house of Judge Frank Johnson's mother was bombed. The gravesite of Judge Richard Rives's son was littered and his tombstone painted red. The judges' crime was to rule in favor of the Montgomery bus boycotters.[48]

Eisenhower and Civil Rights

On the positive side of the ledger, by the late 1950s a rapidly growing northern black electorate showed signs of becoming a sophisticated cadre of swing voters. One sign of black political development was the stronger Republican commitment to civil rights and the punishment of Adlai Stevenson—an estimated 40 percent of blacks voted for Eisenhower in 1956, a significant decline in the support Stevenson had received from blacks in 1952.

Eisenhower would continue a number of Democratic initiatives: (1) accelerating the desegregation of the armed forces by executive action; (2) desegregating public facilities in the District of Columbia; and (3) officially supporting the NAACP's successful court challenge in the *Brown* case. Yet if Eisenhower supported some basic citizenship rights, he did not favor laws that would increase interracial contact. Instead, he made clear his resistance to the use of federal force to support desegregation. "Now I want to say this. I can't imagine any sort of circumstance that would ever induce me to send Federal troops into a Federal Court and into any area to enforce the order of a Federal court."[49]

Eisenhower's administration submitted a friend of the court brief to the Supreme Court that asked the Court to avoid specifying a deadline in its timetable for ending school segregation. Arguably, by temporizing during the desegregation of Central High in Little Rock, Arkansas, Eisenhower emboldened resistance to desegregation. Only after black children were beaten and driven out of school by concerted mob action did the president federalize the National Guard and send troops in to enforce the law. Eisenhower privately informed Attorney General Herbert Brownell "that he strongly disagreed with the [*Brown*] decision." He went on to remark "that since Chief Justice Warren and the Supreme Court had made the ruling, 'let them enforce it.'" In general, the Eisenhower administration's policy of civil rights lacked firmness, vacillating between political advisors urging caution and a Justice Department urging more decisive action. Perhaps the best illustration of the administration's wavering was the submission of the 1957 Civil Rights bill by Attorney General Brownell, rather than, as was customary, by the president himself.[50]

The Civil Rights Act of 1957 would be the first civil rights legislation to pass Congress since Reconstruction. It established a temporary Commission on Civil Rights, an assistant attorney general for civil rights, and a presidential commission to investigate allegations of the denial of voting rights. It also gave the federal government the power to sue local authorities who prevented blacks from voting. Despite its symbolic importance, this Civil Rights Act also showed the tenuous nature of the alliance between organized labor and civil rights activism. Organized labor supported white southerners' insistence that state officials accused of violating court orders on voting rights be entitled to jury trials. Given the certainty that all-white southern juries would not convict state officials for violating black voting rights, many civil rights activists believed that accepting this amendment was tantamount to nullifying the entire bill. President Eisenhower, who certainly lacked any deep commitment to this issue, described the jury trial amendment as one of the most significant setbacks of his administration. Vice President Richard Nixon described the Senate's support for this amendment as a vote against the right to vote.[51]

The bill was also enough of a disappointment that some civil rights activists urged a veto, while both Roy Wilkins and Martin Luther King, who urged support for the bill, were attacked by leading black newspapers. From Wilkins's perspective, the bill was valuable evidence that progress was being made, whereas King saw the issue as a symptom of the civil rights movement's excessive dependence upon white institutions. In spite of these reservations, the 1957 Civil Rights Act brought to a close an eighty-year legislative tradition of avoiding civil rights issues. The Compromise of 1876 no longer held sway; race could no longer be kept off the national agenda as a matter of exclusively regional concern.

The Civil Rights Act of 1960 strengthened the investigating powers of the 1957 Act, and stipulated that court-appointed referees were to ensure that eligible blacks were allowed to register and vote. Eisenhower's commission would find "substantial discriminatory disenfranchisement of Negroes" in approximately one hundred counties in eight southern states. The commission also recognized that the piecemeal strategy of litigating by individual counties was an inadequate remedy for voting rights abuses, since legislatures remained free to gerrymander, adopt at-large elections and run-off elections, and annex neighboring communities in order to dilute black voting strength.[52] Although neither act possessed substantial enforcement power, they were the products of a Republican administration and demonstrated the party's support for civil rights, a view strengthened by Eisenhower's 1957 decision to send federal troops to Little Rock.

The Civil Rights Movement

Notwithstanding the advances of the prior generation, rural black southerners lived in a world that appeared to be frozen in time. They remained an oppressed caste locked to the lowest rungs of employment hierarchies. As late as 1964, black sharecroppers in Wilcox County, Alabama (adjacent to Selma), had never seen U.S. currency. They continued to use scrip provided by plantation owners that restricted them to purchasing from the plantation store.[53]

Discrimination remained widespread throughout the nation. The federal government was largely a bystander on civil rights issues. Resistance to change

in the racial order remained stalwart. With only a few noteworthy exceptions, southern white political leaders were still diehard segregationists. Southern segregationists also benefited from northern apathy. Northern whites
remained on the whole detached from civil rights concerns. Few saw it as a
major issue.

In the late 1950s the civil rights movement was still relatively weak, plagued
by defections on important measures by organized labor and a number of
liberal Democrats. It would, however, soon become the most significant force
in the dismantling of racial barriers. The movement had significant advantages as well as certain disadvantages in its efforts to mobilize a broad constituency for change. In the 1900–30 era, civil rights supporters had shared
disadvantages common to many insurgencies, namely the lack of sufficient
institutional resources to carry out effective action. This resource deficit would
decline dramatically by the 1950s.

During the 1950s southern black organizations were able to more effectively utilize both national and local bases of support by wedding a grassroots
constituency rooted in direct action to an already established elite politics
oriented to judicial and legal activism.[54] Certainly by the 1950s the willingness of many blacks to tolerate the most offensive aspects of white supremacy had lessened considerably, as had the willingness of northern
whites to turn a blind eye to southern practices. Undoubtedly, southern
practices were also becoming an international embarrassment to more en-
lightened Americans and were perceived as greatly hampering the Cold
War struggle against Communism.

The Structural Roots of the Civil Rights Insurgency

White supremacy disintegrated gradually. In fact initially economic reprisals
against blacks increased. Farm tenants were evicted, workers were fired, loans
were denied, and mortgages were selectively foreclosed.[55] The economic
dependency of sharecropping, which made blacks dependent on white credi-
tors, also substantially restricted their political rights. Violence, which was
far more common in rural areas, reinforced white control over blacks.

The conditions of rural life—sporadic communication, overwhelming
poverty, and vulnerability to oppression—imposed significant limitations on
the organizational potential of blacks in a variety of ways. Rural churches
were not strong enough to serve as a source of insurgency because of their
small size and limited funds. Neither the NAACP nor black colleges were
any better positioned to spearhead a potential insurgency. However, each of
these key institutions rapidly grew.

Sharecropping had been in decline since the 1930s. The Great Depression and the drastic decline in the price of cotton on the world market destroyed the livelihood of rural croppers, leading to a mass migration to urban areas. Unlike black migrants leaving the South who would slowly alter the political calculus in northern industrial centers, blacks remaining in the South did not experience any immediate enhancement of their political power. But southern blacks shared in the upgrading of the southern occupational structure and in the benefits of regional economic growth. Furthermore, economic resources could be transformed into political assets.

Urbanization propelled expansion and diversification of the industrial wage-earner class, leading to improvements in the occupational status of blacks in the 1940s and 1950s. Movement into higher-status occupations—clerical and management positions, skilled crafts, and the professions—typified the occupational upgrading of the southern black population. Increased mobility, both residential (from rural to urban areas) and occupational (from agriculture to industry), was vital. Urban environments and industrial occupations did not replicate the total dependency of rural sharecropping. With occupational upgrading came significant increases in income, which in turn fostered an economic and financial independence incomparably greater than what had been possible within sharecropping. Income growth made increased funding of protest organizations possible.

By residing in urban areas blacks were better insulated from the virulent oppression in rural areas. Black relocation to urban areas also made improvements in educational attainment possible. Improved educational status meant a smaller proportion of blacks would be limited to occupations in domestic and personal service, where employer autonomy encouraged personalized despotism.

The Birth of a Movement

By the 1950s a significant core of southern blacks began to possess valuable resources that would potentially strengthen their collective organizations. A key factor responsible for the growing power of southern blacks was the rise of more powerful southern urban churches, whose role in protest began to increase during the 1940s. Church membership itself was increasingly redefined to make movement participation necessary.

Yet, the development of black churches was surpassed by the tremendous growth of black colleges. From 1900 to 1930, total enrollment in black college rose modestly. But from the end of the 1920s black college enrollment rose dramatically, from approximately 14,000 in 1928 to 75,000 by 1950 to 100,000 by 1964. The Supreme Court's support for civil rights was a prime factor in the growth of black colleges. Increasingly, the Court began to rule that the promise of "separate but equal" must be kept—states had either to admit black applicants or provide separate schooling for them.

Southern branches of the NAACP also grew dramatically from the beginnings of the New Deal to the beginnings of the civil rights movement. Between 1934 and 1946, NAACP membership grew from 85,000 to 420,000. Such growth surpassed that of college enrollment or church membership. NAACP growth was concentrated in the South. Churches, schools, and the NAACP were each instrumental in facilitating "bloc recruitment" of movement participants. Through these institutions a wider and larger net was efficiently cast. According to sociologist Doug McAdam, "By building the movement out of established institutions, insurgent leaders were able to recruit en masse along existing lines of interaction."[56]

Student activism reached extremely high levels during the protest era. McAdam argues that "participation in protest activity simply came to be defined as part and parcel of one's role as a student."[57] Not only were the masses of activists disproportionately drawn from the pool of local clergymen, students, and local leaders, but also the pool of leaders came almost entirely from these ranks. Even the National Urban League moved away from its traditional dependence on employers in the 1930s, urging an expansion of federal welfare relief programs, with increases in the benefits provided to blacks. The league began to supplement its investigations of black economic conditions with a more aggressive posture that emphasized protest and pressure. The league lobbied federal agencies and Congress, supported "Don't Buy Where You Can't Work" campaigns, organized demonstrations against Jim Crow, and argued for an end to Jim Crow in the military and in federal programs.[58]

These institutions, especially the NAACP, served as centers of mobilization. Each contributed to what might be termed a hothouse effect—intensifying the commitment of the constituencies pursuing democratization by building loyalties and feelings of solidarity. In a manner not unlike the spread of segregation, activism to overturn it spiraled upward in both extensivity and intensity. Broader groups of people began to join the struggle and committed themselves to a wider range of actions to challenge the fundamentals of white supremacy. Meanwhile, shared exclusion from citizenship fostered an oppositional culture. But this culture did not emerge from a blank slate but rather was based in the most highly developed associational networks in the black community.

A key factor responsible for the role of churches, and to a lesser extent schools, as centers of mobilization was that they enjoyed a higher level of insulation from white control. None was as well insulated as the black church. Of course, insulation was always relative given the capacity of the white power structure to devise methods to penalize the NAACP, the student movement, and the churches. The sanctions imposed by the Alabama courts at the behest of Alabama attorney general Patterson would take eight years to overturn.[59] The counterattack on the NAACP diminished its effectiveness, thereby paving the way for direct action organizations to take center stage.

In the meantime, concerted pressure was brought to bear on administrators at state-financed schools to expel students and fire faculty participating in desegregation protests. Black leaders were threatened with lawsuits to expropriate their assets through libel cases and contempt citations, none more famously than the case of *Sullivan vs. the New York Times*. In this instance police superintendent William Sullivan (and other government officials) brought libel suits against the *New York Times* and others associated with fund-raising advertisements in the *New York Times* (including Martin Luther King, Jr., although he was not personally involved in the ad in question). Assets of prominent civil rights leaders were seized and made subject to forfeiture to satisfy judgments.

Direct Action Begins

The direct action organizations of the modern civil rights movement were spawned by bus boycotts that disrupted Baton Rouge, Montgomery, and Tallahassee, the capital cities of three southern states. Bus boycotts mobilized blacks to cooperate in direct action, while simultaneously providing an alternative to the NAACP's strategy of challenging segregation through the courts. The Southern Leadership Christian Conference (SCLC) brought black churches directly into the movement. Its leadership was dominated by ministers—with just four of its thirty-six formal leadership positions being occupied by laypeople.[60] Montgomery also brought a new figure into the limelight, the Reverend Dr. Martin Luther King. During the evolving civil rights protests, diverse groups would temporarily occupy center stage. The NAACP no longer dominated the national civil rights movement. The charismatic King was readily embraced by the white media as the most important civil rights leader, but his ascension intensified interorganizational rivalries, suggesting that the NAACP no longer spearheaded the movement.

The distinct phases of the early movement would reveal a spiraling process of specialization, as disparate groups improvised, formulated, and refined different techniques.

1. The NAACP's emphasis on legal attacks on segregation went back to its founding. Its domination of civil rights struggles would climax in 1954 with the historic *Brown* case, but would end by 1956.

2. The churches employed direct-action campaigns using boycotts to desegregate public facilities. Out of the activism based in black churches would emerge the SCLC.
3. Black students pioneered the use of sit-ins to protest segregation. This phase began in February 1960 and would spread rapidly throughout the South, especially the upper South. The Student Nonviolent Coordinating Committee (SNCC) would be the result.
4. The Congress of Racial Equality (CORE), founded during World War II, pioneered in the use of nonviolent direct action for civil rights. In 1947, CORE sought to publicize and test the Supreme Court's 1946 *Morgan v. Virginia* ruling, banning segregation in interstate travel. It sponsored a Journey of Reconciliation, a symbolic albeit unsuccessful effort to integrate buses and trains in Kentucky, North Carolina, Tennessee, and Virginia.[61]

There were other bus boycotts that preceded the celebrated Montgomery protest. In 1953, blacks began to boycott segregated buses in Baton Rouge, Louisiana. This boycott, led by Reverend T.J. Jemison, mobilized the black community and spurred nightly mass meetings of 2,000 to 3,000 people. These activities in Baton Rouge would be overshadowed by the *Brown* case and the more recognized 1955–56 Montgomery boycott. According to sociologist Aldon Morris, it was "the Baton Rouge movement, largely without assistance from outside elites, which opened the direct action phase of the modern civil rights movement."[62]

Rosa Parks was not the first person willing to test Montgomery's bus segregation. On March 2, 1955, Claudette Colvin, a black high school student, had refused to surrender her seat in defiance of the segregation law. However, the predominantly male black leadership decided that Colvin was not an appropriate symbol. At the time Colvin was widely rumored to be pregnant out of wedlock. In October 1955 Mary Louise Smith refused to vacate a seat for a white woman in accordance with the segregation law. But Smith was also considered inappropriate because her father was an alcoholic. However, recent information suggests that Colvin was not pregnant and that class prejudice on the part of Montgomery's black leadership against Colvin and Smith was responsible for their being passed over.[63] On December 1, 1955, Rosa Parks refused to surrender her seat, violating the bus segregation law. She was considered a far more appropriate symbol than Smith or Colvin. On June 4, 1956, three federal judges struck down Montgomery's bus segregation ordinances as unconstitutional. The decision was appealed to the U.S. Supreme Court. On November 13, 1956, the Supreme Court upheld the district court, invalidating segregation on Alabama buses.

CORE emerged as a factor in the South in response to the attacks by white southerners upon the NAACP. Until 1960 its relationship with SCLC and NAACP was cooperative rather than competitive because CORE's financial support came from northern middle-class whites and it was a secular organization. CORE initiated the Freedom Rides beginning in May 1961. Under its auspices integrated groups rode buses from Washington, D.C., to New Orleans to test whether buses and facilities were desegregated. This project captured national attention when Freedom Riders were attacked and beaten in Alabama. The violent response by segregationists, with the tacit support of some southern political leaders, inaugurated a new phase in direct action while elevating CORE to the status of a mass movement. Although the number of protesters in the Freedom Rides was far fewer than the participants in the sit-in movement, their national impact was much greater. The Freedom Rides directly challenged the Kennedy administration's preferred modus operandi of low-key, scarcely visible support for civil rights goals. Due to the media attention Freedom Riders attracted, the administration found itself forced to intervene, albeit grudgingly, with as much backsliding as it could possibly manage.

By the late 1950s the revolution of rising expectations was fully in motion. No longer were black Americans to be pacified with largely symbolic victories. From its initial successes, the movement began to spread like wildfire. During the Revolutionary and Civil Wars slaves had seized freedom by joining enemy forces (British soldiers and Union troops) sweeping past the plantations where they lived. In the late 1950s and early 1960s black Americans mobilized again. Once again individuals took it upon themselves to act, this time by desegregating public accommodations. In time, increased pressure by civil rights leaders and activists would precipitate a national domestic crisis. Such dramatic behavior on the part of mobilized black Americans showed a willingness to take on considerable risk. In part it suggested the uncertainty of those eras in which significant social changes occur, of times when "all that is solid melts into air." Taylor Branch believes "from the Montgomery bus boycott to the confrontation of the sit-ins, then on to the Rock Hill jail-in and now to the mass assault on the Mississippi prisons, there was a 'movement' in both senses of the word—a moving spiritual experience and a steady expansion of scope. The theater was spreading through the entire South. One isolated battle had given way to many scattered ones."[64]

The 1960s: A Decade of Progress

By 1960 civil rights issues were important enough that the platforms of both parties included favorable planks. Southern Democrats objected to the civil rights plank in the 1960 Democratic Party platform, but were unsuccessful in getting it removed. The platform called for establishing a permanent Fair Employment Practices Commission, the continuation of the Civil Rights Commission as a permanent agency, and setting 1963 as a deadline for the commencement of school desegregation plans.

The Republicans responded by announcing their support for: (1) equal voting rights; (2) establishment of a Commission on Equal Job Opportunity; and (3) prohibitions against discrimination in federal housing and facilities. The Republican platform was strengthened partly as a result of a joint negotiating session between leading Republican candidates Richard Nixon and Nelson Rockefeller. Nixon and Rockefeller jointly pledged to strengthen the Republican civil rights plank. The resulting party positions were virtually identical for the last time. Governor Rockefeller sought to ally himself with King and take more liberal positions on civil rights in order to lay the groundwork for the 1964 election. It is not insignificant that Rockefeller's son-in-law was arrested as a Freedom Rider.[65]

Although the civil rights issue was not dominant in the 1960 election, both Kennedy and Nixon had to weigh the alternative rewards and costs of appealing to southern whites or northern blacks and their liberal allies. White liberals' support for civil rights had grown dramatically, and had become something of a litmus test. On balance, the tactics of the parties were roughly similar: both emphasized equivocation—doing as little as possible to upset either southern whites or blacks and their liberal allies—and both selected candidates who competed, quietly, for the black vote.

A strong argument can be made that John F. Kennedy owed his election in 1960 to the phone calls he made to Coretta Scott King. His phone calls received wide publicity in the black press, but were virtually ignored by the white media. Kennedy was the beneficiary of a dramatic shift in the black vote. In 1956, blacks had voted Republican by a 60-to-40 margin, but in the 1960 election they voted Democrat by a 70-to-30 margin. The campaign's clever usage of Kennedy's concern for the jailed Martin Luther King stimulated black turnout, while the white press's neglectfulness prevented a backlash. In comparison, the Nixon campaign used black celebrities to attract black support. Yet what is perhaps most significant about this episode is that the era in which the black vote could be won by symbolic acts alone was rapidly drawing to a close.

The success of the phone calls was an omen of the continued effort by the Kennedy administration to rely upon vague symbolism over concrete measures. The phone calls made by John and Robert Kennedy were a sign of their belief, disturbingly common among white politicians of the era, that they could continue to have it both ways: Kennedy's actions helped gain black support while southern Democratic governors' resistance enhanced their pursuit of the antiblack vote. This episode was reminiscent of Cotton Ed Smith's walkout at the 1940 Democratic convention over Roosevelt's invitation to a black minister to deliver a prayer.

John F. Kennedy's Calculated Passivity

John F. Kennedy was not a race liberal by any stretch of the imagination. His attitude on race was largely one of passive indifference. This indifference was compounded by his belief that segregation was incompatible with modern attitudes, as if racism were largely a vestige of primordial sentiments. His approach was essentially the same as Franklin D. Roosevelt's and for similar reasons. Kennedy, like Roosevelt, treated civil rights issues entirely in terms of political calculations. Kennedy, like Roosevelt, lacked any personal experience with racial discrimination. The result was that white southerners' political support was more important than combating racial injustice.

As late as 1963, President Kennedy would maintain that the country faced no serious divisions regarding race, and that the administration's approach to economic growth and education was sufficient to address whatever problems remained. Nor had he pushed any of the legislation promised in the 1960 campaign platform. Moreover, his difficulties with civil rights issues were frequently self-inflicted, a result of his appointment of numerous segregationist judges. Kennedy's first judicial appointee in the South, Harold Cox, was an ardent segregationist who characterized blacks seeking the right to vote as "niggers who were acting like a bunch of chimpanzees."[66] Judge Cox would dismiss many of the criminal counts against the defendants in the infamous murders of civil rights workers Goodman, Chaney, and Schwerner. The Supreme Court reversed Cox and reinstated the dismissed charges. J. Robert Elliot, another segregationist appointee of Kennedy's, ruled that civil rights protests deprived Albany, Georgia's, white community of equal protection under the Fourteenth Amendment by removing police and public resources from white neighborhoods. Taylor Branch maintains it was well known in the Justice Department that "the best civil rights judges in the South, and indeed the department's only hope for racial justice through the courts, were Eisenhower appointees; the most egregious segregationists were Kennedy's."[67]

Kennedy's initial antipoverty measures were limited to programs with a negligible influence on the condition of black Americans. Among such measures were the Area Redevelopment Agency, intended to stimulate employment in depressed areas through loans and subsidies to small businesses, and the Manpower Development and Training Act, designed to retrain workers displaced by automation. Certainly Kennedy's attitude matched the political climate of the early 1960s. Courts were still deciding cases according to the infamous *Screws* precedent, based on a 1945 Supreme Court ruling that federal prosecutions for violation of civil rights necessitated a showing of a specific intent to deprive an individual of his or her civil rights. This criterion of specific intent was required for both criminal and civil actions. Accordingly, prosecutors were required to show that defendants were contemplating violating a person's civil rights, rather than merely present evidence that they had done so.[68] A more assertive stance on civil rights would have required strong determination on the part of the president and key executive branch officials.

Kennedy was extremely hesitant to move forward on civil rights issues. He decided to postpone submission to Congress of the civil rights legislation that had been promised in his campaign platform. On the positive side of the ledger, Kennedy established a Committee on Equal Employment Opportunity, issued executive orders forbidding discrimination in the federal government and in federally assisted housing, and hired more blacks than any previous administration.[69] Nonetheless, the Kennedy administration was both slow to respond and extremely hesitant to push forward a civil rights agenda. The administration was unwilling to act vigorously even in their preferred area of civil rights activism—voting rights. Attorney General Robert F. Kennedy consistently refused to use federal power to protect the constitutional rights of black southerners.

Certainly Kennedy was trying to walk a tightrope to avoid having to choose between two key Democratic constituencies, southern whites determined to maintaining white supremacy and blacks intent on destroying it. But his passive stance on civil rights could not prevent his administration from being drawn into repeated confrontations as an ensuing spiral of conflict between civil rights activism and white resistance channeled into police and southern mob violence.[70]

Believing that taking risks for integration was political suicide, Kennedy sought to do as little as he could. Once again, much like Roosevelt a generation earlier, he tried to accommodate prejudiced white southerners whose votes he needed by backing down before their political leaders. Most notably, the administration reneged on its promises to protect voting rights. In spite of extensive evidence of voting rights violations, and violence against voting rights organizers, the administration refused to intervene.

However, by this time the Roosevelt/Kennedy style of patrician indifference would no longer suffice. Events were moving too fast for "benign neglect." The administration could not simply ignore the increasing evidence that civil rights issues were gaining prominence. Significantly, public opinion surveys were beginning to register the increasing importance of civil rights. The issue of civil rights was identified as the nation's most pressing problem in a majority of the national opinion polls between 1961 and 1965.[71] Yet only in the aftermath of the most dramatic of the confrontations in Birmingham, Alabama, where Bull Connor, the commissioner of public safety, used dogs, clubs, and fire hoses against peaceful demonstrators, did Kennedy propose a stronger civil rights bill—one that included provisions to guarantee access to public accommodations, permit federal officials to pursue desegregation through lawsuits, and make employment discrimination more difficult.[72]

Lyndon B. Johnson's Civil Rights Activism

On September 15, 1963, the Sixteenth Street Baptist Church in Birmingham, Alabama, headquarters of the local civil rights movement, was bombed. Four girls were killed, and twenty children were injured. A riot ensued in which the Birmingham police killed two more children. Upon assuming office, Kennedy's successor, Lyndon B. Johnson, made enactment of a strong civil rights bill a legislative priority. Johnson used the Birmingham tragedies to push the Civil Rights Act through the House of Representatives by a 290-to-130 margin. Southern Democrats cast 104 of the negative votes. The bill was subjected to the longest filibuster ever, eighty-two days. Eventually Senate minority leader Everett Dirksen marshaled enough Republicans to invoke cloture and pass the Civil Rights Act, 73 to 37. Among the opponents were twenty-one southern Democrats and five Republicans, including soon-to-be Republican presidential nominee Barry Goldwater.

The Civil Rights Act of 1964: (1) prohibited discrimination in public facilities and accommodations; (2) gave the attorney general the power to initiate suits to desegregate schools; (3) forbade job discrimination; and (4) promised that federal funds would be withheld from any federally funded program that practiced discrimination. However, it left voting rights to the discretion of local courts. President Johnson, meeting with civil rights leaders informally after the signing of the bill, stated that he believed the need for direct action protests was over, that the Civil Rights Act eliminated "the last vestiges of injustice in our beloved America, and that further demonstrations were therefore unnecessary and possibly even self-defeating."[73]

The Voting Rights Act: A Quiet Revolution

On March 7, 1965, Selma, Alabama, police violently attacked peaceful demonstrators involved in a voting registration campaign, an event that became known as Bloody Sunday. Coming in the midst of intense media coverage, this helped assure passage of the Voting Rights Act of 1965 by overwhelming margins in both houses of Congress. The Voting Rights Act included: (1) the prohibition of literacy tests and similar voting restrictions; (2) the empowerment of the attorney general to oversee federal elections in seven southern states by appointing examiners to register those denied the right to vote; and (3) instructions to the attorney general to challenge the constitutionality of poll taxes in state and local elections. It at least temporarily abolished literacy tests for five years in those states or subdivisions that used literacy tests or similar devices as voting requirements and in which fewer than 50 percent of voting-age residents were registered. Based upon subsequent interpretation by the Supreme Court, those states and counties covered by the act had their voting laws frozen pending federal approval of any proposed changes.[74]

Accordingly, a voting rights violation occurred whenever total voting registration or turnout in the presidential election of 1964 fell below 50 percent and a literacy test was used to screen potential registrants. The federal government immediately sued to remove all southern poll tax statutes and sent federal registrars to Alabama, Louisiana, and Mississippi.

The impact of the Voting Rights Act over the next generation has been accurately termed a "quiet revolution" due to its effect on registration rates for blacks in southern states. In 1964 the number of registered blacks in the former Confederate states was 43 percent of the voting age population. White resistance to black voting registration was substantially greater in the deep South. In Alabama, Georgia, Louisiana, Mississippi, and South Carolina only 22.5 percent of eligible blacks were registered. Between 1964 and 1988 the percentage of registered blacks in the eleven southern states grew from 43 percent to 64 percent. In the five states of the deep South, black registration rose from 22.5 percent to 65 percent. The largest increases came in the southern states that had voted in 1964 for Goldwater. In sum, the Voting Rights Act swamped the existing systems of disfranchisement.[75] According to Earl and Merle Black, "The Civil Rights Act and the Voting Rights Acts amounted to successful and irreversible federal intervention in southern race relations. Desegregating public accommodations and protecting black voting rights meant that white supremacy no longer defined the southern political order and that black citizens would be an integral part of the community."[76]

The End of an Era

The Civil Rights and Voting Rights Acts were also the summit of Johnson's relationship with the civil rights community. According to Powe, whereas

1964 was a year of big wins for liberals—Johnson, the Democrats, the civil rights movement, and the Supreme Court—1966 ended the progressive political tide. The 1966 midterm elections were the first sign of the coming counterreaction. In 1966, Congress rejected the administration's proposed open housing legislation. This rejection was a clear indication of the gathering power of the white backlash. Ironically, Johnson's landslide victory ushered in both the Great Society, which was meant to eradicate poverty, and a backlash against civil rights reflected in the movement of white southerners from the Democrats to the Republicans. The backlash smothered the antipoverty, antidiscrimination thrust of the Great Society.

The 1964 election also marks the beginning of the end of a bipartisan civil rights agenda. The large-scale replacement of liberal Republicans by liberal Democrats would transform the civil rights agenda into a Democratic agenda. The dramatic increase in southern black registration would benefit primarily the Democrats. As the southern Democrats' legislative opposition to civil rights was rejected by the North, many conservative white southerners questioned their partisan allegiances. Earl and Merle Black believe "most southern Republicans viewed Goldwater as their hero and champion." Goldwater received 55 percent of the southern white vote, more than any Republican presidential candidate had ever received before.[77]

Barry Goldwater's appeal to unreconstructed segregationists gave birth to an alternative governing coalition. Goldwater voted against the historic civil rights bill, implying that black poverty was due to laziness. According to Goldwater, "the problem of discrimination could not be cured by laws alone." He also maintained that Social Security and welfare were un-American.[78] Hence, the 1964 Goldwater campaign is often considered a watershed, reflecting the coalescence of several defining elements of a new political era: (1) Republicans' rapidly growing appeal to white southerners; (2) the end of the solid Democratic South; and (3) the beginning of a persistent alienation of black voters from Republicans.[79]

After Goldwater, Republican presidential candidates began to tailor their messages to appeal to white southerners. Whereas Richard Nixon in 1960 ran on a racially progressive platform and made a strong effort to win black support, the Richard Nixon of 1968 and 1972 adopted a "southern strategy" designed to distance his presidency from the government he presided over. As president, Nixon nominated three southerners with strong conservative views to the Supreme Court (two unsuccessfully), opposed the extension of the 1965 Voting Rights Act without substantial revision, asked federal courts to postpone desegregation of public schools in Mississippi, and requested that Congress place a moratorium on federal-court-mandated school busing. Nixon disavowed any intention of continuing Johnson's Great Society efforts to eradicate poverty. Rather he sought to appeal to conservative white southerners by (1) maintaining a posture of supporting racial equality in theory while impeding the enforcement of civil rights legislation; (2) appointing judges with segregationist leanings; and (3) opposing efforts to desegregate schools.

It might appear that the pro–civil rights side of Nixon ledger should include his administration's implementation of the Philadelphia Plan, which included target goals and timetables for minority hiring, and the proposed Family Assistance Plan, which sought to use a negative income tax to create a guaranteed annual income. However, sociologist John Skrentny has persuasively argued that the intent of the Philadelphia Plan was really to sow divisions between two key Democratic constituencies—blacks and organized laborers—rather than a sincere attempt to address trade unions' racial exclusionary practices.[80]

The Supreme Court Turns Right

In 1969, Warren Burger replaced Earl Warren on the Supreme Court. After the failure of conservative nominees Clement Haynsworth and G. Harrold Carswell, Nixon successfully nominated Harry Blackmun, Lewis Powell, and William Rehnquist. The Burger Court was in many respects an interim between the liberal Warren and conservative Rehnquist Court, in a manner not altogether unlike the contrast that presidents Ford and Carter offered to liberal Johnson and conservative Ronald Reagan.

Initially, the Burger Court hesitated to challenge Brown. The Court defended school desegregation in *Alexander v. Holmes County Board of Education* and *Swann v. Charlotte-Mecklenburg County Board of Education*. In these cases, the Court defended the enforcement of the *Brown* rulings. The Burger Court also rendered a strongly pro–affirmative action ruling in *Griggs v. Duke Power Company*.

The Court's attitude shifted, and its opposition to busing to achieve school desegregation hardened. In 1973, the Court overturned a lower federal court decision in *San Antonio Independent School District v. Rodriguez* allowing school funding to remain locally controlled even when it permitted gross disparities between affluent and poor school districts. The Court ruled that education was not a "fundamental interest" and it refused to challenge cross-district inequality in educational resources. In the pivotal 1974 case of *Milliken v. Bradley*, the Court hardened the line between cities and suburbs, refusing to sanction court desegregation orders that crossed school district lines. According to James Patterson, Milliken was "the first key Supreme Court decision to back away from *Brown*."[81] Then came the Burger Court's controversial 1978 *Bakke* ruling narrowing the permissible limits of affirmative action.

A Changing Political Climate

The national Democratic Party maintained its commitment to liberal racial policies through the mid-1970s, when the issue of busing brought northern practices of discrimination under the purview of federal courts, threatening the electability of northern Democrats. However, the counterreaction against racial democratization would be bipartisan, as George Wallace in 1968 attracted many Democratic voters. Much of Wallace's support came from former Thurmond and Goldwater voters.[82] The 1968 campaign took place in a political spectrum dominated by rising racial apprehensions and more conservative appeals on race. Earlier obsessions with race and crime metastasized into the politics of law and order. According to Tom and Mary Edsall, "Wallace provided a desperately sought after moral justification to those whites who saw themselves as most victimized and most displaced by the black struggle for civil rights. This struggle had in many ways become a contest for limited resources— for a city's quality schools and teachers, for union jobs and apprenticeships, for the first layer of housing outside rusting urban centers, and for social status and community standing in an economy that increasingly devalued working-class employment."[83] Wallace and Nixon received 56 percent of the popular vote.

Although some white southern Democrats were able to appeal to both black and white constituents, more often, Earl and Merle Black argue, incumbent Democrats effectively "smothered" Republican challengers by emphasizing their own racial conservatism and by creating safe electoral districts. Jimmy Carter's election as president came with just 46 percent of the white southern votes, in spite of his ties to the region and his symbolic status as the first president of the twentieth century from the deep South. In hindsight, the 1970s were a transitional era in which experienced white southern Democrats won elections, but the distance between what was acceptable to blacks and conservative whites steadily grew. Growing Republican strength throughout the region made cross-race appeals less effective. Rather, the emergence of clear and distinct differences between the two parties on racial issues had been a long time in building. The crystallization of these partisan ideological differences paved the way to greater polarization.

It would be simplistic to argue that the political movement of white southerners was only about race. But it would be naive to believe it had little to do with race. As argued in Chapters 1 and 2, attitudes involving race form a nexus that anchors a host of attitudes and beliefs. Economic conservatism and comfort with the racial status quo frequently overlap. Whereas 67 percent of southern blacks favor a strong role for government, only 28 percent of southern whites concur.[84] This cleavage is quite informative if one believes that dramatic changes in race relations require strong government action to overcome hostility and inertia.

A Shifting Tide: Resurgent Democratization

Summarizing the role of race in national politics from the beginning of the New Deal through the 1960s, initially neither political party monopolized support from either blacks or white supremacists. Rather, both parties contained a portion of each constituency. The Republicans had grown accustomed to winning black votes for virtually nothing as late as 1932, and had treated black voters with a disdain bordering on contempt. Herbert Hoover, in his desire to build upon the inroads made in the south by the Republican Party in the 1928 election, made a concerted effort to drive blacks out of the party.

By the 1940s the disintegration of the racial state was evident. Central to this disintegration was the decline of sharecropping. Perhaps on balance the collapse of King Cotton was the single most influential factor in the demise of white supremacy. Yet even if the emergence of the civil rights movement occurred due to structural conditions, in isolation structural forces do not fully explain the movement's success or its failures. An activist civil rights movement was needed to ignite the growing potential for collective action of blacks and their political allies within labor and the liberal social movements. Protesters win when the circumstances have made concessions possible.[85] Such concessions became possible in the late 1940s as the issue of race began to appear in national politics once again.

In the 1930s and 1940s black Americans also derived benefits from an alliance between the federal courts and liberal political forces. This alliance, which began during the New Deal, was unprecedented. For most of the nation's history the American judiciary has been far more solicitous of the interests of the privileged against "excessive majoritarianism," rather than a protector of the interests of underprivileged minorities. According to Paul Burstein, "By 1964 when the Civil Rights Act was passed, the Supreme Court had heard 106 discrimination cases since 1936, and had ruled ninety times in favor of those allegedly suffering from discrimination."[86] By the time Earl Warren retired from the Court in 1969, the Court was responsible for fundamental changes in race relations, abolishing constitutional support for de jure segregation, based upon its revitalizing the meaning of the Fourteenth Amendment's promise of "equal protection." But the Court was not content to merely undermine the foundations of the racial state.

The Court also crafted a more robust understanding of democracy, one based on universal and equal suffrage, by its endorsement of the concept of "one person, one vote." In *Baker v. Carr*, the Court held apportionment of legislatures to be "justiciable." In *Gray v. Sanders*, the Court overturned Georgia's "county unit" primary system that overrepresented rural counties. In *Reynolds v. Sims*, the Court disallowed Alabama's districting system, and required apportionment to be on the basis of population. These decisions brought rural domination of legislatures to an end. The Court's activism was aligned with a rising tide of democratization, culminating in the Twenty-fourth Amendment, which banned poll taxes in federal elections and which made them impractical for state and local elections as well. Restrictions on the voting rights of paupers were repealed. By 1975, the right to vote was effectively nationalized. According to historian Alexander Keyssar, "poll taxes, literacy tests, understanding clauses, pauper exclusions and good character provisions had been swept away."[87]

> Between the late 1950s and early 1970s, the legal underpinnings of the right to vote were transformed more than they had been at any earlier point in the nation's history. In a cascading series of congressional enactments and court decisions virtually all formal restrictions on the suffrage rights of adult citizens were swept away, and the federal government assumed full responsibility for protecting and guaranteeing their rights. . . . The Supreme Court fueled by an enlarged conception of citizenship and a willingness to extend the powers of the national government was actively promoting the rights of the disadvantaged. The Federal government assumed full responsibility for protecting and guaranteeing those rights.[88]

Additionally, the Warren Court complemented Johnson's War on Poverty, promoting the establishment, in Powe's words, of a "constitutional shield for the poor from the most elemental consequences of poverty."[89] Major civil rights legislation of the late 1950s and 1960s would be the product of an arduously long period of gestation. The civil rights bills enacted between 1957 and 1965 provided democratic political rights to black Americans. The demise of southern one-party politics would follow the passage of the Civil Rights Act of 1964 and the Voting Rights Acts of 1965.[90] In the South the use of terror to maintain the racial state declined markedly.

And yet, this more favorable racial climate would be an interlude, rather than an era. By the early 1970s, the momentum favoring racial progress had dissipated. The Dixiecrat/Republican alliance successfully mobilized a backlash against the tumultuous civil rights era. Reagan's appointment of three conservative justices to the Supreme Court in the 1980s brought the era of judicial protection for minority rights to a close. The Supreme Court and the federal judiciary have returned to their more traditional role as protectors of the privileged. Exploiting resurgent racial antagonisms and the protection of white privilege would become vital issues for important segments of the new Republican majority. Ultimately Republican domination of the presidency blocked further racial progress.

In spite of Martin Luther King's prestige, neither the SCLC nor any other organization achieved the dominance the NAACP had once enjoyed. One factor explaining this failure was actually instrumental to the movement's success—complementarity. The NAACP, SCLC, and SNCC each dominated a distinct resource and offered a different set of tactics and strengths to the overall movement. In spite of their internecine struggles, during their heyday the whole was considerably more than the sum of its constituent parts. Although external attacks on one group exacerbated the difficulties of coexistence, in all likelihood they gave their opponents so many targets it was difficult for enemies to focus on any one civil rights group at any time.

The late 1960s witnessed a collapse of the consensus that existed in the early 1960s. No longer did the movement possess a dominant issue or perspective. Previously, diversity had fostered success as organizations specialized in domains that fit their strengths and interests. Nonetheless, this diversity became an impediment once internal conflict in the movement—which had always been present—was no longer restrained by a sense of common objectives. Major civil rights groups no longer had a common agenda to temper their squabbling. The NAACP diminished its support for the Voter Education Project. The controversy over seating the Mississippi Freedom Democratic Party at the Democratic National Convention led many SNCC members to turn against Martin Luther King, widening the already deep divide between SNCC and the SCLC. While King and Bayard Rustin argued for accepting the compromise of two at-large seats and a rule outlawing segregated delegations in the future, the MFDP rejected the proposal. According to Fannie Lou Hamer, "We didn't come all the way for no two votes!"

SNCC never recovered from the violence inflicted in Mississippi during Freedom Summer. The toll of casualties included six killed, eighty beaten, two wounded by gunfire, more than a thousand arrested, and thirty-seven churches and thirty-one homes burned or dynamited.[91] This reign of terror carried considerable weight in SNCC's turn to radical separatism.

Racial integration was the primary goal of the movement, and until the mid-1960s it enjoyed a wide consensus. But as portions of the movement began to radicalize, the traditional authority of the preachers no longer sufficed to bond the movement's separate strands. Conflicts began to emerge among those with differing goals and agendas. Perhaps this splintering was an inevitable by-product of democratization. Arguably, one price of the greater integration of blacks into the dominant majority society and culture has been greater differentiation among blacks. After all, greater inclusion within the majority culture entails, perhaps by definition, diminishing identification within a minority culture. Certainly the disintegration of the movement was a factor in the changes occurring in national racial politics, especially in the loss of prestige and support for civil rights around the nation.

However, given the disharmony and conflict of the late 1960s it is easy to overstate the tension between the goals and interests of the variety of organizations that constituted the civil rights movement during the era of intense struggle. The conflicts between such organizations as SNCC, SCLC, and the NAACP among others are well documented. As the most visible aspects of segregation were overcome, it became increasingly difficult to replace the traditional goals or even redefine them in ways that maintained the saliency of the issue. Thereafter, no single issue was able to replace the earlier goal of desegregation.

Within the civil rights movement itself this division was expressed in the opposition between traditional integrationists and the advocates of black power, who rejected integration as their fundamental objective. In part such conflicts reflected the competition among the Big Four—the NAACP, SCLC, SNCC, and CORE—for primacy. Perhaps as well the channeling of activism into traditional electoral politics undermined the legitimacy of protest.[92] Even liberal supporters began to tire of protests employing civil disobedience.

There was also trouble brewing due to the growing dependence of SNCC, CORE, and SCLC upon outside financial support. Such support may have factored into the more moderate demands among the more respectable segments of the civil rights movement. Greater emphasis was given to voter registration and integration over more radical demands. On the other hand, the turn toward the more radical agenda favored by many SNCC activists only led to an increase in repression by the federal government and to the fragmentation and splintering of SNCC. Nor did SNCC's new leaders have the stature or the respect of their predecessors. Bob Moses, John Lewis, and Julian Bond were near icons, celebrated by both black and white Americans. Stokely Carmichael and H. Rap Brown lacked their moral authority and their endorsement of violence alienated many and made them easy targets for civil rights opponents. The symbolic discrediting of SNCC's new direction was confirmed by urban riots, Watts only six days after the passage of the Voting Rights Act and Newark and Detroit the next year. In sum, the riots symbolized the end of an era.

In general, the partial dismantling of segregation created new difficulties for the movement because of its tendency to demobilize and disorganize activists. This is not surprising since once the initial goals were met, albeit incompletely, a certain amount of pressure was lifted. For the civil rights movement this meant the strength of its associational networks, based on black churches, colleges, and NAACP chapters, began to atrophy.

Although it is common to represent schisms and disputes as the reason for failure, I believe the conventional wisdom reverses cause and effect. Schisms and obsessions with petty disputes are often the consequence of increasing irrelevance and a marginalized status, not the cause of it. The internal schisms among movement activists and their respective organizations reflected the very likely possibility that the movement had exhausted its original goals and its remaining goals were beyond the capacity of a movement whose strength resided in an oppositional culture isolated from mainstream political discourse.

In other words, democratic politics does not allow one to serve two masters. To stand outside the arena of political competition is to court irrelevance. To participate leads to the compromise of one's goals perhaps beyond the point where they remain recognizable. For black Americans, participation in the American party system would come with strings attached, some quite constraining. As sociologists Frances Fox Piven and Richard Cloward explain:

> The election of a modest number of southern black officials will clearly not create the political power necessary to secure national full employment policies; nor to secure substantial changes in the hiring and wage and promotion practices of private industry; nor the huge subsidies required to house the southern urban minority poor decently; nor any measures, such as land reform coupled with federal subsidies; . . . nor reform of the welfare system to insure an adequate minimum income for all who cannot or should not work; nor any one of a dozen other policies and programs that might improve the living conditions of the black poor.[92]

Once the Voting Rights Act was passed, activists found it difficult to agree upon either means or ends. The difficulties they faced in addressing the ills of northern ghettoes reveal the inability of Martin Luther King and his advisers to devise a coherent strategy. King eventually came to regard his efforts to combat racial injustice as a failure, and southern tactics of marches and demonstrations as ill suited to northern-style discrimination. It is only fair to point out that nothing else has succeeded either! Moreover, the movement also found it more difficult to act cohesively in the South. One culprit was unfulfilled rising expectations. The expectations of black Americans rose dramatically between 1954 and 1965. As their expectations were not fulfilled, their belief in the usefulness of nonviolence waned.

Yet it is also too simplistic to argue that the civil rights movement had no further successes. SCLC was heavily involved in the voter registration campaign that would allow Carl Stokes to become the first elected black mayor of a major American city. In 1990, the twenty-fifth anniversary of the Voting Rights Act, Virginia would have an elected black governor, there would be 24 black members of Congress, 417 black state legislators, 4,388 black officers of city and county governments, and six of the ten largest cities would have black mayors.[93]

Many would argue that black power adherents and other militant advocates were in themselves responsible for the backlash, as opposition to violence and extremist rhetoric was responsible for energizing opponents and discouraging allies. Although there is no doubt some truth in this, I would argue that the difficulties faced by civil rights activists and their movement bore some resemblance to the paradoxes faced by other social movements that have found their appeal limited to a minority: the difficulty in reconciling the particular interests of their constituents with sufficient numbers outside the core group to approach a majority. This problem is evident in affirmative action. The claims of other disadvantaged groups are not necessarily isomorphic with blacks—and are less clearly a result of systemic discrimination. This is not to say that women, Hispanics, Native Americans, and Asian Americans have not suffered. But the coalition at times has led to outcomes that are difficult to justify, as with the inclusion of Hispanics in the Voting Rights Act in light of an only sporadic history of discrimination. On the other hand, the inconsistencies of such constituency logrolling can be defended as the necessary compromises in a democracy in order to accomplish the greater good of fighting discrimination.

The civil rights movement was in many respects relatively conservative since its goals were simply to attain the rights already held by other Americans. However, the consequence of reaching these goals could hardly be so, given the degree of exclusion of blacks from the dominant society and their status as, until recently, the nation's largest minority.

Certainly the political agenda of black Americans has shifted as well from the issues of formal citizenship to dimensions of citizenship involving economic and material rights of citizens. Some, especially more conservative analysts, believe that such a radicalization of the movement was responsible for the disintegration of the civil rights movement. Yet citizenship is never merely about political rights in the abstract. Invariably the question of enfranchisement becomes one of using the vote toward certain ends. Moreover, when new groups are enfranchised, some reallocation of the existing distribution of material resources is usually necessary, since the prior distribution of resources was based in part on their exclusion.

Hence, the achievement of citizenship is but the end of the beginning of the journey to full integration of black Americans. The passage of civil rights, voting rights, and equal employment legislation was a necessary but insufficient condition for attainment of the full meaning of democratic citizenship. Legal freedom in the midst of substantial material inequality formed what can be seen as a hollow victory, important but inadequate. Since the achievement of citizenship, the political agenda of black Americans can be characterized broadly as one based on pursuing the equalization of life chances. In other words, the struggle for racial equality today reflects the considerable remaining inequality of life chances of black Americans.

The civil rights era witnessed perhaps the last great burst of democratic inclusiveness, going well beyond the issue of race. Clearly influenced by the civil rights struggles are a number of developments for which the movement is directly responsible: (1) the dismantling of impediments to full democratization, such as the overrepresentation of legislative districts favoring rural blocs of voters at the expense of urban voters; (2) the dismantling of considerable elements of a police state apparatus, evinced in the abuses of the McCarthy era, the suppression of antiwar and radical activists—particularly evident in the treatment of the Black Panthers; and (3) the legitimation of civil disobedience and a wider consciousness of rights among women, gays, the elderly, environmental activists, the disabled, and last but not least members of a resurgent Christian right.

Some believe such inclusiveness has spawned an overload of democracy by increasing the weight of demands beyond democracy's ability to respond.[94] However, any overload that has occurred must be evaluated in light of the inclusion of those heretofore neglected and oppressed. If contemporary democracy is experiencing a "tragedy of the commons" problem, to rephrase the overload thesis slightly, the answer cannot be simply to shut the door on more recent claimants, but rather it must involve readjusting all shares.

5

The Changing Dynamics
of Class and Labor

During the American Federation of Labor's era of hegemony (1900–30) relations between black Americans and the union movement were often hostile. The basis of this hostility was the opposition of interests between black Americans and the AFL's constituencies, which relied on exclusionary policies to protect a predominantly craft membership. However, the emergence of the Congress of Industrial Organizations (CIO) in the 1930s initiated an era of converging black and trade union interests and agendas that lasted through much of the 1960s. This convergence was a product of several developments within the CIO: (1) its representation of mass-production workers, many of whom were black; (2) its participation in social reform and social activism, a necessity in organizing many of the unorganized; and (3) its political alliance with the northern wing of the Democratic Party, which was rapidly becoming the home base of black Americans. Concurrently, economic and political inequality declined as economic advances were broadly shared across racial lines.

In the mid-1960s, the relationship between unions and blacks began to fray. Union decline exacerbated the competition between blacks and whites over scarce resources (as discussed in Chapter 1). Heightened competition inflamed racial antagonisms. Although the linkages of industrial unions to major civil rights organizations remained strong at the leadership level, relations between their underlying bases weakened considerably. Among the signs of growing animosity between working- and middle-class whites and black Americans were: (1) George Wallace's success in northern states during the 1968 presidential primaries; (2) the struggle over community control of schools in the Ocean Hill–Brownsville section of Brooklyn where white teachers were dismissed in 1968 by a local board of black residents in the "citadel of Northern liberalism"; (3) Richard Nixon's Philadelphia Plan, which established quotas for black applicants for jobs on construction projects; (4) the outbreak of violence in Boston and other northern cities over school busing and integration; (5) riots in Watts, Detroit, and other northern cities; and (6) the emergence of black power separatists.

Terms such as "racial backlash" and "the silent majority" were becoming familiar in the political lexicon. The nation was becoming aware that racial segregation and discrimination were not only southern problems. Riots in Watts, Detroit, Newark, and a host of other northern cities confirmed this impression. During the summer of 1966, thirty-eight riots occurred.[1] Increasing racial discord between blacks and white "middle Americans" assured that an amicable resolution would be extremely difficult. Racial antagonisms, based upon suspicions and resentments stoked by the harsher economic climate since the 1960s and fanned by opportunistic politicians, began to supplant the close collaboration between black and labor constituencies that were instrumental in the political emancipation of the Second Reconstruction.

This chapter examines the decline of the union movement, the fragmentation of work relations, and their combined role in the stagnating life chances of Americans traditionally identified as working class. The fragmentation of work and the decline of unions generated losses for have-nots in general (many of whom remain disproportionately black Americans), while simultaneously depriving black Americans of what were once their most reliable allies. More difficult economic conditions were the primary culprit responsible for rising antagonisms. In this respect, 1970 signified a watershed in the nation's economic performance. According to economist James Galbraith, the 1960s were characterized by high output and productivity growth, growth that slowed significantly in subsequent years. Before 1970, the growth of real wages consistently tracked the growth of productivity and production. In the 1970s and 1980s, economic recovery did not bring real wage growth, but rather wage stagnation. Economic inequality also began to rise, gradually in the 1970s, and then sharply in the 1980s.[2]

The rising economic inequality of recent years has reinforced the racial and ethnic segmentation of employment. Labor market segmentation pervades the concentration of racial and ethnic groups in particular occupations, especially in the secondary sector. Such ethnic queuing has become especially pronounced in those areas of the labor market dominated by "marginal" or "fringe" workers. True, the willingness of recent immigrants to work long hours and create new markets is undeniable, but such attitudes make them susceptible to abuses such as the violation of child labor laws and sweatshop conditions.[3]

The transformation of work has accentuated the atomization of contemporary class organization due to the decline of the labor movement and the spatial movement of work from sites easily organized to sites considerably more difficult to unionize. These are interdependent rather than independent influences. Based upon these trends, the American labor movement has lost the capacity to fulfill a meaningful role as an effective agent of the interests of the nation's have-littles and have-nots. Moreover, in light of the decline of the Democratic Party as an agent of protection for these groups, any counterweight the union/party matrix might have once provided to domination by business and affluent elites has atrophied. Shrunken as well is the Democrats' ability to unite workers across racial and ethnic cleavages. The diminished power of unions and Democrats also makes less viable the once-dominant political coalition of the 1940–60s era. The net result is to effectively shift the balance of power further in the direction of the haves. This partly explains why the 1980s witnessed such emphatically one-sided class struggles.

The institutional structures that regulate the access of individuals to employment have been in the midst of a profound transformation. This dramatic change, sometimes referred to as the decay of industrial society, has engendered a crisis in the employment system. One manifestation of this crisis is the polarization occurring in the distribution of wages, with average wages rising in well-paying industries and falling in poorly paying ones. This polarization is a prime factor contributing to downward mobility. A second manifestation of this crisis is the decline of organized labor—although pockets of strength remain for organized labor, the decline of the percentage of the workforce unionized is significant: today 7.9 percent of nonfarm private employees, or 12.5 percent of all American workers, are unionized, roughly one-third the peak level at the end of World War II. Unions have lost much of their effectiveness, which is not favorable to further improvement in the quality of life of those in the lower half of American society. Yet organized labor's difficulties did not emerge fully grown. The current predicament is a product of the past and arises from conditions that shaped the development of the labor movement in its formative years.

The Development of American Trade Unions

The survival and consolidation of the American Federation of Labor (AFL) in the first two decades of the twentieth century had a number of important implications: (1) as the first labor organization to survive and develop a bargaining relationship with business and the national state, the AFL established a model for the future; (2) although the organization of industrial workers during the New Deal was quite different in many respects, it nonetheless shared essential similarities with its predecessors, none more so than the original AFL, which had reached an accommodation with industry based upon protecting strong constituencies and ignoring weaker ones; (3) the original principles of accommodation also bear some responsibility for the post–World War II decline of the labor movement and the recent disintegration and near collapse of the absolute minimum of social protection—sometimes referred to as the safety net.

The emergence of the AFL in the 1890s as the dominant labor organization in the United States was based in part on its use of restrictive organizing practices, which separated and divided workers, protecting stronger constituencies at the expense of weaker ones. Commencing in the Gilded Age (1870–1900), the devices used to discriminate against newly arrived immigrants from Europe were more severely and viciously applied to the exploitation of Asians, especially the Chinese, and to a small but growing number of blacks in northern cities. Unionists used such devices as competency exams and hiring halls to frustrate new immigrants' entry into their ranks.

Craft unions were the essential mechanism permitting skilled workers to acquire "property rights" to their jobs, leading to the formation of a separate segment of skilled laborers. But a central consequence of AFL success was the breadth of separation between the lives of skilled and unskilled workers socially, economically, politically, and culturally. Craft unionists could not reach out to semi- and unskilled workers without risking their position as the principal agent of unionization. Nor could they engage in outreach while advocating restrictions on immigration. Sustaining their monopoly power required the exclusion of immigrants. By the end of the nineteenth century, skilled workers were considerably better off than the unskilled in wages and employment stability, and their advantages were growing.[4]

Skilled workers were creating a distinctive, privileged position, which survived across several generations based upon craft unions' ability to insulate skilled workers from competition with unskilled immigrant workers. In effect, the AFL cultivated pockets of privilege. Shared similarities in ethnic backgrounds strengthened the effectiveness of exclusionary union practices. Both the durability of craft unions and the persistent schisms between skilled and unskilled labor and manual and nonmanual labor throughout the twentieth century testify to the strength of these intraclass demarcations.[5] Arguably, by forming a distinctive stratum, craft unions preempted the establishment of potentially broader forms of solidarity.

Furthermore, nativism (anti-immigrant prejudice, especially prejudice against more recent immigrants) brought trade unionism and labor politics together. Because of nativism, craft lines were drawn more sharply, and the benefits of unions and labor politics were restricted to a minority. Nativism reinforced the segmentation between immigrant groups. Organized labor's growing role as a legitimate interest group made it a more powerful advocate of immigrant restrictions. By 1900, the AFL had joined the campaign to use the literacy test as a means of restricting immigration.[6] The growth of nativism and acceptance of racism—initially by the rank and file and then eventually by the leadership—cemented the links between AFL craft workers and racist southern Democrats. Nativism helped to mobilize workers by giving their economic organization a political end. In demonstrating the ripeness of the times for exploitation of race, ethnicity, and immigration *by workers*, nativism helped consolidate a labor aristocracy, strengthening its organizational hold over the working class.[7]

Big city political machines provided a structure for the political mobilization of working class ethnics that paralleled the divisions within labor. Predominantly Irish machines favored their own in distributing valued resources of power and patronage among earlier arriving immigrants. Less valuable rewards, public services, and labor and social welfare legislation were shared by later arrivals from Southern and Eastern Europe. Political machines skewed their benefits in order to overreward previously integrated groups (their insiders) at the expense of newer claimants. Political scientist Steven Erie suggests that the failure of urban labor parties can be traced to their ineffectiveness in competition with political machines.

Machine politics promoted the particularistic organization of narrow constituencies in a pattern that would be replicated in the welfare state (1) by dividing its constituents into ethnic blocs, separating old from new immigrants, and each from blacks, and (2) by discriminating in the kind and quality of services it provided to middle- and lower-class voters. Whereas middle-class support depended on low taxes and homeowner services, closely supervised and strictly regulated welfare state benefits were reserved for the poor. Moreover, within their core constituency—the Irish who received the bulk of the available patronage and power—machines provided individual benefits to individual supporters.[8]

The behavior of a number of big city political machines paralleled and thereby reinforced the exclusionary practices of organized labor. Effective machines depended on the construction of coalitions excluding those whose support was not necessary for victory. Hence, party organizations did not mobilize Southern and Eastern Europeans to any degree comparable to their earlier inclusion of the Irish. Rather, by monopolizing political and economic resources for the benefit of insiders, machines applied a strategy similar to that used by craft unions. Craft unions and machine politics each advanced the interests of skilled laborers.

Thus, the AFL's strategy during its most influential years (1890–1930) was based on organizing only "strategic workers"—those who cost more for a company to replace than to meet their demands. The federation made little effort to organize unskilled or semiskilled mass production workers. This strategy would pose several problems for the organization of industrial workers in the CIO in the 1930s and 1940s. To survive and grow, the CIO not only had to take into account the AFL's prior existence and preeminence, but it also had to fiercely compete with the AFL. Thus the AFL's endurance was a significant factor in the environment with which the CIO had to contend. The CIO had to adapt its behavior in order to compete with the AFL, and had to compete on terms in which the AFL was already proficient. Moreover, the eventual merger of the AFL and the CIO in 1955 would mean the CIO was itself compromised by an alliance with the long-established practitioners of discrimination. The combined AFL-CIO would perpetuate the racially exclusive practices of AFL crafts as blacks were discriminated against in apprenticeship programs that led to employment in craft trades.[9]

The ethnic and racial diversity of American workers hampered efforts to create a more universalistic labor movement in this era just as it had before. Ethnic divisions in the base of the CIO's support plagued it right from the start. Skilled industrial workers of German and Irish descent saw their favored positions being threatened by the improving conditions of newer immigrants due the unionization of core industries.

The CIO's efforts to promote racial integration often faced contradictory pressures. For example, the strong alliance between blacks and industrial unions did not prevent organized labor from sabotaging the 1957 Civil Rights Act by supporting white southerners in their insistence that state officials accused of violating court orders on voting rights be entitled to jury trials. This provision was believed by many to be tantamount to nullification of the entire bill, as discussed in Chapter 4. Furthermore, ethno-religious and racial divisions helped enemies of organized labor promote anticommunist sentiments through much of the postwar era.[10] Last but certainly not least, by concentrating on the most easily organized segments of the labor force, the CIO unintentionally set obstacles to its future growth that would come back to haunt it, much as the AFL had done earlier.

The Labor Movement at Its Apex

The modern era of American industrial relations begins with the New Deal. First, the Norris-LaGuardia Act curtailed the use of court-ordered injunctions to prevent workers from striking and picketing. Next, the National Labor Relations or Wagner Act redefined the boundaries of trade union activity.

Then, the Social Security Act established old age pensions and unemployment insurance. Finally, the Fair Labor Standards Act introduced a minimum wage, and set other minimal labor standards.

The Wagner Act created an independent agency, the National Labor Relations Board (NLRB), to regulate labor relations. The NLRB supported collective bargaining by independent unions. It established procedures for bargaining and consideration of unfair labor practices by management. Organized labor used the NLRB to promote collective bargaining, leading to substantial wage increases for millions of workers.[11]

Unsurprisingly, diminishing economic inequality helped to usher in a more favorable political climate. The tighter labor markets of the postwar years fostered a roughly 25 percent decline in inequality from the late 1940s to the mid-1970s as median family income rose substantially. Within these years is the era of the Great Compression (1930–50s), defined by a narrowing gap between top income earners and those in the middle of the income distribution. Declining inequality occurred primarily during Democratic administrations and coincided with the longest economic expansion of the postwar era. According to economist James Galbraith, "the long boom of the Kennedy-Johnson years was far stronger than any since then. It lasted longer, and produced cumulative gains in gross production more than 20 or 30 percent greater than those of its nearest competitors."[12] During much of this era the iron and steel and auto industries paid high wages to unskilled workers, thereby creating the opportunity for better living conditions and moderate upward mobility for millions of Americans.

New institutional structures shaped the exercise of union power. Pattern bargaining has been perhaps the most significant form of solidarity practiced by organized labor in the postwar era. Under pattern bargaining union negotiations in such sectors as auto, steel, and transportation were coordinated, enabling the homogenization of wages and benefits across these industries. For strong unions, pattern bargaining simulated the national wage indexation offered by some European countries, although at the considerable price of simultaneously widening the earnings disparities between unionized and unorganized workers.

Long-term contracts were another step in the institutional setting of the postwar labor environment. Multiyear pacts, which were virtually unknown before the Wagner Act, reached the level of 25 percent of major labor contracts by 1948, and by 1960 between 70 and 85 percent. Business learned (in time) to accept long-term contracts as a means of reducing bargaining confrontations and strikes.[13]

The postwar era also witnessed the development of "internal labor markets" whose dominant characteristics included promotion from inside rather than outside of companies when possible and the establishment of promotion ladders based on explicit rules. For companies this arrangement was valued because it aided on-the-job training, given the presumption that senior workers must have meaningful security to help younger workers. Such procedures were also cheaper than unscheduled strikes, sit-ins, slowdowns, and sabotage as occurred in the 1930s.

The Origins of Union Decline

By the late 1940s it was clear to labor's allies and enemies that the CIO promoted black empowerment while simultaneously benefiting from it. An alliance of conservative business interests and conservative southern politicians, invigorated by their common opposition to the New Deal during the 1930s, responded with a comprehensive effort to halt and reverse labor's advances. The Labor-Management Relations Act of 1947 or Taft-Hartley Act, limited the right to strike, enforced the signing of anticommunist affidavits by union officers, allowed states to ban closed shops, and recast the NLRB from an agency that promoted union recognition to one that incorporated the often antiunion interests of employers as well. The rights of employers to prevent unionization were given more weight, and union shops were subjected to additional restrictions.

Robert Zieger believes "Taft-Hartley furthered a legalistic conception of the relationship between workers and unions and between unions and employers, modifying the basic orientation of the original Wagner Act." Nelson Lichtenstein believes Taft-Hartley created a legal/administrative strait-jacket that encouraged parochialism, thereby penalizing efforts to utilize more class inclusive strategies.[14] Undoubtedly, Taft-Hartley diminished interunion solidarity and removed radical labor activists from the movement's mainstream. Ultimately, Taft-Hartley's restrictions undermined the effectiveness of unions and contained organized labor within its existing geographic and demographic limits, leading to a decline in union membership in the years following its passage. Government intrusion into industrial relations increased even more once the Landrum-Griffith Act of 1959 passed. This measure allowed the federal government to review unions' internal functioning.

Section 14b of the Taft-Hartley Act let states override federal statutes and create right-to-work laws. This clause allowed the decertification of unions that had won representation elections and made the payment of dues voluntary, thereby undermining unions' financial base. The clause was a clear blow to union organizing in the South. Moreover, by holding unions legally liable for such purportedly unfair labor practices as sympathy strikes and secondary boycotts, Taft-Hartley negated one of the strongest tools available in building class-wide solidarity.

Taft-Hartley also made it much easier for management to modify work rules in older frostbelt factories and to devise plans to rationalize production by closing older plants, thereby releasing corporate resources for southern and global expansion. What economists Barry Bluestone and Bennett Harrison term the "geography of deindustrialization" made it easier for companies to shift capital from older industrial areas to regions with nonunionized labor, lower standards of livings, and weaker voices in the workplace.[15] Consequently, the trade union movement has lost much of its momentum.

The impediments to union growth established by Taft-Hartley have been permanent—effectively bureaucratizing labor relations and calcifying existing divisions. Unions now have great difficulty in expanding their base to: (1) new economic sectors; (2) currently unorganized occupations and trades; (3) relatively unorganized geographic regions; and (4) the fastest-growing demographic groups. Thus the boundary between those arenas where unions are strong and vital and those where they are weak and ineffectual has been sharpened. Although the remarkable economic growth of the immediate postwar era would obscure the weakening position of organized labor, the consequences of these strategic losses would become clearer under more difficult economic circumstances.

Southern Unionism

Another major cause of labor's decline was the failure of Operation Dixie—the drive to bring industrial unionism to the South. Labor federations successfully organized over 800,000 southern workers during the war. In 1946 Operation Dixie began a drive to promote unions throughout the South. According to political scientist Mike Goldfield, Operation Dixie's failure was a consequence of the inherent contradictions within the New Deal coalition. To succeed, Operation Dixie needed to actively recruit blacks by exorcising racism and promoting black equality. However, doing so would invariably alienate Dixiecrats. In this case as with Roosevelt's New Deal and Kennedy's New Frontier, the CIO declined to mount a full-blown attack on white supremacy. A frontal attack on racism would have meant an overt confrontation in the politically critical strongholds of white supremacy. Instead, the CIO downplayed its commitment to racial equality.[16]

Quite possibly, the CIO's participation in the New Deal coalition also caused it to pull its punches in Operation Dixie. At the same time, any advances in southern unionization were constrained by the denial of full citizenship to the most oppressed segment of the southern population. Clearly, to grant full citizenship to blacks (and have them exercise their rights as citizens) would have struck at the heart of the powerful reactionary interests ruling the South—a core constituency of the Democratic Party. The accommodations that New Deal Democrats made to retain white southern support are evident in each of the following examples: (1) the arduous and ultimately unsuccessful efforts to enact national legislation such as an anti-lynching law; (2) the inability to pass any significant civil rights legislation during the New Deal; and (3) the concessions to states rights in setting requirements and benefits for public assistance.[17]

Consequently, the South remained hostile terrain to organized labor: the rate of union membership in the South is roughly equivalent in metropolitan and nonmetropolitan areas, both of which lag behind even the nonmetropolitan North. Such impediments as a longstanding surplus of cheap labor, the hostility of political and economic elites, the dispersion of industrial development into less concentrated populations, and the resulting exploitation of racial cleavages each contribute to the relegation of southern states to the bottom of the national scale in terms of union membership.[18]

The failure of Operation Dixie can only be seen as a devastating setback for organized labor. Historian Mike Davis rightly calls this postwar defeat of southern labor "the Achilles heel of American unionism." Of the twenty states that had right-to-work laws by 1980, eleven are former Confederate southern states, comprising 82 percent of the population of right-to-work states. These states have considerably lower rates of union membership than the United States as a whole, and average hourly wages of production workers are 15 percent below the national average.[19] According to Davis, "The right-to-work states have allowed American capital a unique internal mobility, leaving a vast economic space for the evolution of 'Southern strategies' and the crystallization of new non-union sectors. In virtually every industry the supposedly 'marginal' periphery of non-union production has in fact been the redoubt from which, during the 1970s, major assaults have been launched against wage levels and bargaining patterns."[20]

Southern states tax their middle classes lightly, while limiting the scope of redistributive programs that might help the less affluent. The public services of southern states are targeted to their middle classes. Under such conditions, the needs of more disadvantaged voters are seriously neglected. The South has persistently lagged in the quality of basic social provision, including health care, education, and social welfare. Each element directly affects the quality of life of poor southerners and the entire South as a region.[21] For years, exploiting the local welfare system to support the plantation system was an established southern practice. Elderly and disabled blacks received relief at their landlord's request, but relief was available to the able-bodied only in the winter and spring. Landowners were able to apportion part of their labor costs to the national government. According to Richard Bensel and Elizabeth Sandels, "The dramatic transformation of southern welfare policy that followed in the wake of suffrage expansion did not herald the region's entrance into the national mainstream. . . . Without surplus commodity or food stamp programs, without a general relief program, without subsidized housing, and with a highly selectively eligibility determination for child aid, the working class in the South had little or no alternative to work under whatever conditions employers chose to offer."[22] Even today welfare benefits in the South remain low by national standards.

Organized labor's failure in the South, and the passage of Taft-Hartley, each figured powerfully in the erosion of union strength. This erosion has paved the way for a surge in industrialization nationwide remarkably similar to that which has historically marked the South—on the fringes of metropolitan and rural areas rather than in city centers.

In recent years, the South has led the way in a national acceleration of inequality. Bluestone and Harrison find that "the disparity between rich and poor is becoming increasingly evident throughout the Sunbelt, creating a dualism reminiscent of the pre–Civil War South. . . . The wealthiest fifth of the southern population has roughly nine times as much income as the poorest fifth. In non-southern regions, the disparity is 7.4 to 1."[23] This "southernization" of the United States is partly a result of the use of interregional divide-and-conquer mechanisms—the playing of different regions of the United States off against each other in their efforts to attract industries and affluent wage earners. But the economic and political convergence of southern and nonsouthern regions of the country reflects a competitive downscaling to a least common denominator dictated by low costs: low wages, low taxes, and declining standards of living.

Surging Inequality and Income Polarization

In the 1960s, corporations turned to a strategy pioneered by GE and other nonunionized firms in the 1950s: build smaller factories, decentralize in regions where labor organization was already low, and recruit workers without prior experience in unions. Decentralization and relocation have made American industry much more resistant to unionization. For example, manufacturing plants built in the 1970s were 60 percent smaller than older plants in their respective industries.

For a time declining union strength was attributed to cyclical factors, and it was expected that eventual industrial recovery would lead to union recovery. However, the renewal of economic growth since the 1982 recession—the most severe of the postwar era—has not increased unions' bargaining power. Domestic employment attributable to manufacturing has declined from

27 to 19 percent while a decline in union membership has contributed to longer-term stagnation in real wages.

An important contributor to the decline of unions has been the falling number of workers employed in large companies. As political scientist Andrew Hacker points out, nowadays the largest companies hire fewer workers. "In 1973, the nation's 800 largest firms presented paychecks to 229 of every 1,000 employed Americans. By 1993, the top 800 provided jobs for only 169 of every 1,000." This roughly 25 percent decline in aggregate employment by the nation's largest firms pales in comparison to the decline of employment in the industrial sector. In 1973, the industrial sector employed 184 of every 1,000 American workers; in 1993, it employed only 97 of every 1,000, a decline of roughly 50 percent.[24] Thus employment has fallen in those large manufacturing companies that have typically been the easiest to unionize and that form the core of the unionized and nonunionized good jobs available to many wage earners.

Capital Mobility and Union Decline

A second factor in the decline of unions, relocation, reflects the mobility of employment to more favorable business climates. Bluestone and Harrison believe that a "geography of deindustrialization" reflects the desire of companies to relocate capital out of older industrial areas in order to utilize nonunionized labor with a lower standard of living and less voice in the workplace.[25] Capital's increasing mobility shifted the balance of power against labor. Ultimately, capital flight became a valuable method of disciplining workers.

Thus, interregional mobility enhanced the leverage of corporate management to demand reductions in local taxation that translate into cuts in community services and social services. Employers have become adept tacticians in combating unionization drives. Layoffs enhance the business climate by assisting employers in either rolling back wages or limiting their increase. By using consultants effectively and threatening to close worksites, employers have become more sophisticated and aggressive in their efforts to dissuade workers from unionizing, contributing to those structural trends that promote labor's decline. Hence, capital mobility means unions face "take it or leave it" propositions.

Especially significant among these more sophisticated strategies was the employment of parallel production and multiple sourcing. Parallel production refers to the tactic of replicating production facilities, muting the impact of strikes because production can be readily shifted from unionized to nonunionized locations. Multiple sourcing involves using smaller suppliers, and employing several sources for the same components, thus allowing vendors to be played off against one another, and placing the vendor's labor force under pressure to reduce costs as well. Of course, neither of these tactics is limited by national borders and can be applied internationally, given the emergence of a global economy. Foreign relocation or outsourcing forces unionized labor in one country into competition with the unionized labor force of another. By the 1970s, American corporations had succeeded in reconstituting manufacturing on an interregional and international scale.

Deindustrialization and permanent job loss form part of a vicious cycle. The disintegration of the safety net is reflected in diminished social welfare benefits, loss of health insurance, and the unavailability of unemployment benefits for the long-term unemployed. In combination these conditions raise the specter of long-term downward mobility for affected workers and their families. Bluestone and Harrison believe "the competition between local governments to retain existing capital or to attract new private investment is leading to an extraordinary retrenchment in social programs."[26] Such losses are clearly more than temporary frictional unemployment as indicated by the increased utilization of food stamps and general welfare benefits, including AFDC, at least before such benefits were dramatically reduced in 1996.

The Architecture of Polarization

Deindustrialization provides at best a partial accounting of the increasing inequality of the last generation. Inequality has risen in virtually every sector of the economy in these years. The dramatic changes in the institutional structures that regulate the labor force are confirmed by the declining fortunes of many workers. An overriding phenomenon shared by American workers, especially blue-collar workers in the last quarter of the twentieth century, has been wage stagnation. From the end of World War II until 1973, Americans had been able to count on growing income. Since the late 1970s, however, the proportion of the labor force earning low wages has grown substantially. Although wages and salaries became steadily more equal from 1964 to 1978, since 1978 wage inequality has increased by over 20 percent.

U.S. earnings inequality since the mid-1970s has had the following features: (1) sharp declines for non–college-educated males; (2) higher pay for the well educated across gender, race, industry, and occupational groupings; and (3) a growing gap between the higher educated and high school graduates. From 1970 to 2000, earnings of the lowest-paid male workers declined 20 percent, whereas earnings for the highest-paid male workers increased 30 percent. The implications of increasing inequality for women are less straightforward due to the increasing number of women working full time. Most of the new jobs created in the last twenty years have gone to women. Nonetheless for women, real wages also increased in better-paying jobs and declined in lesser-paying ones. According to the Labor Department, the number of women working has increased by 9 million, to 63 million in the last decade. Thus, for men and women the most recent era has been one of increasing inequality.[27]

An added consequence of growing inequality is its impact on families with children, whose income has declined an average of 6.6 percent. However, this average is considerably skewed as the lowest fifth of the family income distribution has declined 32 percent while the highest fifth has been nearly constant.[28] Meanwhile, the concentration of wealth is as high as it has been at any time since the data began to be collected.

Some analysts have sought to counter such evidence by arguing that any decline that has occurred in middle-class earnings is largely demographic. Consequently, the relative earnings of the large cohort of younger workers (especially males) were depressed as the baby boom generation was absorbed.[29] Undoubtedly, generational crowding has affected income disparities, but this by itself is an inadequate explanation of income inequality. The size of the baby boom cohort may have played a significant role in rising inequality in the 1970s. Yet the percentage of middle-income households has been in decline within every age group, making it difficult to attribute this trend to demographic factors. Economist Gary Burtless argues that less than one-quarter of the recent changes in male earning inequality are due to generational crowding. Rather, it is more plausible that the contemporary economy simply produces a smaller proportion of good jobs than its industrial predecessor did in its heyday. Hence, the declining fortunes of the baby boom generation cannot be dismissed as a temporary condition that will melt away as younger workers gain experience and presumably higher wages.[30]

Certainly union decline, emblematic of the changing institutional environment faced by American wage earners, is as essential as any other single factor in explaining the declining fortunes of American workers. But it too constitutes only one element in the overall picture of surging inequality.

Labor market segmentation promotes inequality by diminishing the extent to which the state of the general labor market affects the demand for labor within particular settings. As such, it favors strong labor and large business against weaker and less-organized segments of labor and capital. Labor market segmentation simultaneously diminishes the prospects for cross-segment unity among stronger and weaker labor segments. Polarization has been especially prevalent in the pension, health, and disability plans negotiated by unions, which have widened the gap between well off and secure workers and those employed in less stable settings. Their insulation has understandably led workers protected by strong contracts with good benefits to be disinclined to pursue political action to expand public programs. Where such contracts are tied to the Consumer Price Index, a supplemental boost is given to those union members whose contracts have clauses in which wages escalated based on the CPI relative to other blue-collar and white-collar workers.[31]

Corporate restructuring augments income polarization in myriad ways. For one, corporate restructuring has led to "devolution" of internal labor markets. Instead of job ladders are arrangements under which more irregular, non–full-time employees are hired, which means more part-time, temporary, and leased employees are hired by larger firms. Meanwhile, pools of low-wage contingent or flexible workers are more intensively utilized, often dispersed to a variety of locations, and not infrequently employed by subcontractors. Such outsourcing adds to the creation of different classes of employees in the large companies that were once the haven of desirable employment. In general terms such actions represent a corporate strategy of enhancing employer flexibility by externalizing the employment relationship.

A long-term effect of such policies is to diminish the job stability and wage premiums enjoyed by employees in traditionally secure jobs. Employment instability has grown substantially for older, less-educated men.[32] According to economist Bennett Harrison, "Lean production, downsizing, outsourcing, and the growing importance of spatially extensive production networks governed by powerful core firms and their strategic allies, . . . are all part of businesses' search for 'flexibility' in order to better cope with heightened global competition."[33] For workers, such flexibility produces increasing inequality in earnings, benefits, job security, workplace safety, and other significant quality-of-life dimensions. According to analyst Kevin Phillips, for low-income and unskilled workers, declining benefits and health coverage that dampened inequality in the 1960s and 1970s were increasingly a part of the "architecture of polarization."[34]

The economic policies that have created the trade deficit also redistribute income. Workers employed in industries that compete with mass-produced foreign imports suffer wage declines when even a rising dollar intensifies competition. According to Galbraith, the enormous tax cuts and swollen deficits that stimulated economic growth after 1981 "raised the value of the dollar, prompted a huge increase in manufactured imports, mainly from low wage countries, and therefore put asymmetric pressure on lower-wage import-competing manufacturing workers." Kevin Phillips finds it to be no coincidence that the beneficiaries of Reagan-era trade policies and the beneficiaries of its tax, budget, monetary, and trade policies were largely the same. Lester Thurow believes "a lack of international competitiveness—manifested in a $150 billion annual trade deficit—is eliminating some of America's best paying jobs. The industries that pay the highest wages and thus help narrow inequalities in income, are suffering the most from our lack of competitiveness. . . . Between 1980 and the middle of 1985, for example, the rise in imports drove the wages of 300,000 American workers below $12,500 a year." Economists Kevin Murphy and Finis Welch found trade deficits in durable manufacturing provide perhaps the single most important reason for the growing gap in earnings between white males with a high school diploma or less and those with a college degree or more.[35]

Workers (and others who live on limited or moderate incomes) have suffered from a perverse scissors effect since the mid-1970s: budget deficits have undermined the social wage while free trade, deregulation, and other government policies undermine private wages. The deregulation of labor relations in the 1980s has promoted capital flight, plant closings, deunionization, and the growth of industries that rely on intensive exploitation of labor.[36] The overall consequence of these trends has been to erode the legal support necessary to sustain moderate, nonradical trade unionism. Each of these factors has made an important contribution to the decline of organized labor.

The New Proletarians?

A consequence of the changing economic environment is the explosive growth in the number of workers, primarily unskilled or semiskilled, who have reasonably continuous work histories but little of the common or shared work environments so instrumental in forging solidarity. Employees in fast food and convenience stores, school bus and cab drivers, clerical employees, janitors, and parking lot attendants are typical occupations for workers in the secondary sector. Their characteristics include low pay, minimal benefits, and unstable employment. This is the sector of the economy in which the growth in employment has been greatest. Many of the workers employed in these occupations make less than $8 an hour. Workers of the twentieth percentile earned $8.31 per hour in 2002. Moreover, a wage of $8 an hour multiplied by a thirty-five- to forty-hour week produces an annual wage of $14,500 to $16,000 a year. This wage does not meet the poverty threshold for a family of four, which is approximately $18,100.[37] These are workers who may be fairly described as the working poor. Such workers may well be most similar in terms of their conditions of life to classic "proletarians," but differ in that their work relations do not lend themselves to the economies of scale necessary for efficient union organization.

For a larger proportion of Americans, part-time and/or temporary work offers the only available work opportunities. Approximately 1 of every 200 Americans were temporary workers in the early 1980s, versus 1 of every 40 Americans by the late 1990s.[38] Although this trend is most common in the retail trade, it is evident in other sectors as well. Companies seek to save money and increase flexibility by employing part-timers. Part-time workers add flexibility; their schedules can be lengthened, shortened, or turned upside down each week to meet an employer's immediate needs. Moreover, the largest increase in the labor force is among involuntary part-timers: those who want but cannot find jobs with regular hours and rewards. According to journalist Peter Kilborn, "While the non-agricultural workforce grew 54 percent from 1970 to 1990, the number of involuntary part-timers jumped 121 percent to 4.9 million, according to the Bureau of Labor Statistics. . . . [By contrast] the ranks of voluntary part-timers grew 69 percent."[39] The rise in involuntary part-time employment and its positive relation to rising unemployment provides a strong indication of rising underemployment.

Although attractive part-time employment is available in such areas as accounting and computer programming, the aggregate disadvantages of part-time employment greatly outweigh its advantages. Only 10 percent of part-timers in retail trade received health insurance through their employment compared to 47 percent of full-time employees. An increasing number of involuntary part-time employees lack health insurance. Some retailers employ people who are part-timers in name only, working beyond the thirty-five hours a week the Bureau of Labor Statistics uses as the minimum for full-time work. According to Kilborn, "No law requires an employer to extend full-time benefits and pay rates to all who work more than 35 hours a week."[40] Part-time male workers receive significant lower returns to both age and education than do full-timers. Both male and female part-timers receive significantly lower wages. Part-timers are also less likely to receive pensions.[41]

The growth of secondary labor markets coincides with the intermittent status of many in the workforce and links many of these intermittently employed to the underground economy. In this category must be included the growth of a "subproletariat"—those whose paid labor is insufficient for subsistence, in other words, the working homeless. Millions of Americans may never be able to afford to purchase a home. Roughly sixty percent of low-wage workers reside on the brink of homelessness.[42]

Increasing part-time employment also influences perceptions of unemployment because unemployment is a social as well as an economic phenomenon. In the nineteenth and early twentieth centuries, when self-employed farmers and small businessman were a large part of the labor force, they were typically not considered unemployed, no matter how great their immiserization. According to sociologist Teresa Sullivan:

> From 1870 to 1930, census enumerators asked each respondent ten years or older if she "usually" pursued a gainful occupation for money or goods, or if the respondent assisted in producing marketable goods and services.

Persons answering "yes" were classified as gainful workers. . . . It provided no measure of current occupational behavior because workers reported their "usual" (not present) occupation, or if retired (their previous occupation). . . . Because there was no information about actual employment, there could be no measure of current unemployment. Entrants with no occupation were the only persons usually counted as "unemployed."[43]

Currently, discouraged workers and those who involuntarily work part time are excluded from official unemployment statistics. Their inclusion would raise the unemployment rate by one-third to one-half. The number of disability recipients has virtually doubled to 5.4 million. Disability recipients are the largest group that has left the labor force and are not counted as unemployed. The increase in disability recipients is greatest among less-skilled men unable to find blue-collar jobs at wages comparable to what they formerly earned. Also 2 million people are in prison today (versus 500,000 in 1980 and 1.1 million in 1990) and are not included in the labor force and not counted as unemployed. If such "statistical nonpersons" were included, today's unemployment rate would rival the rates of the 1970s and 1980s. [44]

Racial and Ethnic Structuring of Employment, Unemployment, and Underemployment

Racial and ethnic identities play a central role in the structuring of employment and unemployment, making the distinction between marginal workers and marginal jobs at times ambiguous. Labor markets generate inequality by allocating work based upon categories of workers. Employers discriminate between potential employees who differ in race, ethnicity, nationality, gender, age, class, and religion. Occupations become identified with particular groups of workers because employers recruit different kinds of workers for them, thus drawing sharp distinctions between kinds of work that are fundamentally similar in nature.[45]

Women and black men disproportionately fill less desirable jobs. Moreover, their abilities are often underutilized relative to the skills they bring to the workforce. Unemployment has always been greater for non-whites than for whites, transforming non-whites (and recent white immigrants) into a reserve of cheap labor. Over the past fifty years, for example, the unemployment rate for black Americans has typically been twice that for white Americans.

Racial differences in unemployment rates obviously lend substance to the perception that unemployment is a problem of race-related individual deficiencies rather than a structural phenomenon. By viewing racial differences in unemployment as due to a culture of poverty, its value as a political issue is diminished. Furthermore, the categories of unemployment not only describe, they also discriminate. Unemployment rates miss hidden or concealed unemployment and underemployment of several types. For example, the size of the labor force is affected by whether women, in particular married women, tend to work outside the home or not. Young people who have never entered the labor force also do not count as unemployed. Generous school allowances, scholarships, vocational and retraining programs, early retirement policies, and reduction of working hours all depress the numbers of job seekers relative to what it would be in the absence of such programs. The definition and measurement of unemployment is, to a degree, arbitrary. For example, measurement problems involving the size of the underground economy modify the perception of unemployment. Distinctions are made between those actively looking for work and "discouraged workers," that is, those who are not actively looking for work. The exclusion of the latter restricts the numbers of the "officially" unemployed.

"Structural unemployment" influences the size and nature of the underground economy because underemployment represents less than full employment in ways not typically captured by conventional measures of unemployment. Since the late 1970s, the bulk of new part-time jobs have been filled by people who would prefer (but cannot get) full-time jobs. Underemployment is a factor in the increase in inequality occurring in full-time year-round low-wage work.[46] Some analysts believe that underemployment has accelerated in recent years, and that underemployment represents a dark side of the positive portrayal of economic growth in the mid- to late 1990s. According to John E. Schwarz, if we add the 4 million workers who in 1996 were employed part time but said they wanted full-time work and are thus underemployed, and the nearly 10 million making less than $7 per hour, to the approximately 7 million unemployed based upon official statistics, there are 21 million workers needing full-time employment, not 7 million. By this calculation, 21 million Americans—roughly a fifth of the workforce—are either unemployed, underemployed, or marginally employed. Martin Carnoy estimated that in 1993, 17.5 percent of Americans worked part time and 2.5 percent were temporary workers, together composing 20 percent of the workforce.[47] This considerable deficit in full-time employment highlights the interdependence of employment, unemployment, and underemployment.

Underground employment is influenced by the number of available legitimate aboveground or mainstream employment opportunities. Underground employment is often therefore involuntary. Employment in the "underground economy" like underemployment has increased in part because of the deterioration of employment opportunities available in the aboveground economy. Of course, some of the increase in employment in recent years reflects the "commodification" of nonmarket household employment, which is a shift from unmeasured to measured employment rather than the creation of genuine new employment. For example, because women are more often in the workforce, they hire paid labor to do domestic and household services and purchase ready-made meals and take-out dinners. Thus unpaid labor becomes paid labor and is now added to gross national product, where it was invisible before.

Recent changes in tax law have allowed some employed persons to gain significant tax advantages by registering as self-employed. But despite significant measurement problems, sociologists Erik Olin Wright and George Steinmetz conclude that self-employment is growing due to a declining quality of employment options in the mainstream economy.[48] Many workers are nowadays being registered as self-employed to reduce costs. By comparison, during the postwar industrial period of 1950–70 there was an intense decline in self-employment, a nearly 3 percent annual rate of decline, dispersed across economic sectors. Self-employment is no longer declining, it is now on the rise, especially in the postindustrial economic sectors. Growth in self-employment is often a "second-best recourse" to paid employment. Self-employment has, however, declined since 1994. In 1994, 10.9 percent of the nonagricultural workforce was self-employed, and 9.9 percent in 1999.[49]

Moreover, economic growth in developed countries tends to favor higher capital intensity over lower—the tendency is for the substitution of high capital-intensive for lower capital-intensive firms to occur in both established and newly emerging industries. In order to counteract the negative effects of high capital-intensive firms on employment growth, growth would have to reach and maintain unrealistically high and accelerated rates. Furthermore, projections of increased employment opportunities based on rapid growth in electronics, computers, and other "high tech" industries reflect the familiar illusion of high growth from a small base. Hence, growth in new industries is unlikely to successfully offset employment declines in much larger older industries over any period of time. Moreover, conservative social policies that undermine the social wage force families to send more members into the labor force to sustain existing standards of living, suggesting the difficulties confronting primary wage earners in earning a living wage.

Perhaps one of the less obvious ways in which the postindustrial division of labor promotes inequality is through the growth of franchising. Franchising diffuses ownership, increasing the difficulty of establishing appropriate bargaining units as well as who is to be bargained with. Franchising also raises labor turnover, stimulates protracted labor relations, and is responsible for much of the growth of low-wage employment.

The political significance of high unemployment has clearly declined. In part the exclusion of many workers from the labor force means unemployment no longer measures what it once did. The weakness of organized labor is also a factor in the general public's greater sensitivity to inflation than unemployment. According to economist Douglas Hibbs, "Only in the United States, is there any evidence of a nonvertical long-run Phillips curve" (trading low inflation for higher unemployment).[50] Rising unemployment rates since the late 1960s coincide with the declining strength of labor. During the recession of 1981–82, unemployment reached double-digit levels, peaking at 10.8 percent, the highest rate since the Great Depression. Of course, official rates of unemployment from the 1930s are not strictly comparable to recent rates due to changes in methods of calculation. Fewer workers then were covered by unemployment insurance, but higher unemployment rates have become less relevant to political deliberations. To be unemployed for any length of time in the United States is a harsher penalty than in any other democratic society.[51] Higher rates and more punitive experiences while unemployed exacerbate the whip of the market, reducing the capacity to organize, and thus forcing workers into anomic and defensive modes where they are unable to push for expansion of social citizen rights, and often are forced to relinquish those rights they have already won. Thus the overall decline in welfare state benefits undermines the social or citizen wage, thereby making unemployment more costly to the life chances of the individual wage earner and his or her family.

Higher rates of long-term unemployment also signify downward mobility. By the beginning of 2003, roughly 1.9 million people looking for work were unemployed six months or more, three times the number of 2001. Roughly one of every five American men experience downward occupation mobility. Yet downward mobility is considered an aberration, a consequence of individual deficiencies. According to anthropologist Katherine Newman, "Downward mobility is a hidden dimension of our society's experience because it simply does not fit into our cultural universe. The downwardly mobile therefore become an invisible minority—their presence among us unacknowledged."[52]

Due to the state of the contemporary labor market, workers are subjected to abuses that once seemed anachronistic for a postindustrial late twentieth-century society. Sweatshops, unsafe working conditions, abuses of child labor, employers who cheat workers out of their wages, as well a wide variety of other abuses are parts of a real if seemingly surrealistic portrait reminiscent of Dickensian England as captured in *Oliver Twist.*

The abuses of child labor appear to have grown dramatically. Such abuse is often difficult to measure since much of it takes place off the books. Even very young children (as young as five) are being used as vendors. Poor immigrant workers in the garment trades are especially likely to be cheated out of their wages. In Chicago, Hispanic children selling gum are known as "chicleros." Exploited by their parents, they are also prey for gangs. Obviously, no one regulates his or her hours. Sweatshop firms have flourished in the high technology sector of the economy as well.[53]

Perhaps no workers are more abused than migrant agriculture laborers. These workers are frequently subjected to dangerous conditions and deprived of access to such basic human needs as toilet facilities and drinking water. Farmers are often not required to tell laborers what pesticides they use, their potential dangers, or first aid procedures. Such conditions are often due to the growing practice of defining migrant laborers as independent subcontractors, rather than employees. By reducing the number of formal employees, farmers avoid health and safety laws, which generally exempt farms with fewer than eleven employees. Farm workers who are defined as subcontractors must pay 15.3 percent of their income in Social Security taxes, rather than the 7.65 percent that regular employees pay. As subcontractors they are ineligible for unemployment insurance or worker's compensation.[54]

A Shifting Tide: Surging Inequality

From the 1940s to the early 1970s, a combination of political, social, and economic conditions promoted a cohesive universalism in the United States. Reducing the racial and ethnic divisions impeding economic progress conferred positive benefits upon middle- and lower-income individuals across racial lines. Declining economic inequality paralleled inequality-reducing political trends, highlighted by the development of the civil rights and labor movements. Essentially, the forces that facilitated improving life chances for black Americans aided improving life chances for all working-class Americans. The net result was greater economic and political equality in the United States. This upsurge in economic and political equality made possible a breakthrough for organized labor (albeit less dramatically) corresponding to the accession of black Americans to citizenship. In part, advances for organized labor aided blacks, because of the strong black participation in the industrial union movement.

For most of this era the relations of black Americans and organized labor were symbiotic. True, the record of many unions in redressing racial imbalances left a lot to be desired, especially in skilled craft and construction trades, where black employment remained minuscule. At the same time, racially tainted practices limiting black upward mobility in both union and occupational hierarchies remained pervasive, affecting even the egalitarian-minded United Auto Workers (UAW).[55]

But since those years, a vicious cycle has emerged in which changes in the workplace have exacerbated the decline of organized labor while the decline of organized labor has undermined the ability of workers to stave off deteriorating workplace conditions. Not infrequently, intentional strategies designed to frustrate effective organization have been the culprit. Deindustrialization has played a role in reducing available options for machinists, machine operators, and craft workers, occupations that form core jobs for skilled blue-collar workers. This core was once the upper stratum of working-class males, considered to be the labor aristocracy.

On balance, public policy implemented during the Reagan-Bush era, notably government-induced deflation, deregulation, regressive tax reform, and privatization, have added new weapons to the arsenal of corporate strategies. The net result has been an episodic civil war between firms and regions competing for job-creating investments that pit workers against each other.[56] According to Mike Davis, "Overall, Reagan's first term witnessed a decline in the density of unionization that was unprecedented in the postwar experience of advanced democratic nations."[57]

By undermining the social wage, workers have been made more quiescent. Communities and states find themselves in competition to create "better business climates" by providing tax breaks, investment credits, loan subsidies, and retrenchments in public benefits. Just the threat of capital movement pressures states to cut program benefits. Recent court rulings have given employers considerable latitude to cut back medical insurance. Employers who operate as self-insurers are frequently exempted from state insurance laws that specify which ailments must be covered. The net effect is that in self-insured companies the sick are separated from the healthy, lowering the cost of insurance for healthy workers, but reducing the coverage available to the sick.[58]

American unions have certainly suffered from self-inflicted wounds. They have generally failed to adequately adjust to shifts occurring in employment from blue- to white-collar work and from manufacturing to services. The proportion of unionized white-collar workers is far lower in the United States than in the majority of its industrialized counterparts. Unions in the white-collar field are weak by comparison to major blue-collar unions. Public sector unions are crippled by laws forbidding or inhibiting the right to strike, as well as the right to struggle for a closed or union ship.

Many white-collar unions came into existence by federal executive order, without the kind of struggle that makes for a militant membership. For the most part they have gained relatively little for their members. Unionized white-collar workers have little clout. Moreover, the courts have limited the matters on which they can bargain. Setting aside the issue of cause or effect, it is also true that white-collar workers have more unfavorable perceptions of what unions do and the extent of union power. Their perceptions often over-estimate the extent of union power.

Perhaps most important, unions have poorly adapted to the increasing feminization of the workforce, reminiscent of the half-hearted efforts to union-ize the South and the at times tepid attempts to eradicate discriminatory ra-cial barriers. The growth of the white-collar stratum is closely associated with the increasing participation of women in the labor force. About half of all white-collar workers are women; over 60 percent of the women in the official labor force are employed in white-collar occupations. Organized la-bor has historically not done well in fields dominated by women: clerical, secretarial, insurance, banking, and white-collar fields. Yet, this should not be surprising since the top levels of union federations, and indeed of most unions, remain dominated by a conservative white male gerontocracy that all too often has opposed any mobilization that threatens its power.[59]

The disintegration of the labor movement as a collective bargaining force for workers coincides with the rise of anti-inflationary macroeconomic poli-cies whose costs are borne largely by wage earners. Rising unemployment to combat inflation has been considerably more harmful to those in the low to moderate ranges of the income distribution than inflation itself. Accord-ing to Doug Hibbs, "the small impact on relative income (and wealth) posi-tions that can be traced to inflation appears to have disadvantaged the rich, not the poor. By contrast, upward movements in unemployment unambigu-ously create significant pain for low- and middle-income groups, further skewing the income distribution away from the bottom two quintiles to-wards the top one."[60]

The decline of labor as an effective institution does not augur well for any near-term resurgence of those forces favorable to improvements in the life chances of black Americans. It also suggests that a cyclical resurgence in the capabilities of America's have-nots to undertake organized action is unlikely, notwithstanding the expectations of Arthur Schlesinger, Kevin Phillips, or anyone else. Arguably, the distribution of opportunities or life chances of lower-class Americans (black and white) has deteriorated to the point that their capacity to participate in American society as meaningful citizens has been severely impaired.

6

Inequality and
Popular Sovereignty

In the words of historian Edward Morgan, the history of popular sovereignty in America can be read as a series of "successive efforts of different generations to bring facts into closer conformity with the fiction."[1]

> Its success rested uneasily on the contradiction always present in representation: the sovereignty of the people could be exercised only through representatives who were at once the agents of particular people in particular communities and the wielders of the supreme power that the people mysteriously conveyed to them. The viability of the fiction depended, in part at least, on the people of particular communities feeling themselves to be a part of one people, their particular interests not incompatible with the interest of the whole as directed by the assembled wielders of power. The interests of a part can seldom be identified with those of the whole, but a people must cease to exist if the persons in whose minds it has its being, cease to consider themselves as belonging to it.[2]

However, this view is incompatible with another influential exploration of democracy. Sociologists Michael Omi and Howard Winant argue that "the broad sweep of U.S. history is characterized not by racial democracy but by racial despotism, not by trajectories of reform but by implacable denial of political rights, dehumanization, extreme exploitation and policies of minority extirpation. Democracy has never been in abundant supply where race is concerned."[3]

Within these contrasting interpretations of American democracy we may understand the influence of race on the democratization of the United States. To begin with, the growth of popular sovereignty in the United States has had in fact several significant paradoxes. The United States was the first nation to extend the franchise beyond the class of notables (in other words a

161

largely inherited elite), but the last (among major industrialized nations) to complete the democratic revolution by enfranchising (actually re-enfranchising) its southern black citizens.

Perhaps because the initial incorporation of the masses into democratic politics was premodern, occurring in advance of industrialization, the American conception of democratization is somewhat archaic. More fully than in any other nation, American democracy embraces the doctrines of classic liberalism, which deny any linkage between political and economic rights. This is perhaps one reason why Americans cling to a rhetoric of equal opportunity while ignoring the substantial equality of results that must exist for opportunities to approach equality. The anachronistic character of American electoral rules is highlighted by the 2000 presidential election. The victory by popular-vote-loser George W. Bush was due largely to the overrepresentation of small states in the electoral college.

This chapter will explore the implications of inequality for popular sovereignty, mindful of the following question: Can the United States still be considered a nation in which popular sovereignty holds? Or has the decline of popular sovereignty been so extensive as to suggest its extinction?

Race and Popular Sovereignty in the Early Republic

Throughout American history race has shaped the contours of American democracy. Racial slavery generated the largest obstacle to popular sovereignty. The establishment of the United States as an independent nation brought forth a version of democracy full of both contradiction and paradox, a paradox that, in the words of historian George Dangerfield, "was handed on from one generation to another, growing more steadily in power until Emancipation itself could not set it at rest."[4] Most obviously, the original constitutional compromise on slavery meant that the declaration that all men are created equal was inconsistent with the gross denial of liberty inherent in slavery. Slavery limited popular sovereignty because the notion that blacks might be treated equally was never seriously entertained in colonial America. The growing belief in the "natural rights of man" did not include blacks.[5] The original constitutional accommodation tolerating slavery severely compromised (if it did not altogether stifle) the growth of democracy in the South while undermining the quality of northern democracy. By counting slaves as three-fifths of a person for districting, apportionment, and taxation, the influence of the slaveholding regions was magnified, and that of non-slaveholding areas was diminished.

Such diminution of the franchise affected both the rapidly democratizing North as well as non-slaveholding "up-country" areas of the South. Since slave-owning regions maintained a political influence out of proportion to the number of their actual (white) citizens for the entire pre–Civil War era, the national government invariably catered to slaveowners' interests. The three-fifths rule allowed the South to dominate each branch of the national government.

Compromises with slavery trampled upon the rights of both whites and blacks. The first national fugitive slave law was passed in 1793. This law and its successors required northern complicity in the maintenance of a slave regime. The Supreme Court upheld such laws, ruling first in *Prigg v. Pennsylvania* that states could not regulate the actions of slaveowners in pursuit of their fugitive human property.[6] The notorious *Dred Scott* decision handed down by the Supreme Court in 1857 reaffirmed the perversion of liberty required to maintain the union. Chief Justice Roger Taney, in arguing "the negro had no rights which white men needed to recognize," threatened to disenfranchise free blacks in order to contain sectional tensions.

Involuntary servitude seeped into the sinews of early American democracy. Even so, the struggle for democratic rights led to expansions of popular sovereignty. By the election of Andrew Jackson in 1828, the United States was arguably the most democratic country in the world. In less than two generations, the nation had been transformed from a society in which a narrow spectrum of notables manned and controlled its politics to one in which the majority of male citizens (excluding blacks and Native Americans) were involved. However, the growth of citizenship for white men paralleled a deteriorating political climate for blacks.[7] The United States was becoming a white man's republic. While the franchise was expanding for white males, free black males were being disenfranchised throughout the nation. By 1840, blacks could no longer vote in the South, while less than 10 percent of northern blacks were allowed to vote. Restrictions on black enfranchisement were enacted in New Jersey, New York, and Pennsylvania. Each new state admitted to the union after 1819 prevented blacks from voting.[8]

The Negro Seaman Acts also reflect the deteriorating status of free blacks in antebellum years. Accordingly, any blacks onboard ships in South Carolina's or Louisiana's harbors were to be imprisoned while the ship was in port. The purpose was to prevent free black seamen from spreading the "contagion of liberty." The ship captains were responsible for paying for their imprisonment and if they failed to do so, black seamen could be sold into slavery.[9]

The deterioration of the political status of blacks was paralleled by the deterioration of their economic prospects. The Irish immigrants who flooded northern cities in the 1840s and 1850s employed an arsenal of tactics both violent and nonviolent to drive blacks out of jobs they desired. They committed murder, burned homes and property, and engaged in riots and strikes to exclude blacks from gainful employment in desirable occupations. The violence of Irish immigrants often intimidated white employers, elevating the economic status of Irish immigrants over that of blacks.[10]

Free Negroes threatened the stability of southern society because black slavery provided a floor beneath which no white could fall. By defining blacks as inferior, regardless of whether they were slaves or free, the status of whites was raised irrespective of their economic position. As long as any white could look down on blacks—all blacks—class divisions among whites appeared less ominous. Thus, free blacks were a threat to the racial foundations of the South in an era of growing class conflict among whites. In the United States North and South, the racialization of citizenship in the American republic was the price for diluting its antebellum class antagonisms.

In numerous respects the requirements of a plantation slave system dominated the southern political economy to the detriment of non-slaveholders:

1. In an era in which land ownership and democracy were regarded as the foundations of a stable democratic republic, a Homestead Act, making free land available to settlers, could not be passed until the Civil War (while the South was out of the Union). A major reason was that southern elites were fearful that the migration of poor whites would reduce their political power. They also feared migration would lead to declines in the price of cotton if the region of cotton growing were expanded.

2. The dualism necessary to maintain a caste regime perverted every aspect of southern society. In learning to deal with free blacks before the Civil War, southern whites developed institutions, standards of personal relations, and patterns of thought that they would apply after emancipation. Segregation, black codes, the convict-lease system, and forms of peonage usually associated with the postbellum South all victimized the antebellum free Negro caste.[11]

3. Urban living intensified racial tensions as poor whites and blacks were brought together. Laws and customs developed in a predominantly agricultural society could not be easily transferred to urban living situations. Thus blacks and whites commingled in living arrangements, work environments, after-hours entertainment, and sexual relationships in defiance of strictures mandating segregation.[12] Suspicions were aroused concerning the unseemly contact between the black and white urban poor, encouraging the aristocratic view that poor whites were not much better than blacks.

4. Free blacks in urban areas of the South undercut the wages paid to white laborers. Often lower wages for blacks meant lower wages for whites as well. White workers' desire to restrict blacks to occupations deemed unsuitable for whites conflicted with employers' incentives to hire as cheaply as possible.

5. Even though slavery helped to uplift the white race, because white

supremacy provided a floor to the status of whites above that of blacks, slavery also promoted internal differentiation within the southern white caste. The dividing line between slaveowners and non-slaveowners was a constant source of conflict in southern political life. Where apportionment of legislative seats was based on the entire population, areas with large numbers of slaves had more representatives than did those with few slaves, thereby increasing the value of the franchise in slave-rich areas and diminishing its value in slave-poor areas. Some southern states used the "federal ratio," counting each slave as three-fifths of a person; others used a combination of population and property values.[13] Southern states imposed meaningful property restrictions on the right to vote through most of the antebellum years. This was true, for example, of North Carolina until 1856 and Virginia until 1850. Slaveowning was also becoming more concentrated during the final antebellum years, elevating the status of the slaveowning stratum while establishing a more inegalitarian economy and society.

6. A staple of liberal democratic theory is that democracy depends upon an educated citizenry. However, the structure of the southern economy proved to be a formidable obstacle to the diffusion of mass education in the South. Perhaps most important, the attitudes of the dominant planter class were shaped by the belief that there was little return for investing in human capital. Consequently, planters vigorously opposed expenditures to educate white southerners.[14] But the South's education deficit reflected not only planters' resistance to higher taxes. The concentration in cotton production, the lack of urbanization, and the increasingly unequal income distribution contributed mightily to the retardation of southern educational opportunities. This trend continued during Reconstruction, when the effort to expand public education met formidable political and financial obstacles.[15]

Ultimately, the blight of slavery diminished the equality of the citizenry, in ways both overt and subtle. Because of slavery, a price of expanding liberties for whites was fewer rights for blacks. The modern variant of this paradox is often termed apartheid.

The Status of Popular Sovereignty in Democratic Theory

According to one interpretation, popular sovereignty is an ideal—the belief in collective control over one's destiny is essential to the legitimacy of the modern form of democracy.[16] Democratic societies rely on a belief that the people are able to collectively make causal choices about their destiny. The credibility of this belief, which at times becomes a necessary fiction, hinges on the ability of the people to collectively make meaningful choices. No polity can last very long that depends exclusively on force. Even so-called totalitarian regimes must be able to provide, at minimum, a rudimentary social contract. Tradition alone is insufficient to maintain legitimacy. For democracies, legitimacy is vital, an asset they must continually maintain—they must retain support by means other than purely distributive or coercive bases.

Popular participation is therefore an essential component of the democratic process. Without legitimacy, a variety of potential threats—for example, from the jeopardizing of procedural safeguards by governing elites seeking to perpetuate their power to the pressing of popular demands that exceed what the system can provide—may prove insurmountable.[17] The legitimacy of modern democratic institutions rests on the credibility of this ideal of popular sovereignty: the people acting are collectively sovereign constrained only by conditions independent of their (or anyone's) will.

> We show a government to be representative not by demonstrating its control over its subjects but just the reverse, by demonstrating that its subjects have control over what it does. Every government's actions are attributed to its subjects formally, legally. But in a representative government this attribution has substantive content: the people really do act through their government, and are not merely passive recipients of its actions. A representative government must not merely be in control, not merely promote the public interest, but must also be responsive to the people.[18]

Popular sovereignty rests upon what Joseph Schumpeter termed the "competitive struggle for people's votes."[19] Universal and equal suffrage is a necessary but not a sufficient requirement. True, it is a major step, one that mandates the dismantling of property and income restrictions on ballot access, for example through the elimination of privileged upper houses and plural voting and gerrymandering through disproportionate allocation of seats (as practiced in the United States until the Supreme Court's 1962 *Baker v. Carr* ruling). Popular sovereignty also presumes the existence of specific institutions of which freedom of speech, a free press, and a depoliticization of the military (civilian control) are perhaps the most prominent.

Yet, democratic procedures do not assure democratic results.[20] Popular sovereignty must allow its citizens to make meaningful choices that lead to meaningful results. People are sovereign when they can alter existing institutions and allocate available resources.[21]

Popular sovereignty thus presupposes that power rests in the citizenry.

But for all citizens to share in this power, each must have an opportunity to be heard and to have his or her views taken seriously. This means in essence that all citizens must be able to participate in a winning coalition at least some of the time. As Bruce Cain has argued, "democracy rests on two principal tenets: popular sovereignty and relative equality. . . . Relative equality requires that when preferences are aggregated into a collective choice, individual preferences are weighted as equally as possible."[22]

A republic may cater to the desires of its most privileged (at least a republic whose principles are shaped by an Edmund Burke or an Alexander Hamilton), it may even systematically exclude some of its residents from influence, but a democracy that does so is imperiled. All men may be created equal, yet ultimately equality before the law means little if their capacity to make or influence the making of laws is greatly restricted.[23] In today's United States it would be hard to argue that all voices are heard, that there are not substantial groups whose concerns are consigned to the margins. It would be even more difficult to argue that in America today, forty years after the end of the Second Reconstruction, black Americans do not remain among the marginalized political constituencies.

Popular sovereignty has long been seen as vulnerable to imperfections of the democratic process and limitations imposed by private property. Political scientists Adam Przeworski and Michael Wallerstein believe that perpetual controversy surrounds "whether people can be collectively sovereign in the presence of specialized institutions that comprise the state and of private property of productive resources."[24] The argument that popular sovereignty is infeasible because of the irredeemable weakness of the people or the inherent vulnerability of democratic institutions has been a staple of conservative criticisms of democracy. More recently, neoconservatives have argued that society suffers from an excess of democracy. Political competition has led to a disaggregation of interests, the decline and fragmentation of political parties, a breakdown of traditional means of social control, the delegitimation of authority, and an overload of demands as government exceeds its capacity. Samuel Huntington, perhaps the best-known theorist of democratic overload, has argued that such overloading of demands is a result of the democratic political process. However, arguments of this type are not limited to neoconservatives. Martin Wattenberg has argued in a similar vein. "One result of the decline of partisanship is that we now have a system that is capable of expressing a wide diversity of viewpoints but is rather poor at aggregating them. With parties increasingly less able to resolve these conflicts, the tone of American politics is becoming more negative and bitter, and policy compromises are much harder to come by."[25] Accordingly, elections often serve as negative referendums, ruling out options to be pursued, rather than choosing courses to be followed.

By contrast, much of the criticism from the left of the political spectrum focuses on the distance separating the formal equality of voting from the cramped reality of the participation available to many.[26] Perhaps the most obvious target here is the impact on political equality of substantial and increasing levels of economic inequality. To political scientists Josh Cohen and Joel Rogers, "material inequalities can subvert a structure of free and equal public deliberation by translating into sharply unequal capacities for political action."[27]

The Economic Theory of Democracy

I argued in Chapter 2 that the convergence of economic inequality and racial segmentation have substantially narrowed the scope of popular sovereignty—by freezing outside the domain of political discourse views not shared by the majority. The result has left the United States treading dangerously close to a line marked by majoritarian tyranny. Here I wish to return to this issue, by reexamining the relevance of the majoritarian tyranny thesis theoretically. I will do this in terms of a prominent perspective in democratic theory, known as the economic theory of democracy.[28] According to the principles of this well-known theory, an outcome of majoritarian tyranny is extremely unlikely and may not even be possible. Thus if the case for majoritarian tyranny can be established within this framework, its plausibility will be enhanced.

Consider the following analogy. The behavior of taxi drivers in New York City and elsewhere has drawn public attention in recent years. Many taxicab drivers refuse to pick up blacks, because of their fear that they will be robbed, beaten, or killed. Even blacks outside the target group (middle-aged men, black women) are refused taxi service out of the fear of taxi drivers that they will have to travel to dangerous neighborhoods where they may be harmed. The discrimination is not personal, nor does the solution lie in greater diversity of the workforce. Black cabdrivers pass by potential black customers, as do the many foreign immigrants who work as taxi drivers. In 1999 this issue received a great deal of publicity because the well-known actor Danny Glover complained, leading to a temporary crackdown, in part due to the senatorial ambitions of Mayor Rudolph Giuliani. Nor is this merely a New York City problem. Similar complaints have surfaced in Washington, D.C.[29] The problem is that given a surfeit of potential riders, it makes little sense for cabdrivers in many urban areas to cater to blacks, who are statistically more likely to take cab rides into less affluent, and perhaps more dangerous neighborhoods. Nor is this behavior likely to be revised by occasional retesting to see if the probability of being assaulted has dropped, even though some believe that such retesting is the antidote to inaccurate stereotypes and prejudices. Although it is conceivable that a serious commitment by the city to stop such behavior could force cabdrivers to change, the city is unlikely to be persistently determined enough to permanently modify the behavior of its cabdrivers.

This example offers a rough illustration of the workings of the economic theory of democracy if we view cabdrivers as voters who are choosing customers representing candidates seeking office from a pool in which their preferred customers/(office seekers) cater to the preconceived notions of cabdrivers/(voters) as to which customers/(office seekers) best serve their interests. The selection criteria for preferred customers/(office seekers) effectively freeze out a minority of customers/(office seekers) who are unable to persuade cabdrivers/(voters) to select them. Nor will cabdrivers/(voters) routinely sample a wider range of customers/(office seekers), preferring to choose customers/(office seekers) who fit their already established viewpoints. At times a few customers/(office seekers) may present an appearance compatible with the preferences of cabdrivers/(voters). However, this is an unsatisfactory solution, because not everyone can readily change their appearance to suit cabdriver/(voters), and there is a constituency out there that needs to be served but cannot get taxi service. Moreover, appearance does not exclude young whites from getting cabs. Of course this analogy, like any other, has its limits, and one limitation here is that there are other forms of transportation available to those denied taxis. A second problem is while office seekers may adapt to the preferences of voters, like customers who upgrade their appearance, the interests of some voters will be continually ignored because they do not fit into the appearance preferences of cabdrivers. For example, some customers work in occupations in which they cannot easily dress as do those in white-collar occupations, meaning their chances of successfully hailing cabs are reduced. Also some cabdrivers will refuse to pick up some blacks, male and female, no matter how well dressed they are because they may end up in an undesirable neighborhood. I believe this scenario expresses the basic premises of the economic theory of democracy reasonably well, a theory that postulates that democracy is a choice exercised periodically by the populace among alternative ruling elites, who are pressured via competition from rival elites to offer policies that will attract electoral support.[30] The political process consequently simulates economic markets.[31]

However, in terms of this model, voters quite often desire echoes not choices. According to political scientist Benjamin Page, "the economic theory of democracy calls for a candidate's policy stands to echo the policy preferences of the public."[32] Based on the logic of the theory, the echoes provided by politicians invariably restrict the range of credible policy alternatives. This may serve the interest of median voters, whose perceived interests lie within the range of policies considered feasible. But for those whose preferences are further from the midpoint of the spectrum, democracy does not as effectively respond to their interests. If differences in policy preferences are strong and stable, those on the margins will lose initially because their opinions are in the minority. Over time information costs (in a stable environment) will dictate a reduction in the effort made to sample marginal opinions, leading to such opinions being ignored. Ultimately, voters whose interests lie beyond the range of mainstream discourse may find responsiveness to their preferences jeopardized because their views no longer matter.

The rational course of action for those individuals is to move toward the middle. But structural factors (much like the need to dress for work may make it unrealistic to dress as if you work in a white-collar office) may impede such movement. For democracy to be viable in this model, preferences must be volitional and highly fungible, much like the assumption made by pluralist theory. But when differences in interests are produced, augmented, and stabilized by persistent cleavages—such as those arising from racial or class barriers—movement toward the center may not be possible. Voters can only move toward the center if the policies of the center respond to their perceptions of self-interest.

The Dilemma of Exit and Voice

Albert O. Hirschman's classic thesis on "exit and voice" might at first seem to provide a way around this problem, as those deficient in resources based upon their exit capabilities (in other words, the capacity to disrupt the system by withdrawal of their resources, for instance, as in a strike by indispensable workers or disinvestment by capitalists), can compensate by using resources based upon their collective voice, that is their capacity to influence events by means of collective pressure.[33] However, when racial and class barriers begin to approach consolidated segments, this option diminishes as well. The reason is that exit and voice are not inverse but conjoined options. In other words, the effectiveness of the voice of citizens depends on their prospects for inclusion within a potential winning coalition. Second, the voice of those deemed respectable counts for considerably more than that of those deemed less so. For example, more attention is paid to tax protesters than to protests by the urban poor (even when their actions are the same). Compare for example the delicate treatment of the Montana Freedmen to that meted out to MOVE (the black activists whose homes were destroyed by the Philadelphia city government in the mid-1980s). The effectiveness of voice is determined partly by whose voice it is.

Exit resources all too often augment voice resources. In democratic polities characterized by considerable disparities in economic resources, some voices are diminished while others are magnified. The contemporary United States has no shortage of plutocratic tendencies. Such forces effectively enhance the voice of those already privileged rather than diminishing it. For example, the U.S. Senate's status as a club of millionaires may not mean the wealthy will invariably be favored, but it certainly suggests that wealthy senators will be less able to imagine what it is like to be poor.

During the 2000 presidential campaign, the major contenders for the Democratic nomination were Bill Bradley and Al Gore and for the Republican nomination, George W. Bush and John McCain. Each was a child of considerably greater privilege than the average American. Each fits former Texas governor Ann Richards's stunningly perceptive description of former president George H.W. Bush as someone who was "born on third base," even if these candidates know better than to appear to believe "they hit a triple" to get there.

Hirschman certainly recognized that affluent Americans could use their enhanced capacity to exit more and more as a means to avoid contact with major social ills, but the tendency has grown into a stampede. Because the nonaffluent are locked into public social services, it is more likely that those services will be inferior. They do not have the option to exit and construct comparable or superior private ones. If mobile consumers of public goods and services, for example, are those most sensitive to differences in quality, their flight to private goods preserves mediocre public goods for the less mobile.

The polarization of income has increased the share of income going to the top 1 percent in the United States, severely straining the bonds of community.[34] In many communities around the nation the wealthy have redirected their money from the support of public spaces and institutions to private services, essentially contributing less to the commonweal. Americans earning $100,000 or more contribute less than 3 percent of their income to charity; by comparison, those making less than $10,000 gave more than 5 percent on average. In aggregate, the American inclination to make charitable contributions has fallen sharply in recent decades. "Americans' sense that they are obliged, as individuals, to care for the community is slipping."[35]

Finally, if the stable majority hypothesis put forward in Chapter 2 is credible, voice cannot supplant exit because the political process will have already registered, weighed, and discounted the interests of its less affluent citizens. In effect, the electoral costs of responding to their views outweigh the benefits. Albert Hirschman has argued that "the role of voice in fending off deterioration is particularly important for a number of essential services largely defining what has come to be called the 'quality of life.' . . . Resistance to deterioration requires voice and since voice will be forthcoming more readily at the upper than at the lower quality ranges, the cleavage between the quality of life at the top and at the middle or lower levels will tend to become more marked."[36]

Economic Inequality and Popular Sovereignty

The belief that popular sovereignty is if not impossible then gravely limited in any society in which productive resources are privately owned is a core proposition of classical socialist ideology. According to E.F. Carritt, "great economic inequality gives influence and power of propaganda which are as destructive of any real equality of political power as censorship itself. . . . Even equality before the law, that is legal justice, is endangered by economic inequality."[37]

Whether politics can ameliorate the undemocratic effects of market power is a central determinant of the threat to popular sovereignty stemming from economic inequality. At the extreme of plutocracy—where the outcome of political contests depends almost entirely upon ownership and control of economic assets—the ideal of popular sovereignty has been extinguished. The United States may not fit this extreme case, yet how much does it veer from a somewhat more modest version, having a political system in which the available options are severely circumscribed to prevent politics from significantly affecting the distribution of wealth? In this case, the influence of the wealthy upon politics may not be definitive, but the influence of politics upon the wealthy is weak indeed.

Representation is undermined by economic inequality—the chain of representative democracy is only as strong as its weakest link. Clear differences in the way information is made accessible to different strata of the electorate often compound economic inequality, thereby systematically biasing the information used to make public decisions. More abstract issue-oriented forms of political communication are paid attention to primarily by elite audiences.[38]

Additionally, the strong relationship between social class, political sophistication, and political participation means that those with the greatest material resources are also the most politically active. Such differences pose a threat to ideologies that favor less affluent citizens. According to political scientist W. Russell Neuman:

> The process of learning from the mass media is best described as the gradual accumulation of information that is repeated frequently and consistently in the different media. There is a pattern of stratification by which the more sophisticated citizens attend to the more political media and are better able to recall and interpret abstract political communication. The process in-

volves a spiraling between increasing levels of interest and increasing knowledge and understanding. But the spiral works in the other direction as well. The bottom know-nothing continues to ignore and perhaps actively fend off the flow of political communications in their environment, judging it to be both uninteresting and irrelevant.[39]

A close analogue to the inequitable provision of information based upon economic inequality is found in the strong relationship between education and political participation. In the United States, education is strongly related to turnout, in fact it may be the most important of major socioeconomic indicators. Educational attainment increases cognitive skills governing (1) the ease with which one can acquire information about politics, thereby reducing the cost of acquiring political information; (2) the gratification of political information; and (3) the frustration of bureaucratic hurdles to political participation, such as filling out forms, waiting in line, and meeting deadlines. Restrictive registration laws and procedures are a prime example. Restrictive laws deter the less educated from voting in ways that do not impede the more educated. Even if the import of registration laws has lessened in recent years, the role of education in political participation may well have increased.[40]

Once upon a time, high rates of political participation were a consequence of the active collaboration of individuals and institutions that sought to gain partisan advantage. Nowadays lower turnout serves the interests of political insiders. But outsiders need more than easier registration laws—they need better reasons to vote (and perhaps even some compulsion to motivate their voting, as is used by Australia).

Hence, economic inequality does not simply have first order or direct effects on popular sovereignty, it generates second order or indirect effects as well. Yet, if the affluent are less affected by inferior public provisions than are those whose limited resources mean they cannot substitute private goods for public ones, their insulation does not protect them from other consequences of inferior and inadequate public service provision. The costs of the production and consumption of inferior education, health services, physical infrastructure, and so on exact a toll on the well-being of affluent and nonaffluent alike: for example, a less productive workforce, higher crime rates, the dramatic growth of an underclass, and the growth of an underground economy that includes activities that offer "public bads" or negative public goods.

Each of these phenomena reflects forces of societal disorder and of an inability to provide meaningful life chances for many citizens. The drug problem and the growth of an autonomous drug culture are indicative of the isolation of many who are often considered to be in the underclass (or at least a part of it) and the larger majority. The paucity of their prospective life chances in the legitimate mainstream economy is an incentive to engage in drug trafficking, reflecting the inability of society to integrate its least well-off citizens. As concern about drugs and crime undermines basic civil rights and liberties, popular sovereignty is diminished. Furthermore, taxes must increase to pay for the increased use of penal and judicial resources. Thus the quality of life that is shared by the great majority deteriorates. Hence, the weaker links of the chain of popular sovereignty undermine the stronger ones.

Although black Americans are no longer subject to direct legal restrictions on their political participation (although one might argue that racial disparities in criminal justice and the disqualification of felons from voting are forms of strong indirect restriction), the political system still diminishes and discounts their preferences. Their political concerns are often neglected due to the distance between their interests and those of the majority. Certainly, black Americans made unquestionable breakthroughs in numerous occupations and many attained middle-class status. However, the socioeconomic status of black Americans overall has not reached a level equivalent to that of white Americans, nor do the trends favor such equalization in the foreseeable future. Rather the prospects are that economic inequality will continue over the very long term and that political inequality will endure also because political participation is strongly related to economic status and the political system is more responsive the higher one's economic status. Perhaps the strongest element in the economic and political inequality of black Americans lies in the existence of a sizable black underclass. That a sizable minority of black Americans is in situations of long-term poverty will only impede black Americans from exercising political power commensurate with their numbers.

According to economist Douglass North, "The incentives that are built into the institutional framework play the decisive role in shaping the kinds of skills and knowledge that pay off."[41] Currently, the incentives being built into the framework of institutions encountered by Americans in blighted urban areas encourage knowledge and facility in illegal activities. The urban poor live in an environment that encourages a very low discount rate in terms of the valuation of present consumption relative to future consumption. Many of the children of urban America are receiving an education that ill prepares them for working in the environment they are likely to encounter. Moreover, according to a recent study by Harvard University's Civil Rights Project, "American public schools are twelve years into a process of continuous resegregation."[42] An increasing proportion of the labor supply may be unable to work effectively at a time when projected demographic ratios suggest that new labor force entrants will need to be more productive than ever before, given falling dependency ratios (the proportion of those working for each nonworker).

Thus, the opportunity structure faced by a considerable segment of non-white Americans directs them toward activities on the margins of the "legitimate economy." To paraphrase North, the institutional framework of the American economy has made contemporary versions of piracy the most profitable economic path for many.

Second, as a disproportionate number of black Americans fall within this underclass, the shifts in social policy in a conservative direction have harmed them more severely. Current trends in social policy favor the incarceration of a sizable minority of black Americans, undermining the living standards of those dependent upon direct government aid (also disproportionately black), and reducing the ability of those privately employed to use the resources of the federal government to assure fairness in hiring and employment. Of special note is the declining support for what are often considered the most effective antipoverty programs—means-tested transfer programs, whose real value has stagnated since the 1970s.

Infant mortality in the United States is higher than that of much of the industrialized world and the gap in life expectancies between black and white Americans is rising. Americans who are both poor and members of a minority have in many respects become inhabitants of another country. In their treatment by the criminal justice system, they have become denizens of what Graham Greene so aptly called the "torturable classes," much like the poor in many underdeveloped countries. No one cares what goes on in the prisons they inhabit.[43] The afflictions of their existence falls under the heading of bothersome inconveniences, rather than scandalously intolerable living conditions. If this characterization seems excessive, remember that the use of governmental repression against blacks was a regularity well into the 1960s and not just in the South. Even today the police cross the line against minorities, especially in the environments of the urban poor, sufficiently often to suggest that the freedom of association of residents of poor communities is immeasurably restricted. Amadou Diallo and Abner Louima are only the most sensational of recent cases involving mistreatment of blacks in urban America.

Third, the middle-class black population is more precariously placed than its white counterpart: blacks (1) are more dependent upon two incomes in the family; (2) are more dependent upon government employment; (3) are more dependent upon utilization of government resources to insure fair treatment; (4) own considerably less wealth than their white counterparts; for example, the median wealth of black households is only 9 percent of the median wealth of white households; (5) work more hours to attain middle-class incomes than their white counterparts; and (6) have more poor relatives than middle-class whites, and thus face greater demands on their incomes from lower-income relatives. This burden was accentuated by the sharply rising black poverty rate in the early 1980s.[44] Moreover, even relatively affluent black families are stretched to meet the income needed for a middle-class lifestyle for a typical family of four, according to calculations of the Bureau of Labor Statistics.[45] The net result is that it is unlikely that the economic disparity between the races will narrow substantially in the near future.

Finally, given the comparatively greater segregation of the black population than that of any other racial group in the United States, accession to middle-class living standards is insufficient for access to opportunities comparable to those available for other Americans. Hence, growing economic and political inequality appears likely to continue.

Gilded Age Redux?

The 1980s and early 1990s have been perceived as in some respects a second Gilded Age, based on the recurrence of a number of parallels to the first Gilded Age, which lasted from the 1870s to the end of the nineteenth century. Perhaps the central similarity is the resurgent Social Darwinism and the emphasis on unfettering the market as the antidote for social ills. The deficiencies of this view are in many ways more obvious, but as a political elixir it has been quite potent. In many respects the ideology is frozen in time, grossly insensitive to current conditions, built on the assumption that what is good for big business is good for America. Social Darwinism is antiquated by not recognizing the structural transformations that have made such notions obsolete for a very long time, not that they were terribly realistic even in their heyday.

Among the notable parallels between the two Gilded Ages of 1870–1900 and 1980–92 are: the dominance of Republican presidents espousing conservative politics; a strong belief in the public and elite circles that government needs to be reduced in size; an exalted view of business and a low regard for organized labor; restructuring of the American economy; reduction in taxes for higher incomes; preference for disinflationary monetary policies; and increasing wealth concentration and income inequality.[46] In the earlier era, franchise restrictions in the South and purportedly good government policies in the North effectively cemented a political regime unresponsive to losing constituencies (and strongly exploitative of those with little or no political influence). In each era the lower-income members of the electorate were marginalized. Political scientist Walter Dean Burnham described the creation in the late nineteenth and early twentieth centuries of a hole in the electoral universe. Suffrage restriction transformed the calculus of political parties.[47] The loss of political influence of the have-nots fostered increasing inequality of wealth and income. Perhaps the greatest common feature of America's nineteenth- and twentieth-century Gilded Ages has been in the insulation of wealth from the influence of politics.

For democracy, regular elections are a necessary, but not a sufficient requirement. Some alternation of parties in power and interests in ruling coalitions is necessary as well. If parties compete for the median voter, but some voters are structurally impeded from assuming median positions, alternation of parties will not provide redress (in the absence of some other means to integrate outsiders' interests within governing coalitions). In some cases stable one-party regimes can lead to grand coalitions (whether explicitly or implicitly) in which all major interests are represented and share, albeit perhaps inefficiently, in the distribution of rewards. In other cases, and especially given the "first past the post" electoral system used in the United States, majoritarian tyranny points toward political segmentation. In the United States, economic, political, and social cleavages are not crosscutting, in the fashion of pluralist theory—they are converging, thereby reinforcing already established fault lines. Thus political and economic haves are ever more firmly divided from political and economic have-nots.

One example of such cleavage formation is the reemergence of racial and ethnic queues in employment. In the first Gilded Age, new immigrants arrived from Southern and Central Europe. Now the bulk of the new arrivals are from the Caribbean, Latin America, Asia, and Africa. Much like a century ago, job searchers rely on networks to find jobs and tend to concentrate in distinct occupational niches—concentrations of workers of common ethnic and racial backgrounds. What is different today is the improbability that a twenty-first-century economic boom will allow many of these new immigrants (especially the poorer ones) to replicate the success of their predecessors, establishing a foothold in the middle class.

Political struggles during the first Gilded Age set limits on American democracy by establishing the terms of the struggle between haves and have-nots. The aftermath of Gilded Age politics—sometimes referred to as the system of 1896—an era of long Republican dominance, profoundly reshaped the American political universe through the political marginalization of wage earners.

In the second Gilded Age, the issues involve both the further narrowing of limits on democracy, as well as the decay and perhaps even the demise of its ultimate promise—popular sovereignty. Perhaps the one saving grace of the immense material inequality of the first Gilded Age was that those who amassed great fortunes invested substantial portions of their earnings in companies whose growth would lead to improved standards of living for the next generation of Americans. There is reason to suspect that this may not be as true this time. It is unlikely that multinational corporations today identify with the majority of the citizens of the nations in which they have their headquarters. Or to paraphrase Lester Thurow, we must ask if the behavior of current elites more closely resembles an establishment or an oligarchy.[48]

Many in the elite nowadays find it difficult to take seriously the notion that they have any obligation of noblesse oblige to concern themselves with the nation's long-term interests. Clearly short-term perspectives dominate American public policy. Viable winning electoral strategies incorporate this shortsightedness. According to Bennett Harrison and Barry Bluestone:

> Instead of exchanging short-term sacrifice for long-term prosperity and more equality, America has been doing just the opposite: buying short-term economic recovery at the exorbitant price of forfeiting long-term social and economic security. . . . [They further point out] building a recovery almost purely on borrowed funds, as the United States has been doing since at least 1983, is equivalent to a publicly sanctioned multibillion dollar Ponzi scheme. Without the gains in productivity required to increase the size of the economic pie, the only way to keep the recovery going is to build the pyramid of debt ever higher.[49]

Such shortsightedness is most clearly shown in the treatment of that most valuable of capital resources—human capital. We currently treat a large portion of our collective human and social capital as if it were entirely disposable. The insistence that markets can produce and reproduce desirable social relations by themselves, one of the benchmarks of Social Darwinism, is an underlying motif in a body politic unable to formulate and carry out more farsighted policies. Perhaps the best illustration that current policies are myopic is demonstrated by the startling fact that a number of states, notably California, are spending more on prisons than on higher education.

The Future of Popular Sovereignty

Race has invariably defined the boundaries of American democracy. The distribution of opportunities or life chances of lower-class American (who are disproportionately black) has deteriorated to the point that their capacity to participate in American society as meaningful citizens is impaired. Contemplating the extinction of popular sovereignty may appear hyperbolic, but it is clearly worthwhile to ask whether we have moved so far from the goal that it is no longer visible. Although contemporary limits on popular sovereignty may seem tame individually, in sum they are ominous. Perhaps inevitably, the quality of democratic life suffers whenever a substantial class of citizens is able to exercise fewer rights than other classes. Arguably, popular sovereignty cannot survive circumstances in which some citizens' political rights are indefinitely abridged. Perhaps this is because undemocratic steps affecting substantial numbers require alterations in basic institutions, for example, the codification of differences through restrictions on the rights of the excluded. The denial of the exercise of rights for some tends to contract the rights of the many. If not arrested, this leads to a quasi-apartheid condition that undermines the quality of life of everyone, not simply those excluded and discriminated against.

If majority rule democracy undermines the life chances of many of its most disadvantaged citizens, representative democracy becomes a shell game, at least for the disadvantaged. The failure to incorporate its most disadvantaged citizens precludes them from sharing "the American dream" of upward mobility and material comfort. The infrastructure of democracy is weakening in ways that undermine its meaningfulness to the lives of have-nots and ultimately for the polity as a whole. However, equality of participation cannot survive in a vacuum. Those forces that have effectively reduced the participation of marginal groups have arguably narrowed the terms of citizenship. Hence, regular elections do not ameliorate the contemporary crisis of American democracy because political equality is necessarily linked to economic equality.

In the United States the domain of social citizenship, perhaps even of the social contract itself, has been jeopardized: private earnings, pensions, health provision, housing, and education, have all been put at risk. Citizens at the bottom of the economic ladder are perhaps as badly off as at any time in the last half century. According to Rolf Dahrendorf, "Citizenship is a set of equal rights, and rights are in one respect chances, opportunities to make choices within given linkages. It is commonplace today that such rights cannot be given by writing them into constitutions and laws."[50] Creating the conditions that enable individuals to exercise their citizenship rights necessitates raising the floor sufficiently to enable those on the floor to take advantage of available opportunities. The resulting limitations in social and economic rights have exacerbated the divisions among the population in ways consistent with the theoretical discussion: (1) in the short run, damaging the life chances of have-nots; but ultimately (2) undermining the life chances of everyone else because of the interdependency inherent in social life.

Most important, the denial of the exercise of rights for some has meant a diminution in the rights of all. Democracy and popular sovereignty are inevitably intertwined. If popular sovereignty atrophies, then democracy will also. If majority rule democracy undermines the life chances of its disadvantaged citizens, the democratic character of American life is jeopardized.

7

Rising Economic Inequality, Racial Polarization, and the Prospects for the Future

I have argued throughout this book that progress in race relations has been strongly determined by the ebb and flow of interdependent political and economic forces. Eras of growing economic inequality stimulate political inequality, impeding progress in race relations. Alternatively, eras of growing economic equality stimulate political equality, promoting rapid advances in race relations. This final chapter will summarize the analysis, look forward to the future, and offer a few speculative predictions. The preceding chapters have examined both the historical development of racial democratization and its contemporary status.

Chapters 1 and 2 examined the chillier climate of race relations in recent years, which is largely the result of less favorable trends in political and economic equality of the last generation. Accordingly, progress in race relations slowed as political polarization rose in the midst of growing economic inequality since the early 1970s. According to William Darity and Samuel Myers, "the widening of the racial earning gap is inextricably linked to the widening of overall inequality and the loss of white middle-class employment opportunities. White males were squeezed out of the vanishing middle-class jobs, which had been their purview, especially well-paid blue-collar jobs. They were then crowded into a lower tier of occupations that they would not otherwise have held. They squeezed black males out of those jobs."[1]

It was not unreasonable to expect the extension of formal political equality to black Americans in the 1960s and 1970s would cause the significance of race in political and economic competition to decline. However, the 1980s saw a reversal of favorable trends in political and economic equality. Growing economic inequality fostered a rightward turn in American politics, which halted the march of racial progress. According to Tom and Mary Edsall, the explosive potency of race as an issue was fueled by the expansion of group rights and the increase in taxes necessary to pay for it.[2] Yet the prime beneficiaries of economic liberalism remained the same as before the expansion of civil rights: the broad (predominantly white) middle and upper-middle classes. I believe a previous work of Tom Edsall's, *The New Politics of Inequality*, more accurately highlighted the core issue: slow growth and a chronic shortage of employment generated a zero sum logic in the process of building a majoritarian coalition.[3] In fact, according to James Galbraith, "transfers to the truly poor are minor and declining" in comparison to transfers to the well-to-do through interest payments and transfers to the elderly via government programs.[4]

Yet, this notion that liberalism abandoned issues near and dear to the white majority is taken as a virtually sacrosanct article of faith. But during Democratic political dominance in the 1960s, per capita income of both whites and blacks increased.[5] Nonetheless, the Democrats were judged by many to have failed to reward their constituents. Frances Fox Piven and Richard Cloward believe "the widely heralded federal programs for the ghettoes in the 1960s were neither designed nor funded in a way that made it possible for them to have substantial impact on poverty or on the traumas of the ghetto life. But the publicity attached to the programs—the din and blare about a 'war on poverty' and the development of 'model cities'—did much to appease the liberal sympathizers with urban blacks."[6]

If, as the Edsalls argue, the burden of economic and political citizenship rights was falling disproportionately on the middle class, the fault lay elsewhere: (1) democratization made impossible continued overt discrimination by government, and (2) positional competition intensified during an era in which economic competition was on the rise. In essence, before the Second Reconstruction (1954–65), black Americans were anchored by law and custom to the bottom of the American economic, political, and social hierarchy. For those who benefited from the exclusion of black Americans, there was a loss in status defined by the decline of white privilege. This status readjustment has been magnified by wage stagnation and exploited by opportunistic politicians as reverse discrimination. Arguably, the incorporation of blacks into universal suffrage set off a different type of chain reaction from that analyzed by the Edsalls: a long-excluded group was allowed into the polity, but its interests were neutralized by their delegitimation.

The years since the early 1970s have been marked by major political changes: (1) the increasing importance of swing voters and the decline of party identification; (2) the growing power of lobbyists; (3) the exploding expenses of campaigning and the associated importance of campaign fundraising; and (4) the decline of the union movement. Such changes have reduced the influence of ordinary Americans—both black and white. Consequently, the ability of the less fortunate to organize effectively—their voice—has seriously diminished.

This recent experience concurs with broad economic and social trends that have prevailed over several historical epochs. During eras of increasing economic equality, those benefiting from equalization seek to promote greater equalization by expanding the arena of democracy, essentially using politics to redress the imbalance in the economic power of less-fortunate Americans. The eras of significant expansion in public services for less-affluent Americans were the New Deal and the Great Society. The establishment and expansion of unemployment compensation, Social Security, and Medicare were the signature achievements of those years. However, the end of these eras also brought an end to the unprecedented gains made by wage-earning Americans.

During periods of increasing economic and political inequality, beneficiaries of increasing inequality (typically in the name of freeing market forces) have sought to secure their gains by insulating markets from politics and altering the terms upon which wage earners offer their labor to the market, in part through undermining their living standards while out of the workforce, in the name of efficiency. The relationship of trends in economic inequality to the changing climate for race relations is nothing new.

In Chapter 3 I argued that the consolidation of economic and political inequality during the post-Reconstruction era was responsible for a worsening climate of race relations. This was shown in the emergence of Jim Crow segregation, which involved a surging tide of economic and political inequality. The growth of sharecropping and the ballot restriction movement facilitated the advance of white supremacy. Together these forces insured that black Americans would remain on the lowest rung of American society. But the effects of surging economic and political inequality were experienced by all Americans. During the long retreat of the post-Reconstruction era, American democracy regressed markedly. The political system of the American South became at best "a broadly based oligarchy," rather than a functioning democracy. This had profound implications for the vitality of democracy throughout the nation. The domination of Congress by conservative southern Democrats was essential in fostering an environment antagonistic to the interests of working- and lower-class citizens. Southern economic conservatives held a firm grip on the House and Senate until the 1960s.[7] Hence, the racial conservatism of southern Democrats helped sustain and anchor policies supporting both laissez faire economics and systematic labor repression until the coming of the New Deal. Between 1876 and 1940, the mainstream political spectrum was defined by competition between a political party that catered to southern conservatives committed to the maintenance of white supremacy while the other major party virtually ignored black Americans.

Chapter 4 examined the reversal of the deteriorating post-Reconstruction racial climate. From the 1930s through the late 1960s, concurrent advances in political and economic equality led to the decline of white supremacy, the collapse of its economic base in the plantation economy, the growing and pivotal importance of northern black voters, and a growing assertiveness of southern blacks. The emergence of this more favorable political climate was predicated on greater economic equality.

The Great Depression and the beginnings of the New Deal initiated an era that lasted through the 1960s. Initially Franklin D. Roosevelt paid little attention to black voters. By the 1940 election the continued black migration out of the South and into a few key northern states ratcheted upward the importance of black voters. Black voters were becoming more important, especially so in states that were at the core of presidential politics—87 percent of the total number of black migrants from the South in the 1910–60 period settled in seven key northern (and western) industrial states: New York, New Jersey, Pennsylvania, Ohio, California, Illinois, and Michigan. These seven states represented 80 percent of the electoral votes necessary to win the presidency in the 1950s and 1960s. Essential to winning the presidency was winning a majority of these states.[8] Even the number of registered southern blacks climbed dramatically in the 1950s, from 900,000 in 1950 to more than 2.2 million by 1965. Furthermore, black Americans were not only a political force to be reckoned with, but by exiting a low-income area—the Southeast—for much higher income areas in the Northeast and Great Lake regions, their economic advancement coincided with growing political power.

In the 1930s and 1940s black Americans benefited from an alliance between the federal courts and liberal political forces. This alliance, which began shortly after the New Deal, was fairly unusual in American history. For most of the nation's history, the judiciary has been far more solicitous of the interests of the privileged against "excessive majoritarianism," rather than of the interests of underprivileged racial minorities.[9] "By 1964, when the Civil Rights Act was passed, the Supreme Court had heard 106 discrimination cases since 1936, and had ruled ninety times in favor of those allegedly suffering from discrimination."[10] In the 1950s and 1960s, the court abolished de jure segregation, expanded the rights of the accused, and strengthened First Amendment protections. Congressional conservatism was eroding as well.

The Supreme Court's 1962 ruling in *Baker v. Carr* weakened conservative rural districts while a growing bloc of liberal northern Democratic senators gained influence.

As the influence of white supremacists lessened, the climate for racial progress began to improve, buoyed not just by improving economic circumstances manifest in declining economic inequality but also in renewed political competition for the black vote. The growing political power of northern blacks in the 1940s and 1950s ignited an era of party competition for the black vote. The key political victories of the civil rights era—the Civil Rights Act of 1964, the Voting Rights Act, and the Equal Employment Opportunity Act—were at least partly a product of the growing political power of northern blacks.

The major civil rights legislation of the late 1950s and 1960s would be a product of this long era of (initially gradual) change. Finally, an increasing majority of the public began to perceive civil rights issues in a more favorable light. As the climate improved for major civil rights legislation, support for equal employment opportunity grew as well, reaching 95 percent by 1972. This probably represented the maximum window of opportunity for civil rights legislation. By the early 1970s, the backlash against civil rights was becoming an important base of support for Republicans. Southern white dissatisfaction with the national Democratic Party accelerated, from Thurmond to Goldwater to Wallace and Nixon and finally to Reagan. Clearly, the election of Ronald Reagan was both a cause and a consequence of the resurgent racial polarization of the American electorate. In particular, with Reagan's appointment of three conservative justices to the Supreme Court, the era of bold judicial protection for minority rights ceased. The Supreme Court has led the federal judiciary back toward their pre-1937 role as guardians of the status quo, a role that augurs poorly for those needing extensive judicial protection.

Chapters 1 through 4 are generally consistent with the work of those who perceive American history as essentially cyclical, that eras of growing economic and political inequality inevitably give way to eras of growing economic and political equality. Such cyclical interpretations have been most prominently advanced by Arthur Schlesinger, and more recently by Kevin Phillips.[11]

However, Chapter 5 argued that even though such cycles have occurred in the past, they are less likely in the future, or at the very least the near future. This pessimistic evaluation is based on the premise that key transformations have occurred in the environment faced by wage-earning Americans, and in particular in the institutions that have allowed working people to protect their collective interests. The decline of unions has made it difficult to perceive the current status of those on the lower rungs of American society as the continuation of a cycle by which a self-adjusting mechanism will eventually turn around. Such cycles depend immeasurably upon collective action—oppositions must be able to coalesce, to organize, and to confront. However, the concurrence of racial polarization, class fragmentation, and surging inequality means that the potential for collective action has diminished greatly. Yet hope springs eternal and in the remainder of this chapter I will sketch out what I believe are the more optimistic portents of the near term.

A New Era of Racial Progress?

If there has been a golden era for racial progress it was in the two decades between 1954 and 1973. During these years black Americans won the right to be citizens. However, citizenship did not mean the material aspirations of black Americans were fully realized. Instead, the civil rights movement fragmented and collapsed. Arguably, the splintering was the inevitable by-product of democratization. One price of the greater integration of blacks into the dominant majority society and culture has been greater differentiation among blacks, in other words the significance of race is no longer what it once was. In spite of the controversy this notion has attracted, I do not believe anyone with even a nodding acquaintance with American history can take seriously the belief that racial identity at the beginning of the twenty-first century is as significant to the life chances and material aspirations of black Americans as it was at the beginning of the twentieth century. Black Americans have made considerable progress over the course of the twentieth century.

Inevitably the political agenda of black Americans has transcended issues of formal citizenship. The issue today is one of how formal rights can be translated into an improved quality of life for ordinary people, an issue that is not solely about race. Yet, race still matters, and in my view the near-term future of racial progress will be determined by the forces that have occupied this analysis.

A central question at the beginning of the twenty-first century is what kind of era are we in today. Do we remain in an era in which economic inequality will continue to surge? If so, then race relations should not be expected to improve, or at the very least improvement may be modest. On the other hand, there is some reason to believe that the long economic boom of the 1990s has finally begun to improve the circumstances of some of the least well-off segments of the American population.

Lower unemployment in the late 1990's—the lowest of the last generation—has finally begun to improve the conditions of life of young black men with limited education and skills.[12] And low unemployment has also begun

185

to dampen crime rates, consistent with the well-established relationship between unemployment and crime. Crime rates have dropped markedly in areas where unemployment has fallen substantially. Labor scarcity has also meant greater work opportunities for those Americans who are usually bypassed during periods when labor markets are slack. This has worked to the advantage of many young black males with criminal records and/or less than stellar work histories. An improving economy has lifted the economic conditions of black single mothers. The median income for black female household heads rose from $13,489 in 1993 to $16,256 by 1996. Although such increases leave them below the poverty line, they offer a strong contrast to the previous twenty years of stagnation and decline. According to James Galbraith, when unemployment is below 5.5 percent, inequality begins to decline.[13] Given the current (March 2005) rate of 5.4 percent, however, the inequality reducing impact of low unemployment may no longer exist.

The tentative effects of the long boom on national politics are not to be ignored. Improved economic conditions quell the economic insecurity that fueled racially charged political flashpoints. Good economic times have dampened racial demagoguery, depriving conservatives of some of their most effective bogeymen, such as Willie Horton and welfare queens. Good times have, at least temporarily, made moot the debate over the impact of the recent changes in welfare law. Although the issue remains of interest to policy analysts, its political resonance has declined. Better economic times have also made it difficult for politicians to get as much traction out of issues such as affirmative action. According to William Julius Wilson, continued economic improvement since 1996 has decreased the intensity and frequency of mean-spirited messages attacking minorities, affirmative action, immigrants, and welfare recipients.[14]

Good times and abating racial tension have caused some reappraisal of the racial disparities of the death penalty. Former Illinois governor George Ryan courageously imposed a moratorium on the death penalty and then commuted the sentences of inmates on death row. Currently Pennsylvania is contemplating a suspension of executions due to questions of racial bias. Moreover, two recent Supreme Court decisions: (1) *Roper v. Simmons* forbidding the execution of defendants for crimes committed when they were under eighteen, and (2) *Atkins v. Virginia* forbidding the execution of the mentally retarded suggest the judicial tide may be turning against the grotesque version of American exceptionalism represented by the death penalty.[15]

In addition, the 2001–2 economic recession severely damaged the fiscal health of many states. Straitened finances have prompted a reassessment of the long jail sentences that have become a cornerstone of criminal justice policy. "After two decades of passing ever tougher sentencing laws and prompting a prison building boom, state legislatures facing budget crises are beginning to rethink their costly approaches to crime. In the past year, about 25 states have passed laws eliminating some of the lengthy mandatory minimum sentences so popular in the 1980s and 1990s, restoring early release for parole and offering treatment instead of incarceration for some drug offenders."[16] Politicians are discovering that it can be more important to be smart on crime than to be tough on crime. Such logic has yet to make any headway with the Bush administration, however, which continues to insist on the irrational and racially discriminatory disparities between sentencing for cocaine and crack.[17]

It is too soon to tell whether the dominant political trends of the last generation are beginning to shift. Only the passage of time will tell if the Democratic presidential victories in 1992 and 1996 mark an end to Republican presidential dominance. It may turn out that the Clinton presidency is analogous to the Woodrow Wilson presidency—an era in which a Democratic president is elected due to a split in Republican ranks, and then is able to use the advantages of incumbency to win reelection. Regardless, the second necessary condition for racial progress is greater political equality. The historical record shows unambiguously that the emergence of a more favorable political environment will promote racial progress. For this to happen, there needs to be greater competition for the black vote. Somehow, enough blacks need to vote Republican to create a constituency that will influence the Republican Party. If we review the last half century, the 1950–70s era of progress appears to have prematurely stalled. Certainly, the Second Reconstruction era (1954–65) was successful in removing explicit racial barriers that prevented blacks from fully participating in the American dream. Yet its promise remains unfulfilled in numerous respects. I believe one very important factor in the stalling of racial progress during this era was the demise of the liberal wing of the Republican Party.

There are some signs of a revival of moderate Republicanism in northeastern states. The defeat of liberal Republicans in the late 1950s and early 1960s was a warning of the impending demise of the Rockefeller/Javits/Lindsay Republicans. This brought to an end the era of competition for the black vote. But if moderate Republicans are beginning to reemerge as they must for Republicans to be competitive in northeastern states, where religious fundamentalism does not provide a cohesive force for conservative political beliefs, it may be possible once again for blacks to consider voting Republican. A mitigating factor in the trend toward liberalism is the evidence that the favorable electoral climate for northeastern Republicans reflects the liberalism of the northeast, a region that Clinton swept in 1996, as did Kerry in 2004. It may be that the northeast is becoming ideologically distinctive and perhaps even isolated from other regions of the country.[18]

Perhaps another historical analogy might be useful here as well. The emergence of two-party competition for black votes began in the New Deal era, not by appealing to blacks on the basis of their particular interests, but through policies attractive to lower-income Americans in general. This was the heart of the broad class-based coalition that many progressives believe is the best hope for black America. The belief of many progressives is that such a broad class-oriented coalition would attract blacks without being stigmatized by doing so.[19]

Moreover, the improved economy that robs racially based politics of much of its saliency also refocuses attention on the volatile culture wars that divide key Republicans constituencies. The image of a Republican Party held hostage to its right wing, consisting in part of Christian fundamentalists, damages the Republican's drive to become a majority party. The mismanagement and overreaching by congressional Republicans in their drive to impeach President Clinton is a symptom of a fundamental Republican problem. It is no accident that Republican members of Congress in the more cosmopolitan areas of the nation—the Northeast, Midwest, and West Coast—were more hesitant to support impeachment than were Republican congress members representing Sun Belt and Bible belt districts. Just recently Republican intervention in the Terri Schiavo case, involving the medical condition of a woman in a persistently vegetative state, led Republican congressman Christopher Shays to argue that "This Republican party of Lincoln has become a party of theocracy."[20]

The current southern tilt of the Republican leadership may be assisting the transformation of the Republican Party into one not unlike the Democrats of the 1890s–1930s, a party whose strongest support was among those most fearful of modernization. The strength of Republicans in the southern and western sections of the country creates a problem for the party because their stands on guns and tobacco that help solidify their base among social conservatives may repel many voters in the middle of the political spectrum, especially women. The ties of prominent southern Republicans with white supremacist groups reinforce the notion that core southern Republicans resemble the Bryan Democrats of the early twentieth century.[21] Trent Lott, Bob Barr, and Jesse Helms are only a few of the prominent Republicans who maintain political relationships with and receive political and financial support from groups like the Council of Conservative Citizens, a successor to the White Citizens Council of the 1950s and 1960s. With leaders like these, it is unlikely that there will be much outreach from black Americans to Republican conservatives or from Republican conservatives to black Americans. These mutual aversions have left the Republicans a "lily white" party.

Yet neither the reactionary orientation of many contemporary Republicans nor the singular commitment of blacks to the Democrats is preordained. Nor is there anything inevitable that mandates only Reagan Democrats can be swing voters. Few Americans under the age of forty who are not scholars are aware that black Americans were if anything more strongly Republican between 1865 and 1932 than they are supportive of Democrats today. My students, for example, have a hard time believing that this was ever the case. And the Republican progressive heritage is perhaps the richer one. Of course this was the Republican Party of Theodore Roosevelt, not today's Reagan Republicans. Moreover, Ronald Reagan became a political force to be reckoned with in the aftermath of the disintegration of Republican liberalism. The demise of liberal Republicanism in the 1950s and 1960s was a powerful determinant of the progressive impasse.

It is highly unlikely that black Americans will be able to vote for contemporary Republicans, given the Republicans' continued allegiance to Ronald Reagan's legacy—a legacy that is abhorrent to most black Americans. Yet consider the past. It was only twelve years from the time Woodrow Wilson left the White House until Franklin D. Roosevelt entered it, and set in motion a New Deal that almost immediately reshaped the political alignments of a majority of Americans, both black and white.

Black political progress was powerfully predicated not simply on membership in Roosevelt's progressive coalition, but also on the existence of serious, sustained competition for black votes. Yet, how are blacks to support Republicans who remain anchored in constituencies that at times covertly as well as overtly court white supremacists? The dilemma here is real, but the antagonism today is no greater than that that coexisted among constituencies of the Democratic Party between 1936 and 1968.

Clearly, Republicans must reach out and convince blacks that they are willing to move beyond not just overt racism but also the covert variety— they must show a willingness to appeal to the current economic and political interests of black voters. Republicans' political prospects at the beginning of the twenty-first century suggest that at least some Republicans are beginning to recognize the need to move beyond hidebound conservatism. The politics of conservatism comes dangerously close to the politics of reaction.

Democrats' appeal has grown in some of the more dynamic portions of the electorate—in cities, suburbs, and on both coasts. This is beginning to leave Republicans (especially outside of the broad sunbelt region) with the left behind and the left out, groups that fear progress more than they welcome it. Racists, antiabortionists, fundamentalists—these are constituencies fighting against long-term historical tides in ways reminiscent of the Democratic base between 1896 and 1932, when farmers and skilled workers sought to retard the forces of modernization.

Democrats' greater attractiveness on both coasts gives them an advantage in the more dynamic economic regions, areas that are home to much of the projected growth of the population. True, Republican domination of the South provides some counterbalance, especially given the tendency of the southern states to vote similarly. Furthermore, it is important to keep in mind that the United States is now a suburban nation. In 2004, the suburbs were 45 percent of the electorate. Since 1980, every candidate elected president has received the larger share of the suburban vote. Bush's 2004 advantage in the suburbs and rural areas was more than enough to offset the Democratic domination of large cities.

Perhaps another reason for optimism is the growing ethnic diversity of the country. Certainly, immigration in the present will not have the impact it did in the nineteenth century, especially between 1870 and World War I. However, what is significant today is that the vast majority of immigrants are non-white. Since non-white immigrants continue to establish themselves in the United States, political adjustments to a changing electorate will be inevitable. This may take some time, however, because it is more or less a general rule that first-generation immigrants concentrate on establishing an economic foothold, ignoring politics. Granted, there have been some exceptions to this truism, but generally as new immigrants begin to vote in larger numbers, their presence complicates the efforts of those who would use nativist demagoguery to win elections.

Recent elections in California illustrate the declining utility of nativism in a nation whose non-white population may pass its white population in size by the middle of the twenty-first century. Pete Wilson, the governor of California from 1990 to 1998, chose to make his outspoken opposition to affirmative action the centerpiece of his bid for the presidency. He then proceeded to target illegal immigration in his effort to win gubernatorial reelection in 1994. Although he succeeded in the short run, winning reelection, his stridently anti-immigrant rhetoric helped to establish the image of Republicans as a party willing to use nativist demagoguery. The image of California Republicans as anti-immigrant has also been heightened by the campaigning of outspoken conservative Robert Dornan, who has been thrice defeated in congressional races, in large measure due to his anti-immigrant ideology.

Turning to the national level, Pat Buchanan's speech to the Republican national convention also stirred the nativist pot in 1992, to the detriment of President George Bush's campaign for reelection. Hence, it may have become increasing difficult to devise an appeal to anti-immigrant prejudice that does not cost more electoral support than it gains. Furthermore, all of the deficiencies of the present Bush administration do not alter the fact that George W. Bush is the first president to appoint black Americans—Colin Powell and Condoleezza Rice—to the positions of secretary of state and national security advisor, respectively. In this limited context, the distance the current president Bush has traveled from the racist appeals of his father's 1988 campaign is not to be denied.

At the same time the belief popular in many progressive circles that a multicolored "rainbow coalition" is in the offing is overly optimistic. Hispanics are a diverse population, spanning affluent and middle-class Cuban Americans to impoverished Central Americans. Many Hispanics are illegal immigrants, but this does not apply to Cubans or to Puerto Ricans (who are American citizens by birth). Higher birth rates among Hispanics also means that their population is younger than other Americans, and age has become an increasingly important factor in accounting for electoral turnout in recent years, especially since the lowering of the voting age to eighteen. Will younger and often poorer Hispanics go to the polls in sufficient numbers to be potential partners in coalition politics? And if they do, might younger Hispanics be inclined to support celebrity candidates, perhaps a Hispanic variant of Jesse "The Body" Ventura, whose election as the governor of Minnesota was attributed to an unusually high turnout by young white male voters enamored of his World Wrestling Federation celebrity status? Admittedly, "browns" and blacks share as common enemies conservatives, who support English-only policies and opposition to affirmative action. Whether they can successfully form a multiracial, multiethnic coalition because they have common enemies is, however, unclear. Although Hispanics identify strongly with the Democrats, they have ideologically diverse views. They are often socially conservative and economically liberal. Moreover, if Republicans can build upon President Bush's success in attracting Hispanic votes in 2004, the Democrats electoral future will be a dim one. In the most recent election Bush received 44 percent of the Hispanic vote, the best Republican presidential showing among Hispanic voters of the last eight elections. It was also the first time Republican support from Hispanics surpassed 40 percent, which some observers believe represents a significant threshold. [22] Bush's appeal to Hispanic voters gives additional credence to his renunciation of the coded racial appeals of the recent Republican past.

For black Americans a key problem remains the absence of vigorous competition for their vote. Even if they are less often demonized by conservatives, the distance between their political attitudes and policy preferences and those of most Republicans, especially the conservative activists who cast critical primary votes, makes it unlikely that any Republican will be able to gain a significant voice in Republican primaries by appealing to black voters, or even by appearing to be a moderate on matters of interest to blacks. According to political scientist Nicol C. Rae, the mobilization of conservative activists dampens the prospects of a moderate Republican comeback. [23]

Economic Inequality Continues to Surge

Better economic times have done nothing (so far at least) to diminish the continued surge in economic inequality. The most recent data available show a continuation of the income polarization that is central to this analysis. According to journalist David Cay Johnston, "The gap between rich and poor has grown into an economic chasm so wide that this year [1999] the richest 2.7 million Americans, the top 1 percent, will have as many after-tax dollars to spend as the bottom 100 million. This ratio has more than doubled since 1977 when the top 1 percent had as much as the bottom 49 percent. . . . Income disparity has grown so much that four out of five households, or about 217 million people, are taking home a thinner slice of the economic pie today than in 1977."[24] Inequality continues to surge. According to a survey by the Federal Reserve, the benefits of economic expansion from 1998 to 2001 were broad but very uneven. While the wealth of the top 10 percent increased 69 percent, the net worth of those in the lowest fifth increased 24 percent. Income in the top 10 percent increased 19 percent, for the bottom fifth, 14.4 percent.[25] Additionally, the percentage of poor Americans has continued to grow. The poverty rate rose in 2001, the first substantial increase in eight years. It continued to surge in 2002, with 24 percent of black households falling below the official poverty line. The poverty rate continued to climb in 2003 to 12.5 percent. According to Sheldon Danzinger there has been no real progress against poverty in the last generation.[26]

Black Americans have made their most sustained progress during eras of declining inequality. Declining economic inequality tends to favor greater political equality and a hospitable climate for progress in race relations. Opinions certainly vary regarding the extent to which the forces responsible for economic inequality are within our influence.

Perhaps the most conventional economic explanations attribute recent surges in economic inequality to increasing returns to skill and/or the increasing globalization of the American economy. Thus these explanations emphasize broad, uncontrollable forces of economic and technological transformation. However, James Galbraith has powerfully dissented from this view, arguing that economic policy has played a significant role in generating inequality. Accordingly, the decisions of economic policy makers have emphasized controlling inflation at the expense of higher unemployment. However, declining economic inequality is only the first step in creating an environment more conducive to racial progress. Perhaps one answer lies not in waiting for an ideal candidate to come along, but in seeking to foster electoral change.

Possibly one way to begin this is by forming an electoral coalition based on the model for grassroots activism discussed by William Julius Wilson in *The Bridge over the Racial Divide*. Essentially, it would mean rewarding Republicans willing to rebel against the dominant conservative mainstream of their party. In other words, given a choice between supporting a Democrat or a Republican whose commitment to a progressive agenda is roughly equal, support the Republican. Progressives might in time be able to supplant Reagan Democrats as the most desirable swing voters.

In closing, I would suggest that if this analysis has demonstrated anything at all it is that progress for black Americans depends upon a combination of fortuitous economic and political circumstances. The golden age for black Americans' progress toward full citizenship came in the two decades between 1954 and 1973. Re-creating this golden era depends on resurrecting both the political and the economic features of those years. Black Americans need a return to an economic environment of diminishing inequality (most importantly based upon low unemployment) and a political environment favoring bipartisan competition for their votes.

In 1959, Martin Luther King, Jr., proclaimed that "hypocritical northern Republicans were more dangerous than bigoted Southern Democrats. The Negro must make it palpably clear that he is not extricably bound to either political party."[27] Substitute Democrats for Republicans and much the same is still true today.

Notes

Notes to Introduction

1. Rachel Lewin, "Mugabe's Aides Declare Him Winner of Zimbabwe Vote."
2. Ronald Dworkin, "A Badly Flawed Election."
3. Paul Rosenberg, "Coup Watch: Racial Voting Rights Violations Also Crucial in Florida."
4. Sheryl McCarthy, "Was Jim Crow in Action at Florida's Election Sites?"
5. Andres Viglucci, Geoff Dougherty, and William Yardley, "Black Votes Were Discarded at Higher Rates, Analysis Shows."
6. Noel Rubinton, "Media Underreported Florida's Obstacles to 'Voting While Black.'"
7. Civil Rights Project, *Democracy Spoiled: National State and County Disparities in Disfranchisement Through Uncounted Ballots*, pp. 1–12.
8. John Mintz and Dan Keating, "A Racial Gap in Voided Votes."
9. Adam Clymer, "Shaping the New Math of Racial Redistricting"; Earl Black and Merle Black, *The Rise of Southern Republicans*.
10. Kevin Sack, "Pressed Against a Race Ceiling." See also Raphael Sonenshein, "Can Black Candidates Win Statewide Elections?"

Notes to Chapter 1

1. Donald Kinder and Lynn M. Sanders, *Divided By Color*; Public Perspective "An American Dilemma (Part 12) Black and White Relations: Contradictions Abound," (data essay), February/March 1996; "Race and Ethnicity," www.PollingReport.com, 2003.
2. Edward Bellamy, *Looking Backward, 2000–1887*.
3. Earl Black and Merle Black, *The Rise of Southern Republicans*, p. 45.
4. John Skrentny, *The Ironies of Affirmative Action*, p. 170; Louis Uchitelle, "Union Goal of Equality Fails the Test of Time."
5. William J. Wilson, *The Declining Significance of Race*, chapter 1.
6. Peter Applebome, "Ex-Klansman Puts New Racial Politics to Test."
7. William J. Wilson, *The Bridge Over the Racial Divide*, p. 33.
8. Frank Levy, *Dollars and Dreams*, p. 62.

9. Kevin Phillips, *Wealth and Democracy*; Kevin Phillips, *Boiling Point: Democrats, Republicans, and the Decline of Middle-class Prosperity*, p. 4.

10. Levy, p. 99.

11. Sheldon Danziger and Peter Gottschalk, *America Unequal*.

12. William Darity, Jr. and Samuel L. Myers, Jr., *Persistent Disparity: Race and Economic Inequality in the United States Since 1945*, p. 51.

13. James K. Galbraith, *Created Unequal: The Crisis in American Pay*, p. 145.

14. Wilson, *The Bridge Over the Racial Divide*, p. 25

15. Andrew Hacker, *Money*, p. 57.

16. Martin Carnoy, *Faded Dreams*.

17. Ronald Mincy, "The Urban Institute Audit Studies: Their Research and Policy Context"; Marc J. Bendick, Jr., Charles W. Jackson, and Victor Reinoso, "Measuring Employment Discrimination through Controlled Experiments."

18. Jason DeParle, "A New Target: Welfare as We Known It"; U.S. Census Bureau, *Statistical Abstract of the United States*, table 77 Vital Statistics.

19. Carnoy, *Faded Dreams*, pp. 24, 122.

20. Levy, *Dollars and Dreams*, p. 139.

21. Galbraith, *Created Unequal*, p. 12.

22. Robert Goodin, Bruce Headey, Ruud Muffels, and Henk-Jan Dirven, *The Real Worlds of Welfare Capitalism*.

23. Edmond Malinvaud, *Mass Unemployment*, p. 71.

24. Fred Block, Richard A. Cloward, Barbara Ehrenreich, and Frances Fox Piven, *The Mean Season*.

25. Levy, *Dollars and Dreams*, pp. 90–93.

26. "America's Shrinking Middle."

27. Marvin H. Kosters, "Schooling, Work Experience and Wage Trends," p. 309.

28. Levy, *Dollars and Dreams*.

29. Robert H. Frank and Philip J. Cook, *The Winner Take All Society*; Fred Hirsch, *Social Limits to Growth*, p. 67.

30. David Roediger, *The Wages of Whiteness*; Noel Ignatiev, *How the Irish Became White*.

31. Levy, *Dollars and Dreams*, p. 123.

32. Darity and Myers, *Persistent Disparity*, p. 58.

33. Wilson, *The Declining Significance of Race*; Richard Freeman, "Changes in the Labor Market for Black Americans, 1948–1972."

34. Galbraith, *Created Unequal*, p. 58.

35. Ibid.

36. Paul Burstein, *Discrimination, Jobs, and Politics*; David Featherman and Robert Hauser, "Changes in the Socioeconomic Stratification of the Races"; Stanley Lieberson, *A Piece of the Pie*.

37. Burstein, *Discrimination, Jobs, and Politics*, p. 138.

38. James Smith and Finis Welch, *Closing the Gap: Forty Years of Economic Progress for Blacks*, p. XIX.

39. Paul Peretz, *The Political Economy of Inflation in the United States*, p. 93.

40. Richard Freeman and James Medoff, *What Do Unions Do?*

41. Steven P. Erie, *Rainbow's End*.

42. Joel Krieger, *Reagan, Thatcher, and the Politics of Decline*, p. 27.

43. Joe R. Feagin and Melvin P. Sikes, *Living with Racism*, pp. 176–77.

44. Andrew Hacker, *Two Nations*, 2nd ed.

45. Louis Uchitelle, "Union Goal of Equality Fails the Test of Time."

46. Glenn Collins, with Monte Williams, "In Restaurants with the High Tips, Black Waiters Are Few."

47. Federal Glass Ceiling Commission, *Good for Business: Making Full Use of the Nation's Human Capital*"; Andrew Hacker, *Two Nations*, 1992 ed.

48. Jonathan Glater, "Law Firms Are Slow in Promoting Minority Lawyers to Partnerships."

49. Peter T. Kilborn, "Women and Minorities Still Face 'Glass Ceiling.'"

50. Feagin and Sikes, *Living with Racism*, p. 152.

51. Rosabeth M. Kanter, *Men and Women of the Corporation*, p. 54.

52. Federal Glass Ceiling Commission, *Good for Business*.

53. Burstein, *Discrimination, Jobs, and Politics*, p. 38.

54. Hacker, *Two Nations*, 2nd ed., p. 103.

55. Carnoy, *Faded Dreams*, p. 123.

56. Darity and Myers, *Persistent Disparity*, p. 51.

57. Reynolds Farley, *Blacks and Whites: Narrowing the Gap?* pp. 13–15.

58. Douglas Massey and Nancy Denton, *American Apartheid*.

59. Feagin and Sikes, *Living with Racism*, p. 21.

60. C. Eric Lincoln, *Coming Through the Fire: Surviving Race and Place in America*.

61. Chris Tilly and Charles Tilly, *Work Under Capitalism*.

62. Robert Solow, *The Labor Market as a Social Institution*, chapter 2.

63. Peter Applebome, "Racial Divisions Persist 25 Years after King Killing."

64. U.S. Census Bureau, *Statistical Abstract of the United States*; U.S. Census Bureau, "Children Below Poverty Line By Race and Hispanic Origin," p. 441.

65. Skrentny, *The Ironies of Affirmative Action*, p. 227.

66. "Affirmative Actions: The Selective History of an American Idea."

67. Steven Holmes, "Administration Cuts Affirmative Action While Defending It."

68. Ronald Dworkin, "Is Affirmative Action Doomed?"

69. Adam Liptak, "Affirmative Action by Any Other Name."

70. "Affirmative Actions."

71. Linda Greenhouse, "The Supreme Court, The Justices: Context and Court."

72. Burstein, *Discrimination, Jobs, and Politics*, p. 157.

73. Abigail Thernstrom, *Whose Votes Count?*, p. 132.

74. Nathan Glazer, *Affirmative Discrimination: Ethnic Inequality and Public Policy*.

75. Nicholas Katzenbach and Burke Marshall, "Not Color Blind Just Blind."

76. George Fredrickson, *White Supremacy*, pp. 199–200.

77. "The Supreme Court: Excerpts from Justices' Opinions on Michigan Affirmative Action Cases."

78. Christopher Jencks, *Rethinking Social Policy*, p. 61.

Notes to Chapter 2

1. Edward Carmines and James Stimson, *Race and the Transformation of American Politics*.

2. Alexander B. Lamis, *The Two-Party South*, p. 42.

3. Anthony Lewis, "The Case of Lani Guinier"; Steven Holmes "Clinton Steers Bumpy Course Between Left and Right."

4. Lani Guinier, *The Tyranny of the Majority*, p. 78.

5. Marjorie Connelly, "Portrait of the Electorate."

6. Steven Holmes, "Administration Cuts Affirmative Action While Defending It."

7. Kevin Phillips, *The Emerging Conservative Majority*; Thomas Edsall, "The Return of Inequality."

8. John R. Petrocik, *Party Coalitions*, p. 148.

9. Earl Black and Merle Black, *The Vital South*, p. 308.

10. Guinier, *The Tyranny of the Majority*, pp. 23–24; Earl Black and Merle Black, *The Rise of Southern Republicans*, p. 215.

11. Donald Kinder and Lynn M. Sanders, *Divided By Color*, p. 22.

12. R.W. Apple, Jr., "G.O.P. Tries Hard to Win Black Votes, But Recent History Works Against It"; Black and Black, *The Rise of Southern Republicans*, p. 218.

13. Sidney Blumenthal, *Pledging Allegiance*, p. 264; Joe Feagin, Hernan Vera, and Pinar Batur, *White Racism*, p. 167; Timothy Noah, "Did Gore Hatch Horton?"

14. Blumenthal, *Pledging Allegiance*, p. 265.

15. Kinder and Sanders, *Divided By Color*; Feagin et al., *White Racism*, p. 168.

16. Carl Hulse, "Lott Faces Growing Attacks Over Praise for Thurmond."

17. Paul Krugman, "Gotta Have Faith."

18. Hulse, "Lott Faces Growing Attacks Over Praise for Thurmond"; Peter Applebome, "Impeachment Republicans, 130 Years Later: Dueling with the Heirs of Jeff Davis"; Peter Applebome, "Lott's Close Walk to the South's History of Segregation."

19. Associated Press, "Ashcroft: Confederates Were 'Patriots'"; Michael Powell "The Rebels of the Right: Some Politicians Still Seek to 'Explain' the Confederacy."

20. Petrocik, *Party Coalitions*.

21. Kinder and Sanders, *Divided By Color*, p. 228.

22. J. Himelstein, "Rhetorical Continuities in the Politics of Race: The Closed Society Revisited."

23. Haya El Nasser, "Helms is Victor in Race-Tinged Negative Contest."

24. John Egerton, *Speak Now Against the Day: The Generation before the Civil Rights Movement in the South*, p. 531; Feagin et al., *White Racism*, p. 161; Black and Black, *The Rise of Southern Republicans*; Kinder and Sanders, *Divided by Color*.

25. Associated Press, "Candidate Won't Press Racist Group on His Photo"; Nicholas Dawidoff, "Mr. Washington Goes to Mississippi."

26. Kinder and Sanders, *Divided By Color*, p. 32; ibid, p. 198.

27. W. Russell Neuman, *The Paradox of Mass Politics*.

28. Martin P. Wattenberg, *The Decline of American Political Parties*; Paul Allen Beck, "The Dealignment Era in America."

29. Robert Weissberg, "The Democratic Party and the Conflict over Racial Policy," p. 205; Elizabeth Drew, *The Corruption of American Politics: What Went Wrong and Why*; Thomas Edsall, *The New Politics of Inequality*, U.S. Census Bureau, *2002 Statistical Abstract of the United States*, no. 482 and no. 483, p. 294.

30. John Livingston, *Fair Game? Inequality and Affirmative Action*, p. 194.

31. James K. Galbraith, *Created Unequal: The Crisis in American Pay*, p. 218.

32. Benjamin Friedman, *Day of Reckoning*, p. 29; Douglas Hibbs, *The American Political Economy*, p. 80.

33. Wilson, *The Bridge Over the Racial Divide*, pp. 36–37.

34. David Cay Johnston, "I.R.S. More Likely to Audit the Poor and Not the Rich."

35. Mary Williams Walsh, "I.R.S. Tightening Rules for Low-Income Tax Credit."

36. Thomas Fogarty, "IRS Data Confirms Low-Income Tax Audits Rising."

37. David Cay Johnston, "Rate of All I.R.S. Audits Falls; Poor Face Intense Scrutiny"; Walsh, "I.R.S. Tightening Rules for Low-Income Tax Credit."

38. Porter, Kathryn, Wendell Primus, Lynette Rawlings, and Esther Rosenbaum. *Strengths of the Safety Net: How the EITC, Social Security, and Other Government Programs Affect Poverty.*

39. Frances Fox Piven and Richard Cloward, *The New Class War*, p. 131; Benjamin Page, *Who Gets What From Government.*

40. Timothy Egan, "States, Facing Budget Shortfall, Cut the Major and the Mundane."

41. William E. Schmidt, "Hard Work Can't Stop Hard Times." See also Lester Thurow, "Forum: The Hidden Sting of the Trade Deficit."

42. Lester Thurow, *Head to Head*, p. 53.

43. Piven and Cloward, *The New Class War*, pp. 15–19.

44. "Children Below Poverty Level by Race and Hispanic Origin: 1970 to 2000," *U.S. Census Bureau Current Population Reports*, no. 669.

45. Thomas Ferguson and Joel Rogers, *Right Turn: The Decline of the Democrats and the Future of American Politics*, p. 129.

46. Helene Slessarev, "Racial Tensions and Institutional Support: Social Programs during a Period of Retrenchment."

47. Michael Wines, "Taxpayers Are Angry, They're Expensive Too."

48. Chris Tilly and Charles Tilly, *Work Under Capitalism*, p. 120.

49. Fox Butterfield, "Prison Rates among Blacks Reach a Peak, Report Finds"; John Broder, "No Hard Time for Prison Budgets"; Fox Butterfield, "Study Finds Steady Increase at All Levels of Government in Cost of Criminal Justice."

50. Orlando Patterson, *Slavery and Social Death.*

51. Andrew Hacker, *Money*, p. 65.

52. Fox Butterfield, "Freed From Prison, But Still Paying a Penalty."

53. Fox Butterfield, "Racial Disparities Seen as Pervasive in Juvenile Justice."

54. Somini Sengupta, "Felony Costs Voting Rights for a Lifetime in 9 States."

55. Randall Kennedy, *Race, Crime, and the Law*; Adam Clymer, "Louisiana Senate Renews Debate on Death Penalty."

56. Lucas Powe, *The Warren Court and American Politics.*

57. Linda Greenhouse, "Death Penalty Gets Attention of High Court."

58. Raymond Bonner and Marc Lacey, "Pervasive Disparities Found in the Federal Death Penalty."

59. Alan Berlow, "The Wrong Man," p. 84.

60. Michael Orestes, "The Political Stampede on Execution"; Richard Willing, "Inmates over 2 Million, a Record for USA."

61. Raymond Bonner and Ford Fessenden, "States with No Death Penalty Share Lower Homicide Rates."

62. David Firestone, "Judges Criticized over Death-Penalty Conference."

63. Berlow, "The Wrong Man," p. 84.

64. Orestes, "The Political Stampede on Execution."

65. Berlow, "The Wrong Man."

66. Joe Conason, "Class Will Tell."

67. Robert Bryce, "Louder Than Words."

68. Fox Butterfield, "Limits on Power and Zeal Hamper Firearms Agency."

69. Sentencing Project, *Does the Punishment Fit the Crime? Drug Users and Drunk Drivers, Questions of Race and Class: Executive Summary.*

70. Joseph B. Treaster, "Is the Fight on Drugs Eroding Civil Rights?"

71. Michael Tackett, "Minor Drug Players Are Paying Big Prices."

72. Michael Coyle, "Race and Class Penalties in Crack Cocaine Sentencing"; Timothy Egan, "War on Crack Retreats, Still Taking Prisoners"; Steven Holmes, "Race Analysis Cites Disparity In Sentencing for Narcotics."

73. Egan, "War on Crack Retreats, Still Taking Prisoners."

74. Treaster, "Is the Fight on Drugs Eroding Civil Rights?"

75. David Kocieniewski and Robert Hanley, "Racial Profiling Was the Routine, New Jersey Finds."

76. David Kocieniewski, "U.S. Wrote Outline for Race Profiling, New Jersey Argues."

77. Andrew Schneider and Mary Pat Flaherty, "Drug Law Leaves Trail of Innocents."

78. Michael Tayton, "Assembly-line Justice Perils Legal System."

79. Egan, "War on Crack Retreats, Still Taking Prisoners."

80. James Alan Fox and Marianne W. Zawitz, "Homicide Trends in the United States."

81. Treaster, "Is the Fight on Drugs Eroding Civil Rights?"

82. Peter Applebome, "Study Faults Atlanta's System of Defending Poor."

83. James Patterson, *Brown v. Board of Education*, p. 56.

84. J. Morgan Kousser, *Colorblind Injustice*, pp. 368, 396.

85. Brooke Thomas (ed.), *Plessy v. Ferguson: A Brief History with Documents*, p. 34.

86. Deborah Sontag, "The Power of the Court"; Neil A. Lewis, "First the Senate, Now the Court of Appeals."

87. Walter Dean Burnham, "The 1980 Earthquake: Realignment, Reaction, or What," p. 113. See also Kevin Phillips, *The Politics of Rich and Poor*, p. 88.

88. Adam Nagourney and David Barstow, "G.O.P.'s Depth Outdid Gore's Team in Florida."

89. Carl Hiaasen, "Rioting by GOP Tourists."

90. Andres Viglucci, "1,700 Dade Voters Mispunched Chads."

91. Roger Roy and David Damron, "Small Counties Wasted More Than 1,700 Votes."

92. John Mintz and Dan Keating, "A Racial Gap in Voided Votes."

93. Organized by a consortium of news organizations that included the *New York Times*, the *Washington Post*, the *Wall Street Journal*, CNN, the Tribune Company, the *Palm Beach Post*, the *Petersburg Times*, and the Associated Press. Ford Fessenden and John Broden, "Study of Disputed Florida Ballots Finds Justices Did Not Cast the Deciding Vote."

94. David Barstow and Don Van Natta, Jr., "How Bush Took Florida: Mining the Overseas Absentee Vote."

95. Civil Rights Project, "Democracy Spoiled: National, State, and County Disparities in Disfranchisement through Uncounted Ballots," p. 8.

96. Robert Lowell, *Public Opinion and Popular Government*, pp. 2–3.

97. Dennis F. Thompson, *John Stuart Mill and Representative Government*, p. 36; Christopher Hewitt, "The Effect of Political Democracy and Direct Democracy on Equality in Industrial Societies."

98. Dennis Mueller, *Public Choice*.

99. Hanna Fenichel Pitkin, *The Concept of Representation*, p. 203.

100. Robert Dahl, *A Preface to Democratic Theory*.

101. Samuel Bowles and Herbert Gintis, *Democracy and Capitalism*, p. 52.

102. Dahl, *A Preface to Democratic Theory*, p. 30.

103. Mueller, *Public Choice*, p. 221.

104. Dahl, *A Preface to Democratic Theory*, p. 59.

105. Joel Krieger, *Reagan, Thatcher and the Politics of Decline*, p. 197.

106. Juan Williams, *Thurgood Marshall: American Revolutionary*, p. 219.

107. Fred Block et al., *The Mean Season*.

108. Robert Dahl, "On Removing Certain Impediments to Democracy," p. 78.

109. Ira Katznelson, "A Radical Departure," p. 314.

110. Martin Shefter and Benjamin Ginsberg, "Institutionalizing the Reagan Regime," p. 191.

111. Mike Davis, *Prisoners of the American Dream: Politics and Economy in the History of the U.S. Working Class*.

112. Kevin Phillips, *The Politics of Rich and Poor*, p. 11.

113. Krieger, *Reagan, Thatcher and the Politics of Decline*, p. 30.

114. William Schneider, "An Insider's View of the Election."

115. David W. Brady and Joseph Stewart, Jr., "When Elections Really Matter: Realignments and Changes in Public Policy."

116. Patterson, *Brown v. Board of Education*, p. 219.

117. Erica Frankenberg, Chungmei Lee, and Gary Orfield, *A Multiracial Society with Segregated Schools: Are We Losing the Dream?* p. 5.

118. Arend Lipjhart, *Democracy in Plural Societies*, p. 28.

119. William Frey, Bill Abresch, and Jonathan Yeasting, *America by the Numbers*, p. 202; Katherine Q. Seelye and Marjorie Connelly, "New York: The Conventioneers: Delegates Leaning to the Right of GOP and the Nation"; Jason DeParle, "Shrinking Welfare Rolls Leave Record High Shares of Minorities."

Notes to Chapter 3

1. Gilbert Osofsky, *Harlem: The Making of a Ghetto*.

2. Allan Spear, "The Origins of the Urban Ghetto, 1870–1915."

3. C. Eric Lincoln, *Coming Through the Fire: Surviving Race and Place in America*, p. 85.

4. Jack Bloom, *Class, Race, and the Civil Rights Movement*.

5. Doug McAdam, *Political Process and the Development of Black Insurgency, 1930–1970*, p. 71.

6. William McFeely, *Grant: A Biography*.

7. Charles Robinson, *The Court Martial of Lt. Henry Flipper*.

8. John Marszalak, *Assault at West Point: The Court Martial of Johnson Whittaker*.

9. Robinson, *The Court Martial of Lt. Henry Flipper*.

10. John Egerton, *Speak Now Against the Day: The Generation before the Civil Rights Movement in the South*, p. 201.

11. Desmond King, *Separate and Unequal: Black Americans and the U.S. Federal Government*, p. 125.

12. Alexander Keyssar, *The Right to Vote: The Contested History of Democracy in the United States*, p. 88.

13. Charles Moskos and John S. Butler, *All That We Can Be*.

14. Adam Nagourney, "Clark Makes It Ten, Roiling Democratic Race."

15. Andrea Stone, "Retired General Enters Democrats Presidential Fray."

16. Paul Finkelman, *An Imperfect Union: Slavery, Federalism, and Comity*.

17. Brooke Thomas (ed.), *Plessy v. Ferguson: A Brief History with Documents*, p. 19.

18. Edward Carmines and James Stimson, *Race and the Transformation of American Politics*, p. 30.

19. Thomas, *Plessy v. Ferguson*, pp. 32–34.

20. Harvard Sitkoff, *A New Deal for Blacks: The Emergence of Civil Rights as a National Issue*, p. 241.

21. King, *Separate and Unequal*, p. 7.

22. Sitkoff, *A New Deal for Blacks*, p. 19.

23. King, *Separate and Unequal*, p. 28.

24. Ira Katznelson, *Black Men: White Cities*, p. 55.

25. King, *Separate and Unequal*, p. 20.

26. Sitkoff, *A New Deal for Blacks*, p. 27.

27. Gerald Jaynes and Robin Williams, *A Common Destiny: Blacks and American Society*, p. 60.

28. For a theoretically relevant comparative analysis, turn to Goren Therborn, "The Rule of Capital and the Rise of Democracy."

29. Stein Rokkan, *Citizens, Elections and Parties*.

30. Bloom, *Class, Race, and the Civil Rights Movement*, p. 29.

31. George Fredrickson, *White Supremacy: A Comparative Study in American and South African History*, p. 182.

32. William J. Wilson, *The Declining Significance of Race*, p. 63.

33. Keyssar, *The Right to Vote*, p. 89.

34. Therborn, "The Rule of Capital and the Rise of Democracy."

35. Eric Foner, *Reconstruction: America's Unfinished Revolution, 1863–77*, p. 60.

36. Ibid., p. 67.

37. Barrington Moore, *The Social Origins of Dictatorship and Democracy*.

38. Ibid.

39. Jay Mandle, *The Roots of Black Poverty*.

40. Jay Mandle, *Not Slave, Not Free*.

41. Foner, *Reconstruction*.

42. Joel Williamson, *A Rage for Order: Black/White Relations in the American South since Emancipation*; Foner, *Reconstruction*; David Montgomery, *Citizen Worker: The Experience of Workers in the United States with Democracy and the Free Market during the Nineteenth Century*.

43. Gerald Jaynes, *Branches Without Roots: Genesis of the Black Working Class in the American South, 1862–1882*, p. 47.

44. Ibid., pp. 179–80.

45. Ibid., p. 175.

46. Gavin Wright, *Old South, New South*.

47. Phillip Wood, *Southern Capitalism: The Political Economy of North Carolina, 1880–1980*, p. 43.

48. Ibid., p. 71.

49. Taylor Branch, *Parting the Waters: America in the King Years*, p. 636.

50. Mandle, *Not Slave, Not Free*, p. 41.

51. Jaynes, *Branches Without Roots*.

52. Wood, *Southern Capitalism*, p. 48.

53. Mandle, *Not Slave, Not Free*.

54. Wright, *Old South, New South*.

55. Fredrickson, *White Supremacy*, p. 215.

56. Bloom, *Class, Race, and the Civil Rights Movement*, pp. 59–60.

57. Ibid., p. 52.

58. Michael Schwartz, *Radical Protest and Social Structure.*
59. Foner, *Reconstruction*, p. 598.
60. Lincoln, *Coming Through the Fire*, p. 16.
61. Foner, *Reconstruction*, p. 588.
62. J. Morgan Kousser, *The Shaping of Southern Politics*, p. 238.
63. Juan Linz, *The Breakdown of Democratic Regimes.*
64. Williamson, *A Rage for Order.*
65. Kousser, *The Shaping of Southern Politics*, p. 32.
66. Bloom, *Class, Race, and the Civil Rights Movement*, p. 29.
67. Earl Black and Merle Black, *Politics and Society in the South*, p. 4.
68. Bloom, *Class, Race, and the Civil Rights Movement.*
69. Edward S. Morgan, *Inventing the People: The Rise of Popular Sovereignty in England and America.*
70. Kousser, *The Shaping of Southern Politics*, p. 151.
71. Mike Davis, *Prisoners of the American Dream: Politics and Economy in the History of the U.S. Working Class*, p. 97.
72. Wood, *Southern Capitalism*, p. 135.
73. Keyssar, *The Right to Vote*, p. 122.
74. Ibid., p. 123.
75. Ibid., p. 145.
76. Ibid., pp. 168–69.
77. Michael McGerr, *The Decline of Popular Politics*, p. 48.
78. Walter Dean Burnham, *The Current Crisis in American Politics.*
79. McAdam, *Political Process and the Development of Black Insurgency, 1930–1970*, p. 67.
80. Egerton, *Speak Now Against the Day*, p. 46.

Notes to Chapter 4

1. Dietrich Rueschemeyer, Evelyne Huber Stephens, and John D. Stephens, *Capitalist Development and Democracy.*
2. Robert Margo, *Race and Schooling in the South*, p. 8.
3. Ibid.; Martin Carnoy, *Faded Dreams.*
4. Gerald Jaynes and Robin Williams, *A Common Destiny: Blacks and American Society*, p. 272.
5. Frank Levy, *Dollars and Dreams: The Changing American Income Distribution*, p. 56.
6. Sheldon Danziger and Peter Gottschalk, *America Unequal.*
7. Thomas Ferguson and Joel Rogers, *Right Turn: The Decline of the Democrats and the Future of American Politics*, pp. 56–57; Thomas Edsall and Mary D. Edsall, *Chain Reaction*, p. 39.
8. Frank Levy, *The New Dollars and Dreams*, p. 93.
9. Ferguson and Rogers, *Right Turn*, p. 100.
10. Judith Stein, *The World of Marcus Garvey.*
11. C. Eric Lincoln, *Coming Through the Fire: Surviving Race and Place in America*, p. 72.
12. Frances Fox Piven and Richard Cloward, *Poor People's Movements*, p. 198.
13. Nancy J. Weiss, *Farewell to the Party of Lincoln*, p. 11.

14. C. Vann Woodward, *The Strange Career of Jim Crow*.

15. Ira Katznelson, *Black Men, White Cities*.

16. Weiss, *Farewell to the Party of Lincoln*, p. 21; Harvard Sitkoff, *A New Deal for Blacks*.

17. Ira Berlin, *Slaves without Masters*.

18. Sitkoff, *A New Deal for Blacks*, p. 332; Doug McAdam, *Political Process and the Development of Black Insurgency, 1930–1970*, p. 84.

19. Paul Burstein, *Discrimination, Jobs, and Politics*, p. 16.

20. Lucas Powe, *The Warren Court and American Politics*, p. 17.

21. Weiss, *Farewell to the Party of Lincoln*, p. 17.

22. Juan Williams, *Thurgood Marshall: American Revolutionary*.

23. McAdam, *Political Process and the Development of Black Insurgency*, p. 111.

24. Sitkoff, *A New Deal for Blacks*, p. 77.

25. Piven and Cloward, *Poor People's Movements*, p. 195.

26. Nicol C. Rae, *Southern Democrats*, p. 155.

27. Sitkoff, *A New Deal for Blacks*, p. 109.

28. Weiss, *Farewell to the Party of Lincoln*.

29. Michael Brown, *Race, Money, and the Welfare State*, pp. 70, 81.

30. Bloom, *Class, Race, and the Civil Rights Movement*, p. 72.

31. Weiss, *Farewell to the Party of Lincoln*.

32. Jill Quadagno, *The Color of Welfare*, chapter 1.

33. Weiss, *Farewell to the Party of Lincoln*, p. 179.

34. Michael Goldfield, *The Color of Politics*, p. 204; Alexander Keyssar, *The Right to Vote: The Contested History of Democracy in the United States*, pp. 236–37; Edward Carmines and James Stimson, *Race and the Transformation of American Politics*, p. 31.

35. Sitkoff, *A New Deal for Blacks*, chapter 12.

36. Burstein, *Discrimination, Jobs, and Politics*, p. 8; Carmines and Stimson, *Race and the Transformation of American Politics*, p. 32.

37. Williams, *Thurgood Marshall*, p. 185.

38. Ibid., p. 195.

39. Burstein, *Discrimination, Jobs, and Politics*, chapter 3.

40. John Egerton, *Speak Now Against the Day: The Generation before the Civil Rights Movement in the South*, pp. 363–64, 397.

41. Ibid., p. 409.

42. Alexander B. Lamis, *The Two-Party South*, p. 9.

43. Bloom, *Class, Race, and the Civil Rights Movement*, chapter 3.

44. Powe, *The Warren Court and American Politics*, p. 74.

45. James Patterson, *Brown v. Board of Education*, p. 56; Egerton, *Speak Now Against the Day*.

46. Piven and Cloward, *Poor People's Movements*, p. 212.

47. Powe, *The Warren Court and American Politics*, p. 61.

48. Bloom, *Class, Race, and the Civil Rights Movement*, p. 134; Patterson, *Brown v. Board of Education*, p. 91.

49. Powe, *The Warren Court and American Politics*, p. 157.

50. Williams, *Thurgood Marshall*, p. 231; Taylor Branch, *Parting the Waters: America in the King Years*.

51. Branch, *Parting the Waters*, pp. 220–21.

52. Jaynes and Williams, *A Common Destiny*, p. 232.

53. Stephen B. Oates, *Let the Trumpet Sound: The Life of Martin Luther King, Jr.*, p. 345.

54. Michael Omi and Howard Winant, *Racial Formation in the United States*.

55. Piven and Cloward, *Poor People's Movements*, p. 213.

56. McAdam, *Political Process and the Development of Black Insurgency*, p. 129.

57. Ibid., p. 130.

58. Weiss, *Farewell to the Party of Lincoln*, pp. 62–66; Sitkoff, *A New Deal for Blacks*, pp. 248–49.

59. Branch, *Parting the Waters*, p. 186.

60. Aldon Morris, *The Origins of the Civil Rights Movement*, p. 87.

61. Harvard Sitkoff, *The Struggle for Black Equality*, p. 90.

62. Morris, *The Origins of the Civil Rights Movement*, p. 25.

63. Richard Willing, "Civil Rights Untold Story."

64. Morris, *The Origins of the Civil Rights Movement*; Claybourne Carson, *In Struggle*; Branch, *Parting the Waters*, p. 485.

65. Carmines and Stimson, *Race and the Transformation of American Politics*, p. 38; Branch, *Parting the Waters*, pp. 488–89.

66. Patterson, *Brown v. Board of Education*, p. 90.

67. Kennedy, *Race, Crime, and the Law*, p. 65; Branch, *Parting the Waters*, pp. 609, 700.

68. Quadagno, *The Color of Welfare*, p. 27; Branch, *Parting the Waters*, pp. 408–9.

69. Jaynes and Williams, *A Common Destiny*.

70. Piven and Cloward, *Poor People's Movements*, p. 231.

71. McAdam, *Political Process and the Development of Black Insurgency*, p. 159.

72. Carmines and Stimson, *Race and the Transformation of American Politics*, p. 41.

73. Oates, *Let the Trumpet Sound*, p. 301.

74. Chandler Davidson, "The Voting Rights Act, A Brief History" in *Controversies in Minority Voting*, pp. 17–21, 44–51; Abigail Thernstrom, *Whose Votes Count*, p. 17.

75. Davidson, "The Voting Rights Act, A Brief History"; Carmines and Stimson, *Race and the Transformation of American Politics*, p. 49.

76. Earle Black and Merle Black, *The Rise of Southern Republicans*, p. 77.

77. Ibid., p. 139.

78. Oates, *Let the Trumpet Sound*, p. 311.

79. Carmines and Stimson, *Race and the Transformation of American Politics*, p. 47.

80. John Skrentny, *The Ironies of Affirmative Action*, p. 220.

81. Patterson, *Brown v. Board of Education*, p. 181.

82. Rae, *Southern Democrats*, p. 47.

83. Edsall and Edsall, *Chain Reaction*, p. 77.

84. Lamis, *The Two-Party South*; p. 219.

85. Piven and Cloward, *Poor People's Movements*, p. 36.

86. Burstein, *Discrimination, Jobs, and Politics*, p. 17.

87. Keyssar, *The Right to Vote*, p. 282.

88. Ibid., p. 256.

89. Powe, *The Warren Court and American Politics*, p. 447.

90. Benjamin Ginsberg and Martin Shefter, *Politics by Others Means*, p. 21.

91. Oates, *Let the Trumpet Sound*, pp. 309–11.

92. Piven and Cloward, *Poor People's Movements*, p. 256.

93. J. Morgan Kousser, *Colorblind Injustice*, p. 13.

94. Samuel P. Huntington, "The United States."

Notes to Chapter 5

1. Lucas Powe, *The Warren Court and American Politics*, p. 275.
2. James K. Galbraith, *Created Unequal: The Crisis in American Pay*.
3. Ivar Berg and Janice Shack-Marquez, "Current Conceptions of Structural Unemployment: Some Logical and Empirical Difficulties"; Richard Levine, "Young Immigrant Wave Lifts New York Economy."
4. Gwendolyn Mink, *Old Labor and New Immigrants in American Political Development*, p. 42.
5. Gavin Mackenzie, *The Aristocracy of Labor*.
6. Melvin Dubofsky, "Organized Labor and the Immigrant in New York City."
7. Mink, *Old Labor and New Immigrants in American Political Development*, p. 98.
8. Steven P. Erie, *Rainbow's End*.
9. Gerald Jaynes and Robin Williams, *A Common Destiny: Blacks and American Society*, p. 87.
10. Steve Fraser, "The Labor Question," p. 73.
11. Robert H. Zieger, *American Workers, American Unions, 1920–1985*, p. 40.
12. Kevin Phillips, *Wealth and Democracy*; Galbraith, *Created Unequal*, p. 73.
13. Mike Davis, *Prisoners of the American Dream: Politics and Economy in the History of the U.S. Working Class*, p. 142; Douglas Hibbs, *The American Political Economy*, p. 25.
14. Zieger, *American Workers, American Unions*, p. 110; Nelson Lichtenstein, "From Corporatism to Collective Bargaining."
15. Barry Bluestone and Bennett Harrison, *The Deindustrialization of America*.
16. Michael Goldfield, *The Decline of Organized Labor*, p. 240.
17. Ira Katznelson, "Was the Great Society a Lost Opportunity?"
18. Earl Black and Merle Black, *Politics and Society in the South*, pp. 65–66.
19. Phillip Wood, *Southern Capitalism: The Political Economy of North Carolina, 1880–1980*, p. 153.
20. Davis, *Prisoners of the American Dream*, p. 137.
21. Black and Black, *Politics and Society in the South*; Stanley Lieberson, *A Piece of the Pie*.
22. Richard Bensel and Elizabeth Sanders, "The Impact of Voting Rights on Southern Welfare Systems," pp. 53–54.
23. Bluestone and Harrison, *The Deindustrialization of America*, p. 87.
24. Andrew Hacker, *Money*, p. 46.
25. Bluestone and Harrison, *The Deindustrialization of America*, p. 165.
26. Ibid., p. 18.
27. Martin Carnoy, *Sustaining the New Economy*; David Leonhardt "Out of a Job and No Longer Looking"; McKinley Blackburn, David E. Bloom, and Richard B. Freeman, "The Declining Economic Position of Less Skilled American Men," p. 31; Gary Burtless, "Earnings Inequality Over the Business and Demographic Cycles"; Gary Burtless, "Introduction and Summary," p. 15; Daniel Altman, "Blunt Portrait Drawn of the U.S. Work Force in 2020."
28. Sheldon Danziger and Peter Gottschalk, "Renewing the War on Poverty: Target Support at Children and Families."
29. Linda Datcher Loury, "Effects of Cohort Size on Postsecondary Training," p. 191.

30. Burtless, "Earnings Inequality over the Business and Demographic Cycles," p. 109; Barry Bluestone and Bennett Harrison, *The Great American Job Machine*; Bennett Harrison and Barry Bluestone, *The Great U-Turn*.

31. Zieger, *American Workers, American Unions*; Hibbs, *The American Political Economy*, p. 69.

32. Chris Tilly and Charles Tilly, *Work Under Capitalism*, p. 224.

33. Bennett Harrison, *Lean and Mean*, p. 190.

34. Phillips, *Wealth and Democracy*, p. 133.

35. Galbraith, *Created Unequal*; Kevin Phillips, *The Politics of Rich and Poor*, p. 143; Lester Thurow, "Forum: The Hidden Sting of the Trade Deficit"; Kevin Murphy and Finis Welch, "The Structure of Wages."

36. Davis, *Prisoners of the American Dream*, p. 139.

37. Robert Pear, "Number of People Living in Poverty Increases in U.S."

38. David Leonhardt, "Equal Opportunity Recession: Almost Everyone Is Feeling It."

39. Peter Kilborn, "Part-time Hirings Bring Drop, Change in U.S. Workplace."

40. Harrison, *Lean and Mean*; Kilborn "Part-time Hirings Bring Drop, Change in U.S. Workplace."

41. Rebecca Blank, "Are Part-time Jobs Bad Jobs?"

42. Madeleine R. Stoner, "Beyond Shelter: Policy Directions for the Preventions of Homelessness."

43. Teresa Sullivan, *Marginal Workers, Marginal Jobs*, p. 30.

44. Hibbs, *The American Political Economy*, p. 46; Leonhardt, "Out of a Job and No Longer Looking."

45. Tilly and Tilly, *Work Under Capitalism*, chapter 9.

46. Harrison and Bluestone, *The Great U-Turn*, pp. 43–47.

47. John E. Schwarz, "The Hidden Side of the Clinton Economy"; Carnoy, *Sustaining the New Economy*, p. 77.

48. Erik Olin Wright and George Steinmetz, "The Fall and Rise of the Petty Bourgeoisie: Changing Patterns of Self-Employment in the Postwar United States."

49. David Leonhardt, "Entrepreneurs' 'Golden Age' Has Failed to Thrive in the '90s."

50. Douglas Hibbs, *The Political Economy of Industrial Democracies*, p. 79.

51. Adam Clymer, "Jobless Issue Proves Puzzle to Democrats"; David E. Rosenbaum, "Unemployment Insurance Aiding Fewer Workers"; Edmond Malinvaud, *Mass Unemployment*, p. 71.

52. Dave Leonhardt, "Hiring in Nation at Its Worst Hiring Slump in Nearly 20 Years"; Katherine Newman, *Falling From Grace*, p. 9.

53. Lisa Belkin, "Abuses Rise Among Hispanic Garment Workers"; Gina Kolata, "More Children are Employed, Often Perilously"; Constanza Montana, "Child Vendors Seek Cash, Find Danger"; Martin Carnoy, *Faded Dreams*, p. 157.

54. Jason DeParle, "New Rows to Hoe in the 'Harvest of Shame.'"

55. Zieger, *American Workers, American Unions*, p. 177.

56. Harrison and Bluestone, *The Great U-Turn*, p. 16.

57. Davis, *Prisoners of the American Dream*, p. 145.

58. Milt Freudenheim, "Employers Winning Right to Cut Back Medical Insurance."

59. Thomas Ferguson and Joel Rogers, *Right Turn: The Decline of the Democrats and the Future of American Politics*, p. 200.

60. Hibbs, *The American Political Economy*, p. 117.

Notes to Chapter 6

1. Edward S. Morgan, *Inventing the People: The Rise of Popular Sovereignty in England and America*, p. 152.

2. Ibid., p. 237.

3. Michael Omi and Howard Winant, *Racial Formation in the United States*, p. 72.

4. George Dangerfield, *The Era of Good Feelings*, p. 235.

5. Joel Williamson, *A Rage for Order: Black/White Relations in the American South since Emancipation*, pp. 5–7.

6. Randall Kennedy, *Race, Crime and the Law*, p. 83.

7. Richard P. McCormick, "Political Development and the Second Party System," p. 107.

8. Michael Goldfield, *The Color of Politics*, p. 90.

9. Kennedy, *Race, Crime and the Law*, p. 81.

10. Noel Ignatiev, *How the Irish Became White*, chapters 4–6.

11. Ira Berlin, *Slaves without Masters*, chapters 5, 7, and 10.

12. Ibid., pp. 261–62.

13. Paul Lewison, *Race, Class, and Party*, p. 9.

14. Douglass C. North, *The Economic Growth of the United States, 1790–1860*, p. 133.

15. Stanley Lieberson, *A Piece of the Pie*, p. 140.

16. Morgan, *Inventing the People*, p. 148.

17. Fred Hirsch, *Social Limits to Growth*, chapters 7–8.

18. Hanna Fenichel Pitkin, *The Concept of Representation,* p. 232.

19. Joseph Schumpeter, *Capitalism, Socialism, and Democracy*, p. 269.

20. Brian Barry, *Sociologists, Economists, and Democracy*.

21. Adam Przeworski and Michael Wallerstein, "Popular Sovereignty, State Autonomy, and Private Property."

22. Bruce Cain, "Voting Rights and Democratic Theory," p. 266.

23. Ralf Dahrendorf, *Life Chances*, p. 124.

24. Przeworski and Wallerstein, "Popular Sovereignty, State Autonomy, and Private Property," p. 4.

25. Martin P. Wattenberg, *The Decline of American Political Parties*, p. 129.

26. Philip Green, "What is Political Equality? A Reply to Dahl," p. 105.

27. Joshua Cohen and Joel Rogers, *On Democracy*, p. 158.

28. Anthony Downs, *An Economic Theory of Democracy*.

29. Anthony Ramirez, "Actor Speaks, and Listens, to Cabbies at Bias Forum"; James Dao, "Report Cites Persistent Bias Among Cabbies in Washington."

30. Downs, *An Economic Theory of Democracy*, chapters 7–8.

31. Barry, *Sociologists, Economists, and Democracy*.

32. Benjamin Page, *Choices and Echoes in Presidential Elections*, p. 29.

33. Albert O. Hirschman, *Exit, Voice, and Loyalty*.

34. Robert H. Frank and Philip J. Cook, *The Winner Take All Society*, p. 5.

35. Peter Passell, "Economic Scene."

36. Hirschman, *Exit, Voice, and Loyalty*, p. 53.

37. E.F. Carritt, "Liberty and Equality," p. 139.

38. W. Russell Neuman, *The Paradox of Mass Politics*, chapters 3–4.

39. Ibid., p. 156.

40. Raymond Wolfinger and Steven Rosenstone, *Who Votes?* p. 36.

41. Douglass C. North, *Institutions, Institutional Change and Economic Performance*, p. 78.

42. Erica Frankenberg, Chungmei Lee, and Gary Orfield, "A Multiracial Society with Segregated Schools: Are We Losing the Dream?" p. 4.

43. Graham Greene, *Our Man in Havana*, p. 151.

44. Martin Carnoy, *Faded Dreams*, pp. 153–54.

45. Jaynes and Williams, *A Common Destiny: Blacks and American Society*, p. 276.

46. Kevin Phillips, *Boiling Point: Democrats, Republicans, and the Decline of Middle-class Prosperity*, p. 35.

47. Frances Fox Piven and Richard Cloward, *Why Americans Don't Vote*.

48. Lester Thurow, *Head to Head*, p. 267.

49. Bennett Harrison and Barry Bluestone, *The Great U-Turn*, p. 140; ibid., p. 156.

50. Dahrendorf, *Life Chances*, p. 128.

Notes to Chapter 7

1. William Darity, Jr. and Samuel L. Myers, Jr., *Persistent Disparity: Race and Economic Inequality in the United States Since 1945*, p. 58.

2. Thomas Edsall and Mary D. Edsall, *Chain Reaction*.

3. Thomas Edsall, *The New Politics of Inequality*.

4. James K. Galbraith, *Created Unequal: The Crisis in American Pay*, p. 14.

5. Reynolds Farley, *Blacks and Whites: Narrowing the Gap?* p. 149.

6. Frances Fox Piven and Richard Cloward, *Poor People's Movements*, p. 31.

7. Nicol C. Rae, *Southern Democrats*, p. 67.

8. Doug McAdam, *Political Process and the Development of Black Insurgency, 1930–1970*, pp. 79–80.

9. Benjamin Ginsberg and Martin Shefter, *Politics by Other Means*.

10. Paul Burstein, *Discrimination, Jobs, and Politics*, p. 17.

11. Arthur Schlesinger, *The Cycles of American History*; Kevin Phillips, *The Politics of Rich and Poor*, and more recently Kevin Phillips, *Boiling Point: Democrats, Republicans, and the Decline of Middle-class Prosperity*.

12. Sylvia Nasar and Kirsten R. Mitchell, "Booming Job Market Draws Young Black Men Into Fold."

13. Galbraith, *Created Unequal*, pp. 148–49.

14. William J. Wilson, *The Bridge Over the Racial Divide*.

15. Adam Liptak, "Suspension of Executions is Urged for Pennsylvania"; Linda Greenhouse, "Supreme Court, 5–4 Forbids Executions in Juvenile Crime"; Stuart Banner, "When Killing a Juvenile Was Routine."

16. Fox Butterfield, "With Cash Tight, States Reassess Long Jail Terms."

17. Neil Lewis, "Justice Department Opposes Lower Jail Terms for Crack." *New York Times* March 20, 2002, A20.

18. Adam Nagourney, "For GOP, Northeast Is Becoming Foreign Turf."

19. Wilson, *The Bridge Over the Racial Divide*, chapters 3 and 5.

20. Adam Nagourney, "GOP Right is Splintered on Schiavo Intervention."

21. Christopher Caldwell, "The Southern Captivity of the GOP." Thomas Edsall, "Controversial Group Has Strong Ties to Both Parties in the South."

22. Lizette Alvarez, "Hispanic Voters Hard to Profile, Poll Finds"; Marjorie Connelly, "How Americans Voted: A Political Portrait"; Kirk Johnson, "Hispanic Voters Declare Their Independence."

23. Rae, *Southern Democrats*, p. 112.

24. David Cay Johnston, "Gap Between Rich and Poor Found Substantially Wider," p. 14.

25. Edmond Andrews, "Economic Inequality Grew in '90s Boom, Fed Reports."

26. Lynette Clemetson, "More Americans in Poverty in 2002, Census Study Says"; David Leonhardt, "More Americans Were Unisured and Poor in 2003, Census Finds."

27. David J. Garrow, *Bearing the Cross: Martin Luther King, Jr. and the Southern Christian Leadership Conference*, p. 119.

Bibliography

"Affirmative Actions: The Selective History of an American Idea." *New York Times*, June 29, 2003: section 4, p. 14.

Altman, Daniel. "Blunt Portrait Drawn of the U.S. Work Force in 2020." *New York Times*, August 30, 2002.

Alvarez, Lizette. "Hispanic Voters Hard to Profile, Poll Finds." *New York Times*, October 4, 2002: A18.

"America's Shrinking Middle." *The Economist*, November 12, 1988: 84–85.

Andrews, Edmond. "Economic Inequality Grew in '90s Boom, Fed Reports." *New York Times*, January 23, 2003: 1, 2.

Apple, R.W., Jr. "G.O.P. Tries Hard to Win Black Votes, but Recent History Works Against It." *New York Times*, September 19, 1996: section B, p. 11.

Applebome, Peter. "Ex-Klansman Puts New Racial Politics to Test." *New York Times*, June 18, 1990: A1, A18.

———. "Impeachment Republicans, 130 Years Later: Dueling with the Heirs of Jeff Davis." *New York Times*, December 27, 1998: section 4, pp. 1, 4.

———. "Lott's Close Walk to the South's History of Segregation." *New York Times*, December 13, 2002: A22.

———. "Racial Divisions Persist 25 Years After King Killing." *New York Times*, April 4, 1993: 16.

———. "Study Faults Atlanta's System of Defending Poor." *New York Times*, November 30, 1990: section B, p. 5.

Associated Press. "Ashcroft: Confederates Were 'Patriots.'" *Miami Herald*, December 27, 2002.

———. "Candidate Won't Press Racist Group on His Photo." *New York Times*, October 18, 2003: A10.

Banner, Stuart. "When Killing a Juvenile Was Routine." *New York Times*, March 6, 2005: section 5, p. 4.

Barry, Brian. *Sociologists, Economists, and Democracy.* Chicago: University of Chicago Press, 1978.

Barstow, David, and Don Van Natta, Jr. "How Bush Took Florida: Mining the Overseas Absentee Vote." *New York Times*, July 15, 2001: 1, A15, A16.

Beck, Paul Allen. "The Dealignment Era in America," pp. 240–66 in Russell J. Dalton, J. Scott, C. Flanagan, and Paul Allen Beck, eds., *Electoral Change in Advanced Industrial Democracies.* Princeton, NJ: Princeton University Press, 1984.

Belkin, Lisa. "Abuses Rise Among Hispanic Garment Workers." *New York Times*, November 28, 1990: A10.

Bellamy, Edward. *Looking Backward, 2000–1887*. Boston: Bedford-St. Martin's Press.

Bendick, Marc, Jr., Charles W. Jackson, and Victor Reinoso. "Measuring Employment Discrimination through Controlled Experiments," pp. 77–100 in James B. Stewart, ed., *African-Americans and Post-Industrial Labor Markets*. New Brunswick, NJ: Transaction Publishers, 1999.

Bensel, Richard, and Elizabeth Sanders. "The Impact of Voting Rights on Southern Welfare Systems," pp. 52–70 in Ginsberg and Stone, eds., *Do Elections Matter?*

Berg, Ivar, and Janice Shack-Marquez. "Current Conceptions of Structural Unemployment: Some Logical and Empirical Difficulties." *Research in the Sociology of Work*, vol. 3 (1985): 99–117.

Berlin, Ira. *Slaves without Masters*. New York: Vintage, 1976.

Berlow, Alan. "The Wrong Man." *Atlantic Monthly* (November 1999): 66–91.

Black, Earl, and Merle Black. *Politics and Society in the South*. Cambridge, MA: Harvard University Press, 1987.

———. *The Rise of Southern Republicans*. Cambridge, MA: Harvard University Press, 2002.

———. *The Vital South*. Cambridge, MA: Harvard University Press, 1992.

Blackburn, McKinley, David E. Bloom, and Richard B. Freeman. " The Declining Economic Position of Less Skilled American Men," pp. 31–77 in Burtless, ed., *A Future of Lousy Jobs?*

Blank, Rebecca. "Are Part-time Jobs Bad Jobs?" pp. 125–64 in Burtless, ed., *A Future of Lousy Jobs?*

Block, Fred, Richard A. Cloward, Barbara Ehrenreich, and Frances Fox Piven. *The Mean Season*. New York: Random House, 1988.

Bloom, Jack. *Class, Race, and the Civil Rights Movement*. Bloomington: Indiana University Press, 1987.

Bluestone, Barry, and Bennett Harrison. *The Deindustrialization of America*. New York: Basic Books, 1982.

———. *The Great American Job Machine*. A study prepared for the Joint Economic Committee. U.S. Congress, 1986.

Blumenthal, Sidney. *Pledging Allegiance*. New York: Harper & Row, 1990.

Bonner, Raymond, and Ford Fessenden. "States with No Death Penalty Share Lower Homicide Rates." *New York Times*, September 22, 2000: A1, A23.

Bonner, Raymond, and Marc Lacey. "Pervasive Disparities Found in the Federal Death Penalty." *New York Times*, September 12, 2000: A18.

Bowles, Samuel, and Herbert Gintis. *Democracy and Capitalism*. New York: Basic Books, 1987.

Brady, David W., and Joseph Stewart, Jr. "When Elections Really Matter: Realignments and Changes in Public Policy," pp. 19–34 in Ginsberg and Stone, eds., *Do Elections Matter?*

Branch, Taylor. *Parting the Waters: America in the King Years*. New York: Simon & Schuster, 1988.

Broder, John. "No Hard Time for Prison Budgets." *New York Times*, January 19, 2003: 5.

Brown, Michael. *Race, Money, and the Welfare State*. Ithaca, NY: Cornell University Press, 1999.

Bryce, Robert. "Louder Than Words." *Salon Magazine*, August 24, 1999. www.salonmagazine.com.

Burnham, Walter Dean. *The Current Crisis in American Politics.* Oxford: Oxford University Press, 1982.

Burnham, Walter Dean. "The 1980 Earthquake: Realignment, Reaction, or What," pp. 98–140 in Thomas Ferguson and Joel Rogers, eds., *The Hidden Election.* New York: Pantheon, 1981.

Burstein, Paul. *Discrimination, Jobs, and Politics.* Chicago: University of Chicago Press, 1985.

Burtless, Gary. "Earnings Inequality over the Business and Demographic Cycles," pp. 77–122 in Burtless, ed., *A Future of Lousy Jobs?*

———. "Introduction and Summary," pp. 1–30 in Burtless, ed., *A Future of Lousy Jobs?* Washington, DC: Brookings Institution, 1990.

Butterfield, Fox. "Freed From Prison, But Still Paying a Penalty." *New York Times,* December 29, 2002: 18.

———. "Limits on Power and Zeal Hamper Firearms Agency." *New York Times,* July 22, 1999: A1, A12.

———. "Prison Rates Among Blacks Reach a Peak, Report Finds." *New York Times,* April 7, 2003: A11.

———. "Racial Disparities Seen as Pervasive in Juvenile Justice." *New York Times,* April 26, 2000: A1, A18.

———. "Study Finds Steady Increase at All Levels of Government in Cost of Criminal Justice." *New York Times,* February 11, 2002: A14.

———. "With Cash Tight, States Reassess Long Jail Terms." *New York Times,* November 10, 2003: A1, A16.

Cain, Bruce. "Voting Rights and Democratic Theory," pp. 261–78 in Bernard Grofman and Chandler Davidson, eds., *Controversies in Minority Voting.* Brookings Institution: Washington, DC, 1992.

Caldwell, Christopher. "The Southern Captivity of the GOP." *Atlantic Monthly* vol. 281, no. 6 (1988): 55–72.

Carmines, Edward, and James Stimson. *Race and the Transformation of American Politics.* Princeton, NJ: Princeton University Press, 1989.

Carnoy, Martin. *Faded Dreams.* New York: Cambridge University Press, 1994.

———. *Sustaining the New Economy.* Cambridge, MA: Harvard University Press, 2000.

Carritt, E.F. "Liberty and Equality," pp. 127–41 in Anthony Quinton, ed., *Political Philosophy.* New York: Oxford University Press, 1967.

Carson, Claybourne. *In Struggle.* Cambridge, MA: Harvard University Press, 1995.

Civil Rights Project. *Democracy Spoiled: National State and County Disparities in Disfranchisement Through Uncounted Ballots.* Harvard University.

Clemetson, Lynette. "More Americans in Poverty in 2002, Census Study Says." *New York Times,* September 27, 2003.

Clymer, Adam. "Jobless Issue Proves Puzzle to Democrats." *New York Times,* April 26, 1991: 1, 26.

———. "Louisiana Senate Renews Debate on Death Penalty." *New York Times,* August 31, 2003: A14.

———. "Shaping the New Math of Racial Redistricting." *New York Times,* July 15, 2001: section 5, p. 16.

Cohen, Joshua, and Joel Rogers. *On Democracy.* New York: Penguin, 1983.

Collins, Glenn, with Monte Williams. "In Restaurants with the High Tips, Black Waiters Are Few." *New York Times,* May 30, 2000: A23.

Conason, Joe. "Class Will Tell." *Salon Magazine*, August 24, 1999. www .salonmagazine.com

Connelly, Marjorie. "How Americans Voted: A Political Portrait." *New York Times*, November 7, 2004, section 5, p. 4.

———. "Portrait of the Electorate." *New York Times*, November 10, 1996: 28.

Coyle, Michael. "Race and Class Penalties in Crack Cocaine Sentencing." The Sentencing Project. Washington, DC.

Dahl, Robert. *A Preface to Democratic Theory.* Chicago: University of Chicago Press, 1956.

Dahl, Robert. "On Removing Certain Impediments to Democracy," pp. 71–98 in Irving Howe, ed., *Beyond the Welfare State.* New York: Schocken, 1982.

Dahrendorf, Ralf. *Life Chances.* Chicago: University of Chicago Press, 1979.

Dangerfield, George. *The Era of Good Feelings.* Chicago: I.R. Dee, 1989.

Danziger, Sheldon, and Peter Gottschalk. *America Unequal.* Cambridge, MA: Harvard University Press, 1995.

———. "Renewing the War on Poverty." *New York Times*, March 22, 1987: Business section, p. 2.

Dao, James. "Report Cites Persistent Bias Among Cabbies in Washington." *New York Times*, October 8, 2003.

Darity, William Jr., and Samuel L. Myers, Jr. *Persistent Disparity: Race and Economic Inequality in the United States Since 1945.* Cheltenham, UK: Edward Elgar, 1988.

Datcher Loury, Linda "Effects of Cohort Size on Postsecondary Training" pp. 165–200 in Burtless, ed., *A Future of Lousy Jobs?*

Davidson, Chandler. "The Voting Rights Act: A Brief History," pp. 7–51 in Bernard Grofman and Chandler Davidson, eds., *Controversies in Minority Voting.* Washington, DC: Brookings Institution, 1992.

Davis, Mike. *Prisoners of the American Dream: Politics and Economy in the History of the U.S. Working Class.* London: Verso, 1986.

Dawidoff, Nicholas. "Mr. Washington Goes to Mississippi." *New York Times*, October 19, 2003: section 6, pp. 48–54.

DeParle, Jason. "New Rows to Hoe in the 'Harvest of Shame.'" *New York Times*, July 28, 1991: E3.

———. "Shrinking Welfare Rolls Leave Record High Shares of Minorities." *New York Times*, July 27, 1998: A1, A12.

———. "Welfare as We Have Known It." *New York Times*, June 19, 1994.

Downs, Anthony. *An Economic Theory of Democracy.* New York: Harper & Row, 1957.

Drew, Elizabeth. *The Corruption of American Politics: What Went Wrong and Why.* Secaucus, NJ: Birch Lane, 1999.

Dubofsky, Melvin. "Organized Labor and the Immigrant in New York City, 1900–1918." *Labor History* 2 (1961): 182–201.

Dworkin, Ronald. "A Badly Flawed Election." *New York Review of Books*, January 11, 2001: 53–55.

———. "Is Affirmative Action Doomed?" *New York Review of Books*, November 5, 1998.

Edsall, Thomas. "Controversial Group Has Strong Ties to Both Parties in the South." *Washington Post*, December 13, 1999: A02.

———. *The New Politics of Inequality.* New York: W.W. Norton, 1984.

————. "The Return of Inequality." *Atlantic Monthly* (June 1988): 86–94.

Edsall, Thomas, and Mary D. Edsall. *Chain Reaction.* New York: W.W. Norton, 1992.

Egan, Timothy. "States, Facing Budget Shortfall, Cut the Major and the Mundane." *New York Times*, April 21, 2003: A1, A18.

————. "War on Crack Retreats, Still Taking Prisoners." *New York Times*, February 28, 1999: 1, 20–21.

Egerton, John. *Speak Now Against the Day: The Generation before the Civil Rights Movement in the South.* Chapel Hill: University of North Carolina Press, 1994.

El Nasser, Haya. "Helms Is Victor in Race-Tinged Negative Contest." *USA Today*, November 6, 1996: 14A.

Erie, Steven P. *Rainbow's End.* Berkeley: University of California Press, 1990.

Farley, Reynolds. *Blacks and Whites: Narrowing the Gap?* Cambridge, MA : Harvard University Press, 1984.

Feagin, Joe R., and Melvin P. Sikes. *Living with Racism.* Boston: Beacon, 1994.

Feagin, Joe, Hernan Vera, and Pinar Batur. *White Racism.* 2nd edition. New York: Routledge, 2001.

Featherman, David, and Robert Hauser. "Changes in the Socioeconomic Stratification of the Races, 1962–1973." *American Journal of Sociology* vol. 82, no. 3 (1977): 621–51.

Federal Glass Ceiling Commission. *Good for Business: Making Full Use of the Nation's Human Capital.* Washington, DC. 1995.

Ferguson, Thomas, and Joel Rogers. *Right Turn: The Decline of the Democrats and the Future of American Politics.* New York: Hill & Wang, 1986.

Fessenden, Ford, and John Broden. "Study of Disputed Florida Ballots Finds Justices Did Not Cast the Deciding Vote." *New York Times*, November 12, 2001: A1, A16–17.

Finkelman, Paul. *An Imperfect Union: Slavery, Federalism, and Comity.* Chapel Hill: University of North Carolina Press, 1981.

Firestone, David. "Judges Criticized over Death-Penalty Conference." *New York Times*, August 19, 1999: A16.

Fogarty, Thomas. "IRS Data Confirms Low-Income Tax Audits Rising." *USA Today*, September 30, 1997: 10B.

Foner, Eric. *Reconstruction: America's Unfinished Revolution, 1863–77.* New York: Oxford University Press, 1988.

Fox, James Alan, and Marianne W. Zawitz. "Homicide Trends in the United States." *Bureau of Justice Statistics Crime Data Brief*, January 1999.

Frank, Robert H., and Philip J. Cook. *The Winner Take All Society.* New York: Penguin, 1996.

Frankenberg, Erica, Chungmei Lee, and Gary Orfield. "A Multiracial Society with Segregated Schools: Are We Losing the Dream?" Civil Rights Project, Harvard University.

Fraser, Steve. "The Labor Question," pp. 55–84 in Steve Fraser and Gary Gerstle, eds., *The Rise and Fall of the New Deal Order.* Princeton, NJ: Princeton University Press, 1989.

Fredrickson, George. *White Supremacy: A Comparative Study in American and South African History.* New York: Oxford University Press, 1981.

Freeman, Richard. "Changes in the Labor Market for Black Americans, 1948–1972." *Brookings Papers on Economic Activity* 1 (1973): 67–120.

Freeman, Richard, and James Medoff. *What Do Unions Do?* New York: Basic Books, 1984.

Freudenheim, Milt. "Employers Winning Right to Cut Back Medical Insurance." *New York Times*, March 29, 1992: 1, 14.

Frey, William, Bill Abresch, and Jonathan Yeasting. *America by the Numbers*. New York: New Press, 2001.

Friedman, Benjamin. *Day of Reckoning*. New York: Vintage, 1990.

Galbraith, James K. *Created Unequal: The Crisis in American Pay*. New York: Free Press, 1998.

Garrow, David J. *Bearing the Cross: Martin Luther King, Jr. and the Southern Christian Leadership Conference*. New York: William Morrow, 1986.

Ginsberg, Benjamin, and Martin Shefter. *Politics by Other Means*. New York: Basic Books, 1990.

Ginsberg, Benjamin, and Alan Stone, eds. *Do Elections Matter?* Armonk, NY: M.E. Sharpe, 1986.

Glater, Jonathan. "Law Firms Are Slow in Promoting Minority Lawyers to Partnerships." *New York Times*, August 7, 2001: A1, C2.

Glazer, Nathan. *Affirmative Discrimination: Ethnic Inequality and Public Policy*. New York: Basic Books, 1978.

Goldfield, Michael. *The Color of Politics*. New York: New Press, 1997.

———. *The Decline of Organized Labor*. Chicago: University of Chicago Press, 1987.

Goodin, Robert, Bruce Headey, Ruud Muffels, and Henk-Jan Dirven. *The Real Worlds of Welfare Capitalism*. New York: Cambridge University Press, 1999.

Green, Philip. "What is Political Equality? A Reply to Dahl," pp. 98–118 in Irvine Howe, ed., *Beyond the Welfare State*. New York: Schocken, 1982.

Greene, Graham. *Our Man in Havana*. London: Penguin, 1958.

Greenhouse, Linda. "Death Penalty Gets Attention of High Court." *New York Times*, October 30, 1999: A1–A10.

———. "Supreme Court, 5–4 Forbids Executions in Juvenile Crime" *New York Times*, March 2, 2005: A1, A14.

———. "The Supreme Court, The Justices: Context and Court." *New York Times*, June 25, 2003: section 5, p. 1A.

Guinier, Lani. *The Tyranny of the Majority*. New York: Free Press, 1994.

Hacker, Andrew. "Black Crime, White Racism." *New York Review of Books*, March 3, 1988.

———. *Money*. New York: Touchstone, 1997.

———. *Two Nations*. 2nd edition. New York: Ballantine, 1995.

Harrison, Bennett, and Barry Bluestone. *The Great U-Turn*. New York: Basic Books, 1988.

Harrison, Bennett. *Lean and Mean*. New York: Basic Books, 1994.

Hewitt, Christopher. "The Effect of Political Democracy and Direct Democracy on Equality in Industrial Societies." *American Sociological Review* 42 (1977): 450–64.

Hiaasen, Carl. "Rioting by GOP Tourists." *Miami Herald*, November 29, 2000.

Hibbs, Douglas. *The American Political Economy*. Cambridge, MA: Harvard University Press, 1987.

———. *The Political Economy of Industrial Democracies*. Cambridge, MA: Harvard University Press, 1987.

Himelstein, J. "Rhetorical Continuities in the Politics of Race: The Closed Society Revisited." *Southern Speech Communication Journal* 48 (1983): 153–66.

Hirsch, Fred. *Social Limits to Growth*. Cambridge, MA: Harvard University Press, 1976.

Hirschman, Albert O. *Exit, Voice, and Loyalty.* Cambridge, MA: Harvard University Press, 1970.

Hofstadter, Richard. *Social Darwinism and American Thought.* New York: Vintage, 1963.

Holmes, Steven. "Administration Cuts Affirmative Action While Defending It." *New York Times*, March 16, 1998: A17.

———. "Clinton Steers Bumpy Course Between Left and Right." *New York Times*, October 20, 1996.

———. "Race Analysis Cites Disparity in Sentencing for Narcotics." *New York Times*, June 8, 2000: A16.

Hulse, Carl. "Lott Faces Growing Attacks Over Praise for Thurmond." *New York Times*, December 11, 2002: A23.

Huntington, Samuel P. "The United States," pp. 59–118 in Michel Crozier, Samuel P. Huntington, and Joji Watanuki, eds., *The Crisis of Democracy.* New York: New York University Press, 1975.

Ignatiev, Noel. *How the Irish Became White.* New York: Routledge, 1995.

Jaynes, Gerald. *Branches Without Roots: Genesis of the Black Working Class in the American South, 1862–1882.* New York: Oxford University Press, 1986.

Jaynes, Gerald, and Robin Williams. *A Common Destiny: Blacks and American Society.* Washington, DC: National Academy Press, 1989.

Jencks, Christopher. *Inequality.* New York: Harper & Row, 1972.

———. *Rethinking Social Policy.* New York: HarperPerennial, 1993.

Johnson, Kirk. "Hispanic Voters Declare Their Independence" *New York Times*, November 9, 2004: A1, A16.

Johnston, David Cay. "Gap Between Rich and Poor Found Substantially Wider." *New York Times*, September 5, 1999: 14.

———. "I.R.S. More Likely to Audit the Poor and Not the Rich." *New York Times*, April 16, 2000: A1.

———. "Rate of All I.R.S. Audits Falls; Poor Face Intense Scrutiny." *New York Times*, February 6, 2001.

Kanter, Rosabeth M. *Men and Women of the Corporation.* New York: Basic Books, 1977.

Katzenbach, Nicholas, and Burke Marshall. "Not Color Blind, Just Blind." *New York Times*, February 22, 1998: section 6, pp. 42–45.

Katznelson, Ira. *Black Men: White Cities.* Chicago: University of Chicago Press, 1976.

———. "A Radical Departure," pp. 313–40 in Thomas Ferguson and Joel Rogers, eds., *The Hidden Election.* New York: Pantheon, 1981.

———. "Was the Great Society a Lost Opportunity?" pp. 185–211 in Steve Fraser and Gary Gerstle, eds., *The Rise and Fall of the New Deal Order.* Princeton, NJ: Princeton University Press, 1989.

Kennedy, Randall. *Race, Crime, and the Law.* New York: Vintage, 1997.

Keyssar, Alexander. *The Right to Vote: The Contested History of Democracy in the United States.* New York: Basic Books, 2000.

Kilborn, Peter. "Part-time Hirings Bring Drop, Change in U.S. Workplace." *New York Times*, June 17, 1991: A9.

———. "Women and Minorities Still Face 'Glass Ceiling.'" *New York Times*, March 16, 1995: C22.

Kinder, Donald, and Lynn M. Sanders. *Divided By Color.* Chicago: University of Chicago Press, 1996.

King, Desmond. *Separate and Unequal: Black Americans and the U.S. Federal Government.* New York: Oxford University Press, 1997.

Kocieniewski, David, and Robert Hanley. "Racial Profiling Was the Routine, New Jersey Finds." *New York Times,* November 28, 2000: A29.

———. "U.S. Wrote Outline for Race Profiling, New Jersey Argues." *New York Times,* November 29, 2000: A1, C24.

Kolata, Gina. "More Children are Employed, Often Perilously." *New York Times,* June 21, 1992: 1, 18.

Kosters, Marvin H. "Schooling, Work Experience and Wage Trends." *American Economic Review* vol. 80, no. 2 (1990): 308–12.

Kousser, J. Morgan. *Colorblind Injustice.* Chapel Hill: University of North Carolina Press, 1999.

———. *The Shaping of Southern Politics.* New Haven, CT: Yale University Press, 1975.

Krieger, Joel. *Reagan, Thatcher and the Politics of Decline.* New York: Oxford University Press, 1986.

Krugman, Paul. "Gotta Have Faith." *New York Times,* December 17, 2002: A35.

Lamis, Alexander B. *The Two-Party South.* New York: Oxford University Press, 1990.

Leonhardt, David. "Entrepreneurs' 'Golden Age' Has Failed to Thrive in the '90s." *New York Times,* December 1, 2000: A1, C2.

———. "Equal Opportunity Recession: Almost Everyone Is Feeling It." *New York Times,* December 16, 2001: A1, A24, A25.

———. "Hiring in Nation at Its Worst Hiring Slump in Nearly 20 Years." *New York Times,* February 6, 2003: A1, C6.

———. "More Americans Were Uninsured and Poor in 2003, Census Finds" *New York Times,* August 27, 2004: A1, A18.

———. "Out of a Job and No Longer Looking." *New York Times,* September 29, 2002: section 4, pp. 1, 4.

Levine, Richard. "Young Immigrant Wave Lifts New York Economy." *New York Times,* July 30 1990: A1, A8.

Levy, Frank. *Dollars and Dreams: The Changing American Income Distribution.* New York: W.W. Norton, 1988.

———. *The New Dollars and Dreams.* New York: Russell Sage, 1998.

Lewin, Rachel. "Mugabe's Aides Declare Him Winner of Zimbabwe Vote." *New York Times,* March 13, 2002: A3.

Lewis, Anthony. "The Case of Lani Guinier." *New York Review of Books,* August 13, 1998: 14–16.

Lewis, Neil A. "First the Senate, Now the Court of Appeals." *New York Times,* December 1, 2002: section 4, p. 3.

———. "Justice Department Opposes Lower Jail Terms for Crack." *New York Times,* March 20, 2002: A20.

Lewison, Paul. *Race, Class, and Party.* New York: Grosset & Dunlap, 1965.

Lichtenstein, Nelson. "From Corporatism to Collective Bargaining," pp. 122–52 in Steve Fraser and Gary Gerstle, eds., *The Rise and Fall of the New Deal Order.* Princeton, NJ: Princeton University Press, 1989.

Lieberson, Stanley. *A Piece of the Pie.* Berkeley: University of California Press, 1980.

Lijphart, Arend. *Democracy in Plural Societies.* New Haven, CT: Yale University Press, 1977.

Lincoln, C. Eric. *Coming Through the Fire: Surviving Race and Place in America.* Durham: Duke University Press, 1995.

Linz, Juan. *The Breakdown of Democratic Regimes.* Baltimore: Johns Hopkins University Press, 1978.

Liptak, Adam. "Affirmative Action by Any Other Name." *New York Times,* January 19, 2003: section 4, pp. 1, 5.

———. "Suspension of Executions Is Urged for Pennsylvania." *New York Times,* March 5, 2003: 15.

Livingston, John. *Fair Game? Inequality and Affirmative Action.* San Francisco: Freeman, 1979.

Lowell, Robert. *Public Opinion and Popular Government.* New York: Longmans, 1913.

Mackenzie, Gavin. *The Aristocracy of Labor.* Cambridge, UK: Cambridge University Press, 1973.

Malinvaud, Edmond. *Mass Unemployment.* Oxford: Basil Blackwell, 1984.

Mandle, Jay. *Not Slave, Not Free.* Durham, NC: Duke University Press, 1992.

———. *The Roots of Black Poverty.* Durham, NC: Duke University Press, 1978.

Margo, Robert. *Race and Schooling in the South.* Chicago: University of Chicago Press, 1990.

Marszalek, John. *Assault at West Point: The Court Martial of Johnson Whittaker.* New York: Collier Books, 1994.

Massey, Douglas, and Nancy Denton. *American Apartheid.* Cambridge, MA: Harvard University Press, 1993.

McAdam, Doug. *Political Process and the Development of Black Insurgency, 1930–1970.* Chicago: University of Chicago Press, 1982.

McCarthy, Sheryl. "Was Jim Crow in Action at Florida's Election Sites?" *Newsday,* November 20, 2000: A28.

McCormick, Richard. "Political Development and the Second Party System" in William Chambers and Walter Dean Burnham, eds., *The American Party Systems.* New York: Oxford University, pp. 90–116.

McFeely, William. *Grant: A Biography.* New York: W.W. Norton, 1981.

McGerr, Michael. *The Decline of Popular Politics.* New York: Oxford University Press, 1986.

Mincy, Ronald. "The Urban Institute Audit Studies: Their Research and Policy Context," pp. 165–86 in Michael Fix and Raymond J. Struyk, eds., *Clear and Convincing Evidence: Measurement of Discrimination in America.* Washington: Urban Institute Press, 1993.

Mink, Gwendolyn. *Old Labor and New Immigrants in American Political Development.* Ithaca, NY: Cornell University Press, 1990.

Mintz, John, and Dan Keating. "A Racial Gap in Voided Votes." *Washington Post,* December 27, 2000: A01.

Montana, Constanza. "Child Vendors Seek Cash, Find Danger." *Chicago Tribune,* August 11, 1991: section 1, pp. 1, 18.

Montgomery, David. *Citizen Worker: The Experience of Workers in the United States with Democracy and the Free Market during the Nineteenth Century.* Cambridge, UK: Cambridge University Press, 1995.

Moore, Barrington. *The Social Origins of Dictatorship and Democracy.* Boston: Beacon, 1966.

Morgan, Edward S. *Inventing the People: The Rise of Popular Sovereignty in England and America.* New Haven, CT: Yale University Press, 1988.

Morris, Aldon. *The Origins of the Civil Rights Movement.* New York: Free Press, 1984.

Moskos, Charles, and John S. Butler. *All That We Can Be.* New York: Basic Books, 1996.

Mueller, Dennis. *Public Choice.* Cambridge, UK: Cambridge University Press, 1979.

Murphy, Kevin, and Finis Welch. "The Structure of Wages." University of Chicago, working paper, August 1988.

Nagourney, Adam. "Clark Makes It Ten, Roiling Democratic Race." *New York Times,* September 18, 2003: A1, A17.

———. "For GOP, Northeast Is Becoming Foreign Turf." *New York Times,* November 14, 1996: B12.

———. "GOP Right is Splintered on Schiavo Intervention." *New York Times,* March 23, 2005: A14.

Nagourney, Adam, and David Barstow. "GOP's Depth Outdid Gore's Team in Florida." *New York Times,* December 22, 2000: A1, A22.

Nasar, Sylvia, and Kirsten R. Mitchell. "Booming Job Market Draws Young Black Men Into Fold." *New York Times,* May 23, 1999: A1, 21.

Neuman, W. Russell. *The Paradox of Mass Politics.* Cambridge, MA: Harvard University Press, 1986.

Newman, Katherine. *Falling From Grace.* New York: Vintage, 1989.

Noah, Timothy. "Did Gore Hatch Horton?" *Slate:* Chatterbox, November 1, 1999. www.slate.com.

North, Douglass C. *The Economic Growth of the United States, 1790–1860.* New York: W.W. Norton, 1966.

———. *Institutions, Institutional Change and Economic Performance.* New York: Cambridge University Press, 1990.

Oates, Stephen B. *Let the Trumpet Sound: The Life of Martin Luther King, Jr.* New York: Harper & Row, 1982.

Omi, Michael, and Howard Winant. *Racial Formation in the United States.* New York: Routledge, 1986.

Orestes, Michael. "The Political Stampede on Execution." *New York Times,* April 4, 1990: A10.

Osofsky, Gilbert. *Harlem: The Making of a Ghetto.* New York: Harper & Row, 1971.

Page, Benjamin. *Choices and Echoes in Presidential Elections.* Chicago: University of Chicago Press, 1978.

———. *Who Gets What From Government.* Berkeley: University of California Press, 1983.

Passell, Peter. "Economic Scene." *New York Times,* January 23, 1991: D2.

Patterson, James. *Brown v. Board of Education.* New York: Oxford University Press, 2002.

Patterson, Orlando. *Slavery and Social Death.* Cambridge, MA: Harvard University Press, 1982.

Pear, Robert. "Number of People Living in Poverty Increases in U.S." *New York Times,* September 25, 2002: A1, A19.

Peretz, Paul. *The Political Economy of Inflation in the United States.* Chicago: University of Chicago Press, 1983.

Petrocik, John R. *Party Coalitions.* Chicago: University of Chicago Press, 1981.

Phillips, Kevin. *Boiling Point: Democrats, Republicans, and the Decline of Middle-class Prosperity.* New York: HarperPerennial, 1994.

———. *The Emerging Conservative Majority.* Garden City, NY: Anchor Books, 1970.

———. *The Politics of Rich and Poor.* New York: HarperPerennial. 1990.

———. *Wealth and Democracy.* New York: Broadview Books, 1994.

Pitkin, Hanna Fenichel. *The Concept of Representation.* Berkeley: University of California Press, 1972.

Piven, Frances Fox, and Richard Cloward. *The New Class War.* New York: Pantheon, 1982.

———. *Poor People's Movements.* New York: Vintage, 1979.

———. *Why Americans Don't Vote.* New York: Pantheon, 1989.

Polling Report.com. "Race and Ethnicity" 2003. www.pollingreport.com.

Powe, Lucas. *The Warren Court and American Politics.* Cambridge, MA: Harvard University Press, 2001.

Powell, Michael. "The Rebels of the Right: Some Politicians Still Seek to 'Explain' the Confederacy." *Washington Post,* January 16, 2001.

Porter, Kathryn, Wendell Primus, Lynette Rawlings, and Esther Rosenbaum. *Strengths of the Safety Net: How the EITC, Social Security, and Other Government Programs Affect Poverty.* March 9, 1998.

Przeworski, Adam, and Michael Wallerstein. "Popular Sovereignty, State Autonomy, and Private Property." Unpublished paper, 1985.

Public Perspective. "An American Dilemma (Part 12) Black And White Relations: Contradictions Abound" (data essay), Vol. 7, No. 2 (February/March 1996), pp. 19–35, 38–42.

Quadagno, Jill. *The Color of Welfare.* New York: Oxford University Press, 1995.

Rae, Nicol C. *Southern Democrats.* New York: Oxford University Press, 1994.

Ramirez, Anthony. "Actor Speaks, and Listens, to Cabbies at Bias Forum." *New York Times,* December 6, 1999: A31.

Robinson, Charles. *The Court Martial of Lt. Henry Flipper.* El Paso: Texas Western Press, 1994.

Roediger, David. *The Wages of Whiteness.* London: Verso, 1999.

Rokkan, Stein. *Citizens, Elections and Parties.* New York: D. McKay, 1970.

Rosenbaum, David E. "Unemployment Insurance Aiding Fewer Workers." *New York Times,* December 2, 1990.

Rosenberg, Paul. "Coup Watch: Racial Voting Rights Violations Also Crucial in Florida." *Los Angeles Independent Media Center,* November 10, 2000: 1–4.

Roy, Roger, and David Damron. "Small Counties Wasted More Than 1,700 Votes." *Orlando Sentinel,* January 28, 2001.

Rubinton, Noel. "Media Underreported Florida's Obstacles to 'Voting While Black.'" *Minnesota Star Tribune,* December 10, 2000.

Rueschemeyer, Dietrich, Evelyne Huber Stephens, and John D. Stephens. *Capitalist Development and Democracy.* Chicago: University of Chicago Press, 1992.

Sack, Kevin. "Pressed Against a Race Ceiling." *New York Times,* April 5, 2001.

Schlesinger, Arthur. *The Cycles of American History.* Boston: Houghton-Mifflin, 1986.

Schmidt, William E. "Hard Work Can't Stop Hard Times." *New York Times,* November 25, 1990: 1, 12.

Schneider, Andrew, and Mary Pat Flaherty. "Drug Law Leaves Trail of Innocents." *Chicago Tribune,* August 11, 1991: section 1, pp. 1, 13.

Schneider, William. "An Insider's View of the Election." *Atlantic Monthly* (July 1988): 29–57.

Schumpeter, Joseph. *Capitalism, Socialism, and Democracy.* New York: Harper & Row, 1962.

Schwartz, Michael. *Radical Protest and Social Structure.* Chicago: University of Chicago Press, 1976.

Schwarz, John E. "The Hidden Side of the Clinton Economy." *Atlantic Monthly* (October 1998): 18–21.

Seelye, Katherine Q., and Marjorie Connelly. "New York: The Conventioneers; Delegates Leaning to the Right of GOP and the Nation." *New York Times* August 29, 2004: section 15, pp. 1, 13.

Sengupta, Somini. "Felony Costs Voting Rights for a Lifetime in 9 States." *New York Times*, November 3, 2000: A18.

Sentencing Project. *Does the Punishment Fit the Crime? Drug Users and Drunk Drivers, Questions of Race and Class: Executive Summary*. Washington, DC, May 1993.

Shefter, Martin, and Benjamin Ginsberg. "Institutionalizing the Reagan Regime," pp. 191–203 in Ginsberg and Stone, eds., *Do Elections Matter?*

Sitkoff, Harvard. *A New Deal for Blacks: The Emergence of Civil Rights as a National Issue*. New York: Oxford University Press, 1978.

————. *The Struggle for Black Equality*. New York: Hill & Wang, 1993.

Skrentny, John. *The Ironies of Affirmative Action*. Chicago: University of Chicago Press, 1996.

Slessarev, Helene. "Racial Tensions and Institutional Support: Social Programs during a Period of Retrenchment," pp. 357–80 in Margaret Weir, Ann Shola Orloff, and Theda Skocpol, eds., *The Politics of Social Policy in the United States*. Princeton, NJ: Princeton, University Press, 1988.

Smith, James, and Finis Welch. *Closing the Gap: Forty Years of Economic Progress for Blacks*. Santa Monica, CA: Rand Corp., 1986.

Solow, Robert. *The Labor Market as a Social Institution*. Cambridge, UK: Basil Blackwell, 1990.

Sonenshein, Raphael. "Can Black Candidates Win Statewide Elections?" pp. 307–24 in Theodore Rueter, ed., *The Politics of Race: African-Americans and the Political System*. Armonk, NY: M.E. Sharpe, 1995.

Sontag, Deborah. "The Power of the Court." *New York Times*, March 9, 2003: section 6, p. 44.

Spear, Allan. "The Origins of the Urban Ghetto, 1870–1915," pp. 153–66 in Nathan I. Huggins, Martin Kilson, and Daniel Fox, eds., *Key Issues in the Afro-American Experience*. New York: Harcourt Brace Jovanovich, 1971.

Stein, Judith. *The World of Marcus Garvey*. Baton Rouge: Louisiana State University Press, 1986.

Stone, Andrea. "Retired General Enters Democrats Presidential Fray." *USA Today*, September 18, 2003: 16A.

Stoner, Madeleine R. "Beyond Shelter: Policy Directions for the Preventions of Homelessness." *Social Work Research and Abstracts* (December 1989): pp. 7–11.

Sullivan, Teresa. *Marginal Workers, Marginal Jobs*. Austin: University of Texas Press, 1978.

"The Supreme Court: Excerpt from Justices Opinions on Michigan Affirmative Action Cases." *New York Times*, June 24, 2003: A24.

Tackett, Michael. "Minor Drug Players Are Paying Big Prices." *Chicago Tribune*, October 15, 1990: section 1, p. 9.

Tayton, Michael. "Assembly-line Justice Perils Legal System." *Chicago Tribune*, October 14, 1990: section 1, pp. 1, 12.

Therborn, Goren. "The Rule of Capital and the Rise of Democracy." *New Left Review* 103 (1977): 3–43.

Thernstrom, Abigail. *Whose Votes Count?* Cambridge, MA: Harvard University Press, 1989.

Thomas, Brooke, ed. *Plessy v. Ferguson: A Brief History with Documents.* New York: Bedford Books, 1997.

Thompson, Dennis F. *John Stuart Mill and Representative Government.* Princeton, NJ: Princeton University Press, 1979.

Thurow, Lester. "Forum: The Hidden Sting of the Trade Deficit." *New York Times,* January 19 1986: F3.

———. *Head to Head.* New York: Warner, 1993.

Tilly, Chris, and Charles Tilly. *Work Under Capitalism.* Boulder, CO: Westview Press, 1998.

Treaster, Joseph B. "Is the Fight on Drugs Eroding Civil Rights?" *New York Times,* May 6, 1990: E5.

U.S. Census Bureau. "Children Below Poverty Level by Race and Hispanic Origin. 1970–2000." *Current Population Reports* no. 669. 2002. Washington, DC.

———. *Statistical Abstract of the United States.* 2002. Washington, DC.

Uchitelle, Louis. "Union Goal of Equality Fails the Test of Time." *New York Times,* July 9, 1995: A1–A10.

Viglucci, Andres. "1,700 Dade Voters Mispunched Chads." *Miami Herald,* January 6, 2001.

Viglucci, Andres, Geoff Dougherty, and William Yardley. "Blacks Votes Were Discarded at Higher Rates, Analysis Shows." *Miami Herald,* December 12, 2000.

Walsh, Mary Williams. "IRS Tightening Rules for Low-Income Tax Credit." *New York Times,* April 25, 2003: A1, C4.

Wattenberg, Martin P. *The Decline of American Political Parties.* Cambridge, MA: Harvard University Press, 1986.

Weiss, Nancy J. *Farewell to the Party of Lincoln.* Princeton. NJ: Princeton University Press, 1983.

Weissberg, Robert. "The Democratic Party and the Conflict over Racial Policy," pp. 204–20 in Ginsberg and Stone, eds., *Do Elections Matter?*

Williams, Juan. *Thurgood Marshall: American Revolutionary.* New York: Times Books, 1998.

Williamson, Joel. *A Rage for Order: Black/White Relations in the American South Since Emancipation.* New York: Oxford University Press, 1986.

Willing, Richard. "Civil Rights Untold Story." *USA Today,* November 28, 1995: A1–A2.

———. "Inmates over 2 Million, a Record for USA." *USA Today,* April 7, 2003: A13.

Wilson, William J. *The Declining Significance of Race.* Chicago: University of Chicago Press, 1978.

———. *The Bridge Over the Racial Divide.* Berkeley: University of California Press, 1999.

Wines, Michael. "Taxpayers are Angry, They're Expensive Too." *New York Times,* November 20, 1994: E5.

Wolfinger, Raymond, and Steven Rosenstone. *Who Votes?* New Haven, CT: Yale University Press, 1980.

Wood, Phillip. *Southern Capitalism: The Political Economy of North Carolina, 1880–1980.* Durham, NC: Duke University Press, 1986.

Woodward, C. Vann. *The Strange Career of Jim Crow.* New York: Oxford University Press, 1974.

Wright, Erik Olin, and George Steinmetz. "The Fall and Rise of the Petty Bourgeoisie: Changing Patterns of Self-Employment in the Postwar United States." *American Journal of Sociology* vol. 94 (5) (1989): 973–1018.

Wright, Gavin. *Old South, New South.* New York: Basic Books, 1986.

Zieger, Robert H. *American Workers, American Unions, 1920–1985.* Baltimore: Johns Hopkins University Press, 1986.

Index

About the Author

Antoine L. Joseph has a Bachelor's degree in Economics from Swarthmore College and a PhD in Sociology from the University of Chicago. He is currently a professor in the Department of Social Science at Bryant University. He has published articles in *Politics and Society*, *Ethnic and Racial Studies*, and the *British Journal of Sociology*. His previous book, *Skilled Workers Solidarity: The American Experience in Comparative Perspective*, was published in 2000.